TRUTH, TORTURE, AND THE AMERICAN WAY

TRUTH, TORTURE, AND THE AMERICAN WAY

THE HISTORY AND CONSEQUENCES
OF U.S. INVOLVEMENT IN TORTURE

JENNIFER K. HARBURY

BEACON PRESS
BOSTON

11/05
14.00

Beacon Press
25 Beacon Street
Boston, Massachusetts 02108-2892
www.beacon.org

Beacon Press books
are published under the auspices of
the Unitarian Universalist Association of Congregations.

08 07 06 05   8 7 6 5 4 3 2 1

This book is printed on acid-free paper that meets the uncoated paper
ANSI/NISO specifications for permanence as revised in 1992.

Text design by Bob Kosturko
Composition by Wilsted & Taylor Publishing Services

Library of Congress Cataloging-in-Publication Data

Harbury, Jennifer.
  Truth, torture, and the American way : the history and consequences
of U.S. involvement in torture / Jennifer K. Harbury.— 1st ed.
     p.   cm.
  Includes bibliographical references and index.
  ISBN 0-8070-0307-7 (pbk. : alk. paper)
  1. Human rights—Government policy—United States. 2. Human rights—
Latin America. 3. Torture. 4. Political prisoners—Abuse of. I. Title.

  JC599.U5H272 2005
  323'.0973—dc22   2005011578

*This book is dedicated to Sister Dianna Ortiz
and to all those in secret torture cells
who have come face to face with the CIA.*

CONTENTS

AUTHOR'S NOTE

Of the many difficult issues facing American society today, one of the most crucial is the use of torture by our intelligence agencies. Torture has, of course, been abhorrent in this country since the framing of the Constitution and is prohibited by our domestic laws and treaties. Yet as the photographs of Abu Ghraib made clear, it has been used as an interrogation tool since the September 11 attacks on the World Trade Center.

We have heard a number of responses from our government leaders on this matter. On the one hand, we are told that the abuses were carried out by individual and undisciplined soldiers who have now been court-martialed. Since there is no official policy in question, no further action is necessary. As documented throughout this book, however, the use of torture has in fact been widespread, with the same startling methods revealed not only at Abu Ghraib but also throughout Iraq, Afghanistan, and Guantánamo. Worse yet, these techniques can be tracked back to U.S. operations in Central and Latin America and even Vietnam. This information strongly suggests a covert and illegal policy. If such a policy exists, it requires urgent attention. Moreover, legal responsibility sits squarely on the shoulders of top U.S. officials.

We are also told that harsh methods must be permitted in order to prevent another terrorist attack. To be sure, September 11 ushered in a new era of national security concerns. Yet as the war in Iraq rages onward, it is equally clear that such harsh practices are sowing the seeds of rage and hatred against us abroad. Does the use of torture protect us, or does it endanger us?

These hard questions must be asked and answered. It is hoped that the evidence and analysis set forth in these pages proves useful in reaching informed decisions. Our national future is at stake.

FOREWORD

It was June 6, 1991. Guatemalan general Hector Gramajo proudly approached the entrance of Harvard University's Kennedy School of Government. Dressed in his black robe, he would soon join the other students as they excitedly prepared for the big moment. It was graduation day at Harvard. But just before the general made it inside, a process server called out his name. He looked up. Minutes before getting his diploma, he was slapped with a lawsuit...for crimes against humanity. He was being sued by nine Guatemalan torture victims or their surviving family members. Armed with a tape recorder, I ran up to the general and asked his thoughts on this special day. He was no longer smiling. He said he was no tin pot dictator. "I am," he said angrily, "a product of the American educational system." And then, proving his point, he strode onto the big lawn along the Charles River, and, together with hundreds of his classmates, he was awarded a Harvard diploma.

A week later, he would be served with yet another lawsuit. This one was on behalf of Sister Dianna Ortiz, an American nun who had been dragged from her convent in rural Guatemala and brutally raped and tortured. This time Gramajo was a little more prepared. He spit on the process server and left the United States. But he would be back. Six months later, the U.S. military invited the general to address Latin American soldiers training at the School of the Americas at Fort Benning, Georgia.

Once a year, thousands gather outside the gates of Fort Benning to protest the U.S. Army's School of the Americas (renamed in 2001 the Western Hemisphere Institute for Security Cooperation, or WHINSEC, to counter the rising movement to close the school). *"Presente!"* the protesters intone as they solemnly chant the litany of names of people who died in Guatemala, in El Salvador, in Honduras, in other Latin American countries at the hands of military men trained at Fort Benning. By invoking the names of the dead, their memory is kept alive.

Jennifer Harbury embodies the word *presente*. After her husband, Everardo—a Mayan *comandante* in the mountains of Guatemala—disappeared, she demanded answers. If he couldn't be present, she would be. She risked her life, protesting outside the National Palace in Guatemala and fasting for over thirty days.

She traveled back and forth between the country where her husband was born and in which he disappeared and the country of her birth, the United States of America, where she thought the answers to his disappearance lay. She was relentless. She took her protest from the National Palace to the White House then headed to the Guatemalan army base where she was told he'd been buried. As she fasted, she brought to light the plight not only of her husband but also of the Guatemalan people. More than 150,000 of them had died or disappeared at the hands of successive military regimes backed by the United States.

I remember one of the first times I met Jennifer Harbury. It was late. I had boarded the train in New York, headed to Washington, D.C. I saw across the aisle from me a woman stretched out over two seats, sleeping. As the train rolled along, she raised her head. I saw it was Jennifer, whose campaign I had just begun covering. She was exhausted, sick, but determined as ever.

Harbury's vigils and hunger strikes were a direct confrontation with one of the world's most notorious human rights–abusing regimes. Her courageous campaign did not succeed in gaining the release of her husband, but it gained instead the tragic information that he had been tortured and killed by the Guatemalan military. Many loved ones, as she writes, never even learn that detail, never get the closure that knowledge brings. The spotlight she focused on that regime no doubt saved others in similar straits as Everardo from further torture. But her work then, we now know—as so eloquently laid out in the book before you—was just beginning.

I continued to follow Jennifer Harbury's story as she painfully pieced together what had happened to her husband, tracing his torture and death to Guatemalan military officers on the CIA payroll. She didn't stop there but continued to demand an end to U.S. government sponsorship of torture and extrajudicial executions. She made remarkable strides, and legislative checks and balances were imposed on the conduct of U.S. government entities, especially the Central Intelligence Agency.

U.S. sponsorship—financing, training, arming—of brutal regimes was by no means limited to Latin America. Independent journalist Allan Nairn is well known for exposing U.S. support for the Guatemalan military. But I traveled with him to East Timor to investigate the U.S.-backed Indonesian occupation. On November 12, 1991, we witnessed the Indonesian army—armed with U.S. M-16s—gun down more than 270 Timorese. The soldiers beat us and fractured Allan's skull. But we believe they decided not to kill us because we were from the same country their weapons were from.

Government policy since September 11, 2001 has disregarded both recent and historical laws against torture, including the advances gained by Jennifer Harbury and the movement she helped build. The signs were all around us, as the days and months passed from late 2001: special registration of Arab American and South Asian men and boys; mass detentions in the U.S.; secret deportations in the middle of the night to countries known to use torture; the creation and expansion of offshore prisons like Cuba's Guantánamo Bay, Bagram Air Base in Afghanistan, the remote island of Diego Garcia in the Indian Ocean, and, of course, Abu Ghraib in Iraq. The 2004 release of the photos from Abu Ghraib confirmed the fears and suspicions of so many that people held in these prisons, beyond the reach of courts, defense attorneys, and the media, were being abused. Then followed the release of a string of U.S. government memorandums from 2002 that included then–White House counsel Alberto Gonzales's assertion that the "new paradigm" of the war on terror renders obsolete and "quaint" certain protections of the Geneva Conventions.

Most Americans don't understand how the rest of the world sees us. While the iconic image of the U.S. invasion of Iraq remains for most Americans the video of the statue of Saddam Hussein being pulled down (by U.S. Marines) in Firdos Square on April 9, 2003, for most of the world the iconic image of the invasion is probably the famous torture photo from Abu Ghraib, the hooded Iraqi prisoner, his arms outstretched in Christlike fashion, electrical wires attached to his fingertips.

I recently chanced upon a gathering of World War II veterans who had been prisoners of war under Nazi Germany. They were celebrating the sixtieth anniversary of their liberation. These men had all been pilots, shot down over occupied France or Germany, and ultimately ended up at the same luft stalag. Among the group were two veterans of the Tuskegee Airmen, African American pilots. I approached one and struck up a conversation, curious about how he had been treated in detention.

"Better than I was treated in Mississippi," he replied.

Another captured pilot narrowly avoided indicating on his POW intake form that he was Jewish. When a fellow prisoner saw him writing "J," the man took his form from him, changed it to a "P" and wrote "Prot." for Protestant. I asked him what he thought of the images and stories of abuse coming out of Abu Ghraib and Guantánamo. He said they reminded him of what the SS did: tortured and executed people. He said he had been saved by the Geneva Convention (the first convention, expanded in 1949 into the multiple conventions we are familiar with now). The Luftwaffe, he said, abided by the international standards for the detention of POWs. He added that he feared that abusive U.S. treatment of Iraqi and Afghan prisoners put any captured U.S. soldier at risk.

It is an observation echoed by a number of people in the military. Retired brigadier general James Cullen joined more than a dozen retired generals and admirals in writing a letter to the Senate opposing the confirmation of Alberto Gonzales as attorney general. Cullen asserted that Gonzales had endangered U.S. servicemembers around the world by saying that the Geneva Conventions do not apply.

Each of us is closer than we think to the distant interrogation cells we are learning more about daily. As a journalist, it is my responsibility to seek out this news, to get as close to the story as possible, to expose official policy and official lies. But it is not only journalists who have a stake and a role in determining the truth. Each of us has a role. Talk to your neighbors. If you know soldiers who have returned from overseas, ask to hear their stories. Look for the immigrants' rights groups in your region and speak to them about their experiences. What you learn, who you meet, and the decisions you make do matter. Your decision to pick up this book might lead to not much more than a thought-provoking moment in a library or bookstore before the demands and hassles of workaday life retake your attention. The clear insight and hard-earned wisdom of Jennifer Harbury that follow, however, may serve to inspire you, as they have inspired so many others, to take action to make the world a safer place.

As you read these words someone, somewhere, is in pain, in the midst of torture, or perhaps wrongly detained. Maybe a family member is wracked with anxiety, wondering where their loved one is who they last saw hours ago dragged away in handcuffs and a hood. It is with them in mind that I leave you to consider this book, which is a testament to the life work of Jennifer Harbury as she joins thousands in a growing global movement to stop torture.

Amy Goodman, with Denis Moynihan
New York City, 2005

INTRODUCTION
AN EARLY GLIMPSE

Sister Dianna Ortiz and I share a passionate love for the people of Guatemala, but when we met in 1994 we were both marked by the ongoing horror there. Sister Dianna had survived torture at the hands of the notorious Guatemalan military and was struggling to heal and recover her faith. My husband, Everardo, was being secretly detained and tortured, and I was trying to save his life. Meanwhile, the Guatemalan army was continuing its brutal rampage across the country, leaving death, destruction, and terror in its wake. Sister Dianna and I were in Washington, D.C., trying to speak out about what we had learned, to sound the alarm, to rally assistance. We both met with the same implacable foe: the United States Central Intelligence Agency. The harsh truth about our own government's torture practices would forever alter the rest of our lives.

Sister Dianna was a young Ursuline nun from New Mexico who had been teaching Mayan children to read and write in rural Guatemala. Inexplicably, she began to receive death threats in 1989, which intensified until many people urged her to flee the country. As she knelt in a convent garden to pray for discernment, she was assaulted by strangers who dragged her through the hedge and took her to a clandestine military detention center. There she was battered, raped, burned with more than one hundred cigarettes, and subjected to other unspeakable abuses. There were many other prisoners suffering there as well. Her ordeal ended when a tall, fair-skinned man, an obvious American, entered the room. He began speaking on a first-name basis with her torturers, demanding that she be dressed and released to him. He clearly spoke with authority, and he was obeyed. As he drove her away, he told her to forgive her abusers because they were fighting Communism and said that he would take her to his friend at the U.S. Embassy. He spoke in poor Spanish with a heavy American accent. She leaped from his car and ran for her life.

Haunted by the screams of the Guatemalans left behind to die, Sister Dianna begged embassy officials to send their friend to rescue the others. She was told that no such American existed. For many years, the embassy made it clear to Congress and human rights networks alike that Dianna Ortiz was unstable and that her story could not be trusted. When I met her, she was struggling with her personal trauma, her despair for the others, and the agony of being silenced by lies when she tried to speak out about the "silent holocaust" in Guatemala.

I was driven by the specter of Everardo's continuing torture and imminent murder.[1] He was a high-ranking Mayan resistance leader who had fought from the mountains for seventeen years. On March 12, 1992, he had vanished under mysterious circumstances during a brief battle. Guatemalan army intelligence officers reported that they had found his body at the combat site and had buried him in Retalhuleu. They also reported that he had shot himself through the mouth with his own rifle to avoid being captured alive. Six months later a young prisoner of war, Santiago Cabrera López, escaped from a military base and told us that Everardo had in fact been taken prisoner. Because of his intelligence value, the goal was to subject him to long-term torture until he broke psychologically. Great care was taken to avoid his accidental death. To prevent an international human rights outcry, the army officers staged his death, placing the body of a different person in the Retalhuleu grave, then sending us a precise physical description of Everardo when we made inquiry.

One of the last times Santiago had seen my husband alive was in June of 1992. He was chained to a cot, with an unidentified gas tank nearby. He was stripped naked and his entire body was extraordinarily swollen, with one arm and leg heavily bandaged, as if they had hemorrhaged. He was raving. Colonel Julio Roberto Alpirez, a graduate of the U.S. School of the Americas, was bending over him, taking careful notes. A physician stood in the doorway, on hand to prevent an accidental death.

In despair over this news, I flew to Guatemala and opened the grave. There I found the body of a frail eighteen-year-old who had been battered to death.[2] Everardo was thirty-five when he vanished and had quite different dental characteristics. Like Sister Dianna, I approached the U.S. officials at the embassy and the Department of State, only to be told again and again that they had no information at all about Everardo. Concerned members of Congress also made numerous inquiries on my behalf and received official form letters in response bearing the same message: there was no information about Everardo, nor any independent evidence that secret military prisons existed in Guatemala. Meanwhile, time was running out. The peace negotiations were in the final stages. When the war ended, the army would have no need for Everardo's information. Nor would they ever let him live to tell of the torture he had endured at their hands. If I did not find the key to his rescue, he would soon be killed.

By 1994, both Sister Dianna and I had sought refuge and support at the Guatemala Human Rights Commission in Washington, D.C. Driven and sleepless, we understood only too well the unbearable pain in each other's eyes. Somehow, we had to find a way to help bring the horror to an end.

Toward the end of the year, the sand had run through the hourglass for Everardo. Despite the strong support of Congress, the OAS, and many human rights networks, we had been unable to glean even the slightest information about his whereabouts. Nor had he been turned over to any court of law. Spreading out banners and candles in the National Plaza in Guatemala City, I declared a hunger strike to the death and simply sat down to wait. I had no place else to go, and there was no time left. After thirty-two days I was gaunt and staggering but still determined that Everardo and I would either survive or die together. A *60 Minutes* broadcast had just revealed that the U.S. Embassy, despite its long denials, in fact possessed a CIA report confirming Everardo's capture and secret detention by the army. This crucial information had never been shared with me or with the inquiring members of Congress. The public response was vociferous.

Embarrassed U.S. officials hastily invited me to meetings with high-level National Security advisors to discuss the case. Believing that serious help was at last at hand, I returned to Washington only to have all doors slam shut after a brief but unhelpful tête-à-tête with then–National Security advisor Anthony Lake. Sensing betrayal, I resumed my hunger strike on March 12, 1995, this time in front of the White House. After twelve long days, then–U.S. representative Robert Torricelli courageously shared information that he had just received. Everardo was indeed dead. He had been killed upon the orders of Colonel Alpirez, who was also a paid CIA informant or "asset."

In the ensuing political scandal, still more information came to light, although it was hardly the news I had hoped to hear. Everardo had been the captive of a select group of high-level Guatemalan intelligence officials who decided to fake his death and subsequently carried out his torture. Several of these officers were also assets of the CIA. Colonel Alpirez himself had received $44,000 from the agency in June 1992, the same month Santiago saw him bending over Everardo's bound and swollen body. The CIA, although well informed of his plight, continued to seek and pay for further information, though they knew it would be extracted from him by torture. According to the most reliable reports, Everardo survived into the spring of 1994, and during those two years he was repeatedly drugged, battered, and held in a full body cast to prevent his escape. Eventually his tormentors realized that he would never speak, and either had him thrown from a helicopter into the sea, or dismembered and scattered across a sugar cane field.

The public outcry over these disclosures was fierce. The idea of U.S. tax dollars being paid to a broad network of known death squad members and torturers throughout the hemisphere provoked fury from all sectors of society. Members of Congress, too, were outraged that their repeated inquiries and efforts to assist had met with lies and obstructions from their own U.S. agencies. Articles and editorials filled the press and interviews and commentaries aired repeatedly on the radio and television networks.

For a while, it seemed that serious reforms might be possible. President Clinton ordered an in-depth investigation by the Intelligence Oversight Board (IOB) of CIA misconduct in Guatemala. The Senate Intelligence Committee took action as well, holding a public hearing on the CIA's involvement in the murders of both Everardo and the innkeeper Michael Devine, a U.S. citizen. There were dramatic promises that many more hearings on the matter would soon take place. The CIA, for its part, enacted a new policy requiring any agent hiring a known torturer as an asset to report that fact to his higher-level supervisors. Small steps, these, but at least they led in the right direction.

Given all this, we took it for granted that Sister Dianna's tireless efforts to expose the "North American connection" would at last be vindicated. After the extensive disclosures about the very close relationship between military torturers and the CIA, the existence of the tall, fair man speaking with a heavy American accent and exercising authority over her tormentors hardly seemed open to question. Yet U.S. officials continued to stonewall. While her lawyers battled to obtain her files, the agencies balked, releasing mostly press clippings, copies of letters from her supporters, and other useless information. When she approached sympathetic members of Congress for support, a none-too-discreet campaign of veiled threats and smears was resumed by State Department officials and others. She suffered daily, growing ever more sleepless and emaciated, yet ever more determined. The truth about U.S. involvement in torture was a matter of life and death for many in Guatemala and around the world. She would not be silenced.[3]

Meanwhile, the oft-promised hearings on Capitol Hill never materialized, and the entire question of human rights abuses by the CIA faded from the press. The IOB investigation bogged down again and again, and rumors abounded that even when completed, it would never be released to the public or to any of us. With that news, Sister Dianna took action. In the freezing March rains of 1996, she began a grueling vigil and fast in front of the White House, demanding answers. After five weeks had passed she had grown dangerously frail, and her health was threatened by the cold, sleepless nights in the open. Yet she endured. In the end the government had to yield, promising that the IOB report would soon be completed and that most of it would be made public. Meanwhile, a police artist had worked closely with her to develop sketches of her two Guatemalan abductors and of the North American who had come to her cell. The frightening images of those faces went out around the world. In turn, more than one hundred members of Congress signed onto a letter of support for her cause. She had forced the issue back into the public eye and, fragile but determined, she returned home to rest at last.

The IOB report was released in June of 1996, and to no one's surprise it evaded all major issues. While confirming that the CIA operated a large network of well-paid assets and liaisons, including known torturers, and that CIA reporting to Congress about human rights abuses had been evasive to the point of deception, the report stopped short of the obvious. No specific finding of intentional participation or collusion in torture or murder was included. In short, although abusive and even illegal practices were recognized de facto, CIA officials were carefully shielded from any criminal prosecutions.

Yet the genie could not be stuffed back into the bottle. As the world grew to know and love Sister Dianna through her appearances, interviews, and public statements, the questions as to her credibility simply vanished. No one could hear her and doubt the truthfulness of her story, or the clarity of her gentle mind. The official "questions" began to sound downright foolish if not sinister. Eventually, a photograph of a CIA agent who had worked in Guatemala at the time of Sister Dianna's abduction found its way into our hands. We compared it to a sketch of the North American drawn by the professional artist for Sister Dianna long before. The resemblance is startling, despite CIA claims that the agent was out of the country that day.

Most telling of all, however, are the voices of other survivors. Most of the "*desaparecidos*," or "disappeared," of Latin America did not live to tell their stories; like Everardo, they lie in unmarked graves across the continent. Those who did survive spent many years in hiding or on the run. Moreover, they too had to somehow work through the devastating trauma that had been inflicted upon them. Irked by the official refusal to openly admit the truth about Dianna's case, I turned to the tools of my own trade, lawyering. I began my own slow investigation, reading old files and testimonies and contacting longtime friends throughout the Latin American human rights network.

Disturbing but clear patterns began to emerge. One by one, survivors began to surface and tell us that yes, strange North Americans had entered their torture cells, too. Yes, a "gringo" had observed the wounds inflicted during the "interrogations," but no, he had not offered any help. In some cases the American spoke good Spanish, in some cases very poor, but always with a marked U.S. accent. Sometimes he asked the questions himself, and sometimes he even supervised the torture. Always he had authority over the torturers. Always he simply left the victim to his or her fate.

I began to keep files, startled by how often this had in fact occurred, and the significance of the testimonies. The CIA officials had long insisted that their agents had never knowingly supported or in any way been involved in torture. Individual agents caught in public human rights scandals were quickly written off as a few "bad apples" or "rogue operators" or even "mercenaries." This had been the immediate response in Everardo's case. Moreover, while it was admitted that information is and must be purchased from "unsavory characters," CIA spokespersons vehemently denied that its agents ever knowingly paid for information extracted through torture. Yet the more I heard from the survivors, the more it seemed that exactly such a direct collaboration was in fact a standard operating procedure for the CIA. Agents were not simply purchasing information from unsavory characters, they were wandering in and out of the torture cells and handing out cash. In short, their actions transgressed the boundaries between acceptable intelligence gathering and outright criminal conduct. Like any lawyer, I kept on asking questions and I kept on reading.

Gradually, the scandal over the cases of Everardo and Sister Dianna simply dissipated. There were no further hearings and the press moved on to other stories. The declassification of other U.S. files concerning human rights violations in Central America slowed. Sources inside the CIA reported that the new policies were having little real effect and that authorization had not once been denied for the hiring of assets, no matter what their backgrounds. I filed a civil suit against various U.S. officers, including implicated members of the CIA, only to encounter endless legal loopholes providing them with protections quite unavailable to any other government officials.[4]

Nonetheless, remarkable advances were taking place in the field of human rights. Sister Dianna started a new organization, the Torture Abolition and Survivor Support Coalition (TASSC),[5] and was leading international efforts to abolish torture and to assist and empower the survivors. General Pinochet was arrested in Britain on charges of war crimes carried out in Chile, and international tribunals were convened to hear the cases of "ethnic cleansing" from Bosnia and Rwanda. At long last, the Convention Against Torture was ratified and put into effect by the United States. In 2000, the Inter-American Court on Human Rights of the OAS issued a lengthy and unanimous ruling in Everardo's case against the Guatemalan government, holding that his status as a URNG commander in no way negated his fundamental rights. Meanwhile, various international truth commissions published blistering reports on the "dirty wars" from around the world. The report on Guatemala, for example, found the military responsible for genocide and for 93 percent of the war crimes that had occurred, including 200,000 civilian murders and "disappearances" and 660 massacres.[6] One by one, the generals of Central America found themselves facing civil suits in the United States, brought by their own victims under the Alien Tort Claims Act. It began to look as though fundamental human rights, long relegated to mere political lip service, might at last become an enforceable reality.

Then came the horrors of the September 11 attacks on the World Trade Center. As we watched, appalled, from our offices and living rooms around the globe, human beings waved for help from high above the inferno, then leaped one after another to their deaths far below. Members of the police and fire department, showing extraordinary valor, rushed into the blazing buildings hoping to rescue at least some of the thousands trapped within. Then, amid the shrieks from the people still on the streets, the towers came crashing downward in a cloud of smoke, debris, shoes, shreds of paper, and office furniture. In the grim silence that followed, a few survivors staggered through the choking dust, cloaked in white like specters from Pompeii. Of those inside, only their haunting last words remained, transported in those final moments to the cell phones of relatives left behind.

These brutal images will be with us for the rest of our lives. They should be, but we must take care to learn the right lessons from them. As I walked through a New York train station not long afterwards, I could hardly stand to look at the photographs of the missing lining the walls, placed there by frantic relatives still searching the morgues and hospitals. The faces were of bright and interesting human beings, playing with their children, hiking in the woods, smiling up from their busy desks. They brought back too many memories, though, of Guatemala and so many other countries; the mothers of the "disappeared" filling the streets and plazas, sobbing and holding up pictures of loved ones they could not bear to live without. I had known that pain myself since 1992 and did not wish to be reminded. Now the agony had arrived in New York City.

All too swiftly the public reaction in this country turned to rage, justifiable enough, but also dangerous. These were the times when lynch mobs, vigilantism, and government excess were all too likely a response. Sadly, that response was not long in coming. The requirements of our laws, treaties, and religious tenets exist to hold us firmly within civilized boundaries during just such an emotional crisis. But could they hold us here in the United States?

The answer was no. Although hate killings by the people themselves were mercifully few, our government officials, in the mad scramble for national security and revenge, began to toss aside some of the nation's most time-honored principles of human rights and civil liberties. Despite the memories of the internment of Japanese Americans during World War II, many innocent people with connections to the Middle East were dragged from their homes and imprisoned for prolonged and frightening interrogations. Prisoners captured in Afghanistan were taken to Guantánamo to be held indefinitely and without any legal charges, contact with attorneys, or hearings. As for the benefits of the Geneva Conventions, we were hastily assured that they were not "deserved" by terrorists.[7] Many urged that John Walker Lindh, the "American Taliban," should be shot despite his obvious youth and the utter lack of evidence linking him to the September 11 attacks.

Together with so many others, Sister Dianna and I listened in horror while leaders in the Bush administration made it clear that basic human rights would take a back seat to all defense efforts at home and abroad. Many officials and respected jurists, including

Professor Alan Dershowitz, suggested that torture, abhorred in this country since the drafting of our Constitution, was in fact legal, or should be.[8] Again and again the press bombarded us with stories about the "ticking bomb"—cases in which the world was saved from a massive explosion because heroic agents were willing to carry out torture when it was needed. As it turned out, all of these stories were merely hypothetical, and such a situation had never actually occurred. However, this was never made clear, and the story terrorized the public much as Orson Welles's "War of the Worlds" broadcast did so long ago.

Meanwhile, within days of September 11, high-level administration leaders were naming me in the press, stating that my campaign against torture had somehow prevented the CIA from gathering the needed intelligence to prevent the attacks.[9] For several months, when journalists asked if the disaster in fact represented the worst intelligence failure in United States history, CIA officials would point to me and other human rights activists, insisting that we had tied their hands. The ban on racial profiling was yet another scapegoat, used to explain the failure to arrest and question obvious suspects. Later, of course, it would become all too clear that voluminous information about the pending attacks had long been received by the FBI, the CIA, and other agencies, but never properly coordinated or analyzed.[10] Worse yet, agency whistleblowers recounted their desperate efforts to get information through the red tape to higher officials, only to find themselves blocked outright.[11] Mere weeks before the disaster a bulletin entitled "Al-Qaeda Determined to Attack Inside the United States" was circulated, but it received no urgent attention.[12] In short, there had been enough information but too little intelligence.

Clearly, the war on terror was about to proceed on two fronts, one in Afghanistan against al-Qaeda and the Taliban, the other at home, against human rights activists and immigrants. Members of Congress, fearing to appear "soft on terror," passed the rather draconian Patriot Act without a struggle. The longtime ban on assassinations abroad was lifted, as President Bush called for Osama Bin Laden to be captured dead or alive. Chillingly, there was little discussion as to how serious an effort should be made to seize him alive and bring him to a fair trial. Next to go was the rather weak CIA policy requiring agents to notify their superiors when hiring assets known for human rights violations. Good intelligence gathering, the agency declared, required working with unsavory characters. Intriguingly, anonymous insiders from the CIA spoke out, noting that no requests to work with such persons had ever been denied under the policy, and that in fact it promoted internal communications and discipline. Their words went unheeded.

Meanwhile, the real issue behind the "unsavory character" question was never addressed at all. There can be little argument that information could properly be purchased from an Al Qaeda member willing to report, in return for a small fee, on a plan to hijack another jet or to poison a public water supply. However, a very different and serious question is also raised here. Specifically, should CIA agents be permitted, on a routine basis, to provide a large sum of money and a cattle prod to a known torturer, then ask him to "interrogate" the prisoner across the hall? The first situation prevents terror while the second promotes it. Yet our intelligence leaders, in their appeals to the public, carefully concealed the one behind the other.

As members of our intelligence and defense networks boasted openly that the "gloves were off" in the war on terror, and that torture had become a necessary evil, Sister Dianna and I could only shake our heads in disbelief. Our national principles of human rights were hurtling backwards in time, past the framing of the Bill of Rights and the Constitution and into the era of the Star Chamber, the rack, and the screw.

Demonstrators in Pakistan held up banners, asking if we Americans knew why we were so hated throughout the world. President Bush was quick to respond. It was merely envy, he said; others were jealous of our flourishing democracy. Meanwhile, and somehow without a blink, administration leaders declared that anyone questioning the U.S. government was "un-American," a phrase all too reminiscent of the embarrassing McCarthy era. As pressure built to expand the war into Iraq, many experts on the Middle East warned that such an invasion could be perceived as an attack on the Islamic world. This would increase hatred against the United States and result in other long-term consequences for both the war and national security. The administration did not listen. Our soldiers would be greeted with flowers by cheering crowds as soon as Saddam Hussein was gone. We had only to show how tough we were, to use our weapons of "shock and awe," and all would be well again.

Show the world we did, hurling a rain of deadly firepower into the streets of Baghdad at the cost of untold numbers of civilian lives. Our stated justification, the existence of weapons of mass destruction, turned out to be baseless, but even now the war in Iraq rages onward. To be sure, for a few sweet days there were many Iraqis who, delighted with the overthrow of Saddam Hussein, flocked into the streets to topple his statues and throw blossoms to U.S. troops. Today, a growing number of Iraqis throw bombs instead.

Why has such a change occurred? In part, of course, because no nation enjoys bombardment, military defeat, and occupation by a foreign army, and that is precisely the reality in Iraq. To make matters worse, our claimed justification of nuclear and biological weapons turned out to be false, and we have shown utter disregard for the Iraqi people by failing to plan for the aftermath of Saddam Hussein's defeat. Instead we left them to suffer chaos and the lack of basic living requirements such as water, electricity, and medical supplies.

Another reason for the growing rage against us, however, is clearly reflected in the photographs from Abu Ghraib, which depict the sexual humiliation and physical torture of Iraqi prisoners by U.S. soldiers. Since the inception of the wars in Afghanistan and Iraq, human rights organizations had been denouncing the frightening and excessive methods used in carrying out arrests and seizures. The photographs revealed what had long been hinted at by our own officials: our intelligence agents were using torture to interrogate the detainees. This harsh reality has been repeatedly confirmed by an ever increasing number of survivors, witnesses, and government files. If such tactics were used against our own people by an occupying force, we would no doubt respond in exactly the same way. We would be outraged and we would fight back.

The Bush administration has insisted that torture is indeed both un-American and forbidden by our laws and treaties. Our national leaders have also insisted that the abuses were merely the individual actions of a few low-level soldiers, not the result of any official policy. For those of us who remember precisely the same torture practices from Latin America, this assertion rings hollow indeed.[13] The distinction is an important one. If the abuses were indeed cases of individual excess, then the court-martial and imprisonment of the few soldiers involved is adequate. But if the torture techniques really were a standard operating procedure for intelligence work, authorized and ordered by high-level officials, then persons like Secretary of Defense Donald Rumsfeld must also stand trial. Otherwise a secret and illegal policy remains in force, and our servicemen and -women are serving jail sentences alone for simply following orders.

This issue raises more than moral and legal questions. Our leaders have repeatedly asserted that harsh methods are necessary to keep our citizens safe during the "war against terror." However, the broad use of torture and humiliation by our own intelligence agencies also creates serious national security problems. These horrific practices obviously foment rage and hatred against the United States, and the consequences are already evident. Sadly, our young servicemen and -women bear the brunt. Not only must they face the ever growing number of deadly suicide attacks against them, they now also face the possibility of torture should they fall captive. By casting aside the Geneva Conventions, we have stripped our own troops of crucial protections as well. Moreover, we have endangered our own citizenry. By fomenting hatred against us, these policies have greatly increased the risk of future attacks in the United States.

The time has come for us to think carefully about these issues. It is certainly tempting, when faced with such complex and frightening questions, to continue with our daily lives and "leave things to the experts." In the end, however, this is our government, and torture is being utilized in our names and supported by our tax dollars. We are responsible. We must become informed, weigh the issues carefully, and take a stand. Our decisions will determine our collective future.

TRUTH, TORTURE, AND THE AMERICAN WAY

CHAPTER ONE

THE FALL OF ABU GHRAIB

As the grim photographs of the prisoner abuse at Abu Ghraib came to light, the public reaction across the United States was one of near universal outrage. This furious response was appropriate, and it was heartening to see that our national values could withstand the test of fear, at least at the grass-roots level. The constitutional standard for acceptable official conduct is whether or not the actions would shock the conscience of the American people. Faced with the images of frightening dogs, battered and naked prisoners, and leering guards, the U.S. public gave a loud and clear response to the question of acceptability: "Hell, no!"

In the end, however, we must share some of the blame for the human rights violations that occurred. Appalling as the photographs were, not one of us should have been surprised. Our national leaders and officials had long been telling us outright that the detainees were being tortured. True enough, sanitized language was used in order to keep the abuses in our peripheral vision and prevent public protest. Moreover, access to the prisoners was nearly impossible for journalists and human rights networks alike. Nevertheless, the press for the most part failed to ask the obvious questions or to challenge evasive or egregious official statements. Bland assertions that interrogation techniques stopped "just short" of torture, for example, were simply accepted at face value. But we must also face the fact that most U.S. citizens simply did not want to see or hear the obvious. Frightened and searching for personal safety, the public chose to avert its eyes.

The signs were clear enough from the very beginning. As *Washington Post* journalist Dana Priest concluded after her interviews with U.S. officials, "The picture that emerges is of a brass-knuckled quest for information, often in concert with allies of dubious human rights reputation, in which the traditional lines between right and wrong, legal and inhumane, are evolving and blurred." Priest reports that Cofer Black, then head of the CIA's Counterterrorist Center, told the House and Senate Intelligence Committees that the agency had new "operational flexibility" in dealing with detainees, and that after September 11, the "gloves came off." Other officials openly discussed the "extraordinary rendition" procedures by which a captured suspect was transferred, together with a list of questions from the CIA, to a third country known for its brutal interrogation methods. As one agent noted, "We don't kick the (expletive deleted) out of them. We send them to other countries so they can kick the (expletive deleted) out of them." The use of "stress and duress," such as painful positions and sleep deprivation, was openly admitted. So was the selective use of painkillers for prisoners like Abu Zubaida, who had been shot through the groin during his capture. As one official source stated grimly, "Pain control is a very subjective thing."[1]

Quite apart from such sinister comments, concrete evidence of torture by U.S. intelligence agents began to mount. Yet public outcry remained quite weak.

THE PRISONER MASSACRE OF KONDUZ, AFGHANISTAN

Early on, *Newsweek* journalists reported the discovery of a large mass grave located in Afghanistan, where numerous prisoners of war lay buried. The victims were Taliban and al-Qaeda members who had surrendered at Konduz after fierce battles with the combined Northern Alliance and U.S. forces. Under the orders of General Dostum they had been transported to the Sheberghan prison in sealed metal containers. During the long journey they received no food or water, and the containers had no ventilation openings.

Crowded together, the prisoners began to die of dehydration and suffocation. Some drivers, hearing the screams, punched small air holes in the walls and passed through water. Others would have done the same, but they were beaten or otherwise prevented by the guards. One driver reported that when his container truck was finally opened, all 200 of the prisoners inside were dead: "They opened the doors and the dead bodies spilled out like fish." According to the Afghan Organization of Human Rights, more than a thousand prisoners died in this manner.[2]

Disturbing questions about the U.S. role in this massacre have never been adequately answered. U.S. Special Forces, specifically the 595 A-team, were certainly involved in the fierce fighting in that area and were working closely with General Dostum and the Afghan troops. They were together at the Konduz negotiations and at the surrender at Yerganak. According to one spokesperson cited in *Newsweek*, American soldiers were constantly at Dostum's side during the entire period. Significantly, the source also noted that but for the earlier uprising at Qala-i-Jangi prison, during which CIA agent Mike Spann was killed, the prisoners might have been transferred more "peacefully." Other sources reported that a U.S. intelligence team in full combat gear had received and screened the prisoners, including John Walker Lindh, as they arrived at Sheberghan prison. An Afghan translator for the U.S. forces, Said Vasiqullah Sadat, admitted that he had quickly heard of the container deaths. While evasive as to just what he told the Americans, he states, "I think they found out soon. They were at Sheberghan prison from the very beginning."[3]

Newsweek approached this issue cautiously, noting that U.S. personnel were in the prison when the trucks arrived, but "probably" did not watch as they were unloaded. An explanation from U.S. officials was also sought. However, according to the journalists, Pentagon, Defense, and administration, officials either evaded the questions raised or made false statements in response.[4]

It would seem impossible, however, that the highly trained U.S.

intelligence officials present at the prison knew nothing of a thousand prisoners arriving dead and tumbling out of the containers. This is especially difficult to credit in light of the fact that U.S. agents were themselves using such containers. John Walker Lindh, for example, was held in a shipping container by U.S. forces.[5] Moreover, the CIA was also using containers to hold prisoners under punitive conditions in Afghanistan.[6] This is a rather stark reality since it was well known that such containers were used in the past as an instrument of torture and mass murder in Afghanistan.[7] Certainly a number of very serious legal questions as to joint responsibility are raised by this case. Yet even now, long after the scandal and investigation of prisoner abuse at Abu Ghraib, the massacre has never been properly investigated or explained.

THE CASE OF JOHN WALKER LINDH

The treatment of John Walker Lindh, the "American Taliban," should have served as yet another warning to the U.S. public. The twenty-one-year-old from Marin County had become deeply involved in Islam, eventually ending up in a military camp in Afghanistan where he was trained to fight the Northern Alliance. He arrived at the front lines only a week before September 11, knowing nothing in advance of the World Trade Center attacks and receiving only sketchy information after they occurred. As American forces arrived in the country, his unit was caught up in the ferocious battles near Konduz. The survivors, including Lindh, tried to flee, but they were poorly provisioned. One third of their members died along the trails,[8] and in the end they surrendered to General Dostum. Believing they would be freed, they were instead herded into the basement of the Qala-i-Jangi prison in late November 2001.

John Lindh, emaciated and bound, was soon detected by CIA agents Mike Spann and Dave Tyson, who tried to interrogate him. They were interrupted by a spontaneous mass uprising of the other prisoners, who apparently feared for their lives. Tyson escaped,

Spann was killed, and Lindh was shot through the leg during the battle. After feigning death for nearly twelve hours, he was dragged back to the basement with the other survivors. For a week they remained there while Northern Alliance members threw grenades into the basement, then flaming diesel fuel, and finally freezing water, which drowned many. Of the original three hundred prisoners, only eighty-five survived to surrender, including John Lindh.[9]

Lindh was then transferred to Sheberghan prison, where he was immediately separated from the others by U.S. Special Forces personnel. His ordeal did not come to an end, however. Although he was given basic medical care, including morphine, a decision was made by the U.S. agents to leave the bullet in his leg. Even in this condition, he was interrogated by the agents. He was later hooded, bound, and taken to a separate facility at Mazar-i-Sharif. There his intensive questioning continued with the bullet remaining in his leg, the wound becoming, according to his attorneys, "seeping and malodorous."[10] On December 7 he was blindfolded again, and in an eerie preview of the Abu Ghraib abuses, the soldiers scrawled the word "shithead" across the blindfold and posed with him for photographs. They also threatened to kill him. His hands were then cuffed so tightly he suffered extreme pain, and he was transported to Camp Rhino. He was bound to a stretcher with duct tape and placed in a metal shipping container about fifteen feet long, seven feet wide, and eight feet high. The interrogations continued despite his request for a lawyer. Moreover, the lawyer his father had hired was not permitted access. Lindh suffered greatly from the cold and the tight bindings. It was not until December 15 that he had surgery for his wounds, and the bullet in his leg was removed.[11]

Although Attorney General John Ashcroft attempted to charge John Lindh with a number of high-level criminal acts, in the end there was simply no evidence to link him to Mr. Spann's death or to the planning of the World Trade Center attacks. Instead, Lindh finally agreed to plead guilty to aiding the Taliban, and all remaining government charges were dropped. In return, the officials nervously insisted that he relinquish all claims of official mistreatment and abuse.[12] Although the case certainly signaled that very serious misconduct was taking place, there were few questions asked on the Hill, and even less outcry from the public.

THE EXTRAORDINARY RENDITION OF MAHER ARAR

Yet another warning sounded with the "extraordinary rendition" of Maher Arar, a Canadian citizen of Syrian birth. On September 26, 2002, Mr. Arar was returning home from a brief family vacation in Tunis. He was attempting to change flights at Kennedy International Airport when he was seized by U.S. officials. He was searched, fingerprinted, and subjected to intense interrogation, in particular about his Syrian-Canadian friends, including a Mr. Abdullah Almalki. When he asked to speak with a lawyer, or even to make a phone call, he was told he had no such rights. After five days he was permitted to contact his mother-in-law and to meet with a Canadian consular officer and an attorney. They promised to help, but he was abruptly deported, not to Canada, where he had lived since his teens, but to Syria. There he was held for the next ten months.[13]

After hours of questioning by Syrian intelligence agents when he arrived, Mr. Arar was taken to his cell, which was six feet long, three feet wide, and seven feet tall, with a heavy metal door. Faint light came through a small opening in the ceiling. He called it "the grave." Throughout the first two weeks of his imprisonment, he was beaten continuously and intensely. Often the interrogators used electrical cables to whip him across his entire body, leaving deep blue marks. Many blows were directed to the sensitive palms of his hands. During other sessions they beat him with their fists. Often they would place him in a "waiting room" between beatings, allowing him to spend long periods listening to the screams of other prisoners. They asked him again and again about his friends and relatives, pressing him to confess that he had trained in Afghanistan. To stop the torture, he finally "confessed" although he had never been to that country. On October 23, he received his first

6

consular visit. The guards nervously warned him not to speak of the beatings. Out of fear he held his tongue. Over the next many months he thought he would go mad.[14]

In August, Maher Arar was forced to sign a lengthy statement, as dictated by a Syrian investigator. When he protested the contents, he was kicked. He decided to simply sign and was taken to the Sednaya prison. He had lost nearly forty pounds and had not seen sunlight in many months. At Sednaya he saw his friend Abdullah Almalki, who had been held in a similar "grave" and very severely tortured.[15] Thanks to Mr. Arar's wife, who had carried out a remarkable battle to rescue him, he was released and returned to Canada in October 2003. He had not seen his children for a year, his good name was in tatters, and he suffers still from unspeakable nightmares.[16]

In the glare of the publicity accompanying his release, U.S. officials scrambled to justify their actions. Conspiracy to commit torture is, after all, a serious crime,[17] and Maher Arar's deportation to Syria, as opposed to Canada, was approved by a top Justice Department official.[18] Although one anonymous source insisted that Mr. Arar had the names of many al-Qaeda members in his pockets, this has never been substantiated.[19] Moreover, according to Mr. Moustapha, a high-level Syrian diplomat, the U.S. never presented any such evidence. Indeed, the Syrian intelligence officials were unable to confirm any of the U.S. accusations while Mr. Arar was in their custody. Although they carried out their own investigation, they found nothing.[20] Nor had Syria requested the extradition of Mr. Arar; indeed, they had never heard of him until the United States deported him to their country. Significantly, the interrogation there focused on matters of interest to the U.S., such as al-Qaeda supporters and activities, and not his lack of military service in Syria or his Sunni background.

Other U.S. officials claimed that Mr. Arar was deported only upon assurances from Syria that he would not be tortured.[21] However, this seems rather disingenuous, since the State Department has often denounced the use of torture in Syria.[22] Moreover, if torture was not the U.S. objective, why was Maher Arar sent on a costly flight to Syria instead of simply returned to Canada, where he held citizenship?[23]

Disturbingly, Mr. Arar's case is hardly unique, although he is one of the very few to return to the West to speak out and demand justice. Rather, his experiences fit squarely within the "extraordinary rendition" practices that U.S. officials have admitted are now in effect.[24] This practice permits suspects and detainees to be transferred from the United States, or from their home countries, to third nations known for their brutal interrogation methods, such as Jordan, Egypt, Morocco, and Syria. Often the prisoners are turned over by U.S. agents together with a list of questions compiled by the CIA.[25] Although a clear violation of U.S. law, the practice was apparently authorized by a secret directive signed by President Bush shortly after the September 11 attacks.[26]

CIA participation in these cases varies, with U.S. agents sometimes observing the interrogation sessions through two-way mirrors and sometimes receiving summaries of the information gleaned. According to *Newsweek,* much of what the CIA knows of al-Qaeda comes from other intelligence services which do not observe "democratic niceties," and the CIA keeps a pipeline to the secret police in various Middle Eastern countries "well lubricated with large amounts of cash."[27] Although some officials insist they only send detainees to countries where they are "wanted," others admit that "sometimes a friendly country can be made to 'want' someone we grab." As acknowledged by yet another official with direct involvement in these renditions, "I do it with my eyes open."[28]

According to intelligence sources, more than a hundred terror suspects have been transported from their homelands to Middle Eastern nations known for their use of torture.[29] This includes two men who were seized and handed over to hooded Americans in Sweden's Stockholm airport. The agents cut off the men's clothing, sedated them, chained them, then placed them on a jet to Cairo, where they were tortured.[30] Similarly, Mamdou Habib, an Australian citizen, was seized and brutalized in Pakistan by interrogators with U.S. accents, then flown to Egypt where he, too, was severely tortured. He was eventually transferred to Guantánamo.[31] One U.S. official explained, "The temptation is to have these folks in other hands because they have different standards."[32]

These matters raise grave legal questions. The U.N. Convention against Torture, which has been ratified by the United States, flatly prohibits the deportation of any person to a nation where he or she might face torture. U.S. criminal laws, moreover, make it a felony punishable by up to twenty years in prison for any U.S. official to conspire to torture a person abroad.[33] The actions of U.S. officials in the Maher Arar and other extraordinary rendition cases more than meet the legal definitions of both civil and criminal conspiracy. Yet there has been no serious official investigation of Maher Arar's case, and the Bush administration defends and continues the practice of extraordinary renditions.

TORTURE AND DEATH IN AFGHANISTAN AND IRAQ

Prisoners in U.S. custody abroad did not fare much better. Early on, it was difficult to evaluate their treatment, since access to the press, human rights organizations, and even attorneys was fiercely obstructed by U.S. officials. In a number of off-limit detention centers like certain bases in Afghanistan, or the Diego Garcia interrogation center, the U.S. even denied access to the International Committee of the Red Cross for some time.[34] Nonetheless, there were many warnings that were all too quickly overlooked and forgotten.

In 2002, knowledgeable sources of the *Washington Post's* admitted that newly captured prisoners of the U.S. forces were being beaten, confined to tiny rooms, blindfolded, thrown against walls, bound in painful positions,[35] subjected to loud noises, and deprived of sleep.[36] Some prisoners were stripped and doused with cold water in chill weather.[37] In Iraq, for example, Khraisan Al Aballi was stripped naked, hooded, kept awake for more than a week, and forced to either stand or kneel. He begged to die.[38] His brother Dureid, captured with him, had not returned home many months later. As noted earlier, when Abu Zubaida was apprehended in Pakistan, he suffered a bullet wound in the groin and was selectively denied painkillers as part of his interrogation process.[39]

In one particularly disturbing case, a prisoner's two elementary-school-aged children were also captured and reportedly held within American military "access."[40] Were they harmed? Was their father threatened with their death or injury? Either of such actions would be unlawful. Although these questions have not been answered, it was later learned that an Iraqi general was forced to watch his seventeen-year-old son shivering uncontrollably. The boy had been soaked in water and mud by U.S. agents, then exposed to extreme cold in order to "soften up" his father.[41]

In other early cases, it was revealed that detainees had been killed outright by their U.S. interrogators. In December 2002, two Afghan men were detained at Bagram Air Base and died after ten days in custody. Official reports indicate that the cause of death was a blood clot in the lungs of one and a heart attack caused by a clot for the other.[42] An American pathologist found that the men died of blunt trauma, ruling the cause of death in both cases to be homicide.[43] A third Afghan prisoner died in June 2003 of unexplained causes.[44] An official investigation was promised, but as months dragged on, no explanations were provided.

A grim report of another obvious murder was made by a young Afghan American immigrant. Eighteen-year-old Hyder Akbar of the San Francisco Bay area had gone to visit his father in Afghanistan during the summer of 2003. While he was there, word went out that a certain Abdul Wali was a terror suspect and should be captured and turned over to the Americans. The Akbars located the frightened man and, firmly believing in American justice, convinced him to turn himself in and simply tell the truth. To Hyder's shock, when they returned to the U.S. base a few days later, Mr. Wali was dead. The Americans claimed he had struck his own head against the wall.[45] This story on its face was ridiculous, and, as noted by young Hyder, made the "good guys" look very bad indeed. Moreover, U.S. officials were already admitting that prisoners were being beaten and thrown into walls by MPs. Yet no autopsy was performed, and this case, for a while, slipped into oblivion.[46]

In response to these startling reports, administration and Defense officials repeatedly promised investigations but curtly reminded everyone that such matters required time and patience, especially during times of war. Matters faded from the press and from public awareness.

The human rights network, on the other hand, was far from silent. Legal defense networks were battling the government through the courts, insisting on the detainees' rights to a hearing and to counsel. The International Committee of the Red Cross, albeit in private, was vehemently protesting to U.S. officials. Despite the formidable obstacles, human rights organizations like Amnesty International, Human Rights Watch, and Human Rights First published report after report, documenting U.S. abuses as best they could and demanding a halt to the use of torture.[47] As the outcry mounted, President Bush finally denounced both torture and cruel and degrading punishment on June 26, 2003, the International Day in Support of the Survivors of Torture.[48] Those words would come back to haunt him soon enough.

THE ABU GHRAIB REVELATIONS AND BEYOND

The scandal over prisoner abuse at Abu Ghraib burst forth after the riveting broadcast by *60 Minutes* on April 28, 2004.[49] The program was swiftly followed by massive press coverage. Photographs were published showing the naked, bound, and hooded prisoners with electrodes attached to their bodies, piled into human pyramids, terrorized by dogs, forced to masturbate or wear women's underclothes or to pose in simulated or actual homosexual acts. Leering U.S soldiers, male and female, stood nearby pointing and giving the thumbs-up sign.

Such actions, shocking enough in Western cultures, were both unthinkable and sacrilegious in traditional Muslim societies. As one military officer stated, "We will be paid back for this."[50] His words proved to be prophetic. Nicholas Berg was beheaded a few days later, specifically in retaliation for the Abu Ghraib violations. Meanwhile, rage swept the Islamic world. As Abu Ahmad, who had personally suffered the abuses at Abu Ghraib, told the *New York Times*, "The Americans are an occupation force, not liberators, and we should fight to drive them out."[51]

The abuses were not limited to psychological fear or gross humiliation. Many of the photographs show severe physical assaults and battery by U.S. guards. In one image, a naked man lay bleeding after a dog attack. Ensuing reports disclosed that chemical lights were broken and the liquid poured over one prisoner, while another was sodomized with either the light or a broom. Many detainees were slammed headfirst against the walls. Hayder Abd suffered a broken jaw during just such a session.[52] Two prisoners were photographed dead and bloodied. According to one soldier, a prisoner was punched in the chest so hard he went into cardiac arrest. Other prisoners were held in tiny cells and denied access to toilets for days on end. General Taguba, who was asked to investigate the Abu Ghraib situation, found "sadistic, blatant, and wanton criminal abuses."[53]

Members of Congress were shown eighteen hundred additional photographs and videos not made available to the public, depicting yet worse abuses. They emerged shaken and ashen from the room.[54]

As access to the prisoners was at last obtained, more details of the tortures emerged, including the affidavit of a prisoner forced to curse his religion after guards struck him on his broken leg.[55] New photographs showed a hooded man, his head held in the arms of a beefy MP about to deliver a powerful blow to the man's face. They are surrounded by other hooded prisoners lying limp on the floor.

Predictably, President Bush and his administration officials scurried to declare the abuses to be "un-American" and the work of a handful of bad apples, in this case a few poorly trained MPs. The systematic use of torture or other abuses was fiercely denied, and the young servicemen and -women in the photographs quickly found themselves in the traditional role of government scapegoats, facing court-martials alone. While they admitted to abusing the prisoners, they also insisted that they had simply been following the orders of higher-level intelligence officials, both CIA and military, who were in charge of actual interrogations.[56] It was swiftly confirmed that the use of frightening dogs was approved by military intelligence officials.[57] As stated to *Newsweek* by one torture specialist, the hooded man on the box with cables attached to his finger, toes, and penis was the victim of a well-known and long-standing torture method called "the Vietnam" by experts in interrogation.[58] " 'Was that something that an [MP] dreamed up herself? Think again. That's a standard torture. . . . But it's not common knowledge. Ordinary American soldiers did this but someone taught them.' " Many lawmakers viewing the additional films and photographs agreed.[59]

Sadly, when defense attorneys sought to locate the CIA and intelligence officials on duty during the periods of abuse, they found the logs poorly kept, with the officials often signing in with rather sarcastic names like "James Bond" and "John Doe."[60] Once again, the intelligence officials had done the dirty work through intermediaries, then quietly slipped into the shadows when the time came to face justice.

Torture and interrogation specialists were not the only ones who found the photographs to be rather familiar. On the other side of the world, Latin American survivors were suffering from chilling memories of precisely the same abuses. Sister Dianna Ortiz and Honduran citizen Ines Murillo remembered all too well being terrorized by vicious dogs during their captivity. They remembered more than that. Ines's shoulder joints were permanently injured by the agonizing hours she spent hanging in "uncomfortable positions." Sister Dianna winced at the memory of her tormentors filming her torture, laughing, and threatening her with future blackmail.

The MPs were not simply being foolish in taking those photographs. It was part of the psychological torture inflicted, a standard intelligence-gathering technique. As noted by U.S. senator John Warner, "They staged those photographs, which I understand were going to be shown to the prisoner's families by way of threats unless he came forward with some valuable information."[61]

All of the Latin American torture survivors also remembered the hoods, the constant beatings, the nakedness, the electrodes, and the rapes and sexual humiliations as well. Browsing through my old files from my time in Central America, I found sketches depicting the tortures endured by prisoners at Mariona, in El Salvador during the 1980s. The drawings, posted at www.tassc.org, show naked men, in frightening hoods, hanging limply from metal bars; they are indistinguishable from the photographs from Iraq. Worse yet, these same memories were shared by the core group of survivors I had interviewed earlier, following up on the cases of Sister Dianna and Everardo. The survivors not only recognized the torture techniques at Abu Ghraib, they also remembered the North American intelligence officials standing in their cells, sometimes asking questions, sometimes giving orders, and sometimes even laughing.[62] All of us remembered the prompt official story about rogue operators and bad apples. We had heard it all before, together with the promises of intensive investigations and serious reforms. Obviously, these had never taken place.

Nevertheless, the low-level MPs remained the only ones facing actual jail time. Surprisingly, they received support from one of their own prisoners, Mr. Saddam Saleh Aboud. Noticing what he thought might be a bomb in a parked car, twenty-nine-year-old Mr. Aboud had reported what he saw to the Iraqi police, only to be arrested and turned over to the Americans at Abu Ghraib. He was stripped, hooded, beaten, urinated on, and left with his arms and legs tied together behind him in the excruciating "scorpion" position. He had also been chained to the bars of his cell for twenty-three hours and forced to urinate on himself. A laughing MP threatened him with rape. Loud music was left on for hours at a time. Battered and exhausted, he admitted to anything he was asked in order to avoid more torture, once even confessing that he was Osama Bin Laden himself in disguise. Furious though he is, Mr. Aboud confirmed that the MPs seemed to be following orders, and that higher-up officials routinely visited, especially a military intelligence agent named "Steve" who told the others what to do. In the end, Mr. Aboud was released. Asked by a journalist if he planned to become an insurgent, he responded, "What would you do if I occupied your country, tortured people, and violated all the laws of your country? Would you resist me?"[63]

The report by Maj. Gen. Antonio M. Taguba confirmed that a civilian interrogator named Steven Stephanowicz was responsible for ordering MPs to use improper methods.[64] According to General Taguba, there were in fact two military intelligence officers as well as two civilian contractors involved in the prisoner abuse cases. He supported the MPs' claims that they were told by military and "other intelligence" officers (usually a reference to the CIA), to help "soften up" the prisoners for questioning.[65] General Taguba also cited direct abuses by military intelligence officers and members of the Joint Interrogation and Debriefing Center at the prison.

As the scope of the scandal and investigations broadened, the CIA and other intelligence networks became ever more deeply implicated. Early on, for example, it was disclosed that the CIA had utilized far harsher interrogation methods than the military, including a technique called "water-boarding." This practice consists of strapping the prisoner down and pushing him under water until, in the Machiavellian phrasing of the CIA, he is "made to believe he might drown."[66] Once again, the Latin American survivors had to cringe, as they all had firsthand experience with this technique. They had been held under water until they had in fact begun to drown and lost consciousness, only to be revived by their torturers and submerged again. It is one of their worst memories.

While admitting that the CIA tactics "simulated" torture, officials insisted that their agents had stopped short of any "serious injury." As the *New York Times* reported, however, the methods were so shocking that the FBI ordered its agents to stay out of any such interviews. Moreover, as the investigation intensified, many CIA officials became concerned about their own potential legal liability. Some of the methods approved by the CIA included hoodings, beatings, soaking the prisoners with water, and depriving them of food, light, sleep, and medications. Apparently, many of the torture techniques were taken from the training course for U.S. Special Operations soldiers, designed to prepare them for possible capture and torture by an enemy.[67] One of the techniques in the course is the water pit, in which prisoners must stand on tiptoe to avoid drowning.[68] On reading this I was struck again by a grim sense of déjà vu. The water pit was often used at the Retalhuleu military base in Guatemala, according to the Department of Defense reports on Everardo's case.[69] Did the death squads there just happen to think up the identical technique? Or did they learn it from the U.S. Special Ops forces? Apparently the CIA had also sought permission to utilize "mock burials," although the administration declined to comment on whether or not this technique was approved.[70]

The official assertions that the Abu Ghraib MPs were but a few bad apples was further eroded as the investigation continued, revealing the widespread use of similar torture and degradation throughout U.S. bases in both Iraq and Afghanistan. One prisoner in Iraq died when he was left gagged with his hands tied to the top of his cell door after being questioned by U.S. Special Forces. Another prisoner at a "secret" Baghdad facility died in the interrogation chair after a blow to the head.[71] Iraqi general Abed Mowhush was gagged, stuffed into a sleeping bag, and flipped rapidly back and forth. An interrogator then sat on his chest and covered his mouth. The prisoner died several days later, after the CIA handed him over to the military.[72] Later disclosures indicated that certain marines set fire to a prisoner's hands, carried out a mock execution of juveniles, and applied electrical shocks to others.[73] Similarly, Special Operations agents were reported to have used electrical shocks.[74] In some cases, lit cigarettes were inserted into the detainees' ears.[75]

Treatment of the detainees in Afghanistan was much the same. At one location, prisoners were kept in scorching hot shipping containers as a form of punishment.[76] The CIA's secret interrogation center in Kabul, Afghanistan, was called "the Pit" because of its terrible conditions.[77] Abdul Wali, who had fought the Soviets in Afghanistan and, as described above, had turned himself in for questioning at Hyder Akbar's urging, died in the hands of a CIA contractor from CACI.[78] Sayed Nabi Siddiqui was taken prisoner after he attempted to report police corruption. He too was battered, held naked, doused with cold water, humiliated, and photographed by the Americans at various bases. At one base he was crowded into a wire cage with twenty to thirty other prisoners, with only a bucket as a communal toilet.[79] His experiences were not unique. Eighteen-year-old Afghan citizen Jamal Naseer and his friends had been taken to a Special Operations base where they were hung upside down and beaten with cables, rubber hoses, and sticks. They were also immersed in cold water, forced to lie in the snow, and given electrical shocks. Naseer, severely bruised, died after complaining of abdominal pains.[80] Two other Afghan prisoners held with a Mr. Dilawar, similarly described their treatment at the Bagram compound. One had his hands chained to the ceiling for seven to eight days until they turned black. The other was kept naked and hooded, his legs shackled so tightly that the circulation was cut off and he could no longer walk. Mr. Dilawar, twenty-two years old, died.[81] It was later disclosed that his leg had been "pulpified" by some thirty blows from his U.S. interrogator.[82]

Conditions at Guantánamo were no better. As recent disclosures obtained by the ACLU show, prisoners were often placed in a chair, then chained hand and foot to a bolt in the floor ("short-shackled") and left for as long as twenty-four hours, while being blasted with strobe lights and loud music, subjected to severe cold and heat, and denied toilet privileges. According to one FBI agent, "On a couple of occasions, I entered interview rooms to find a detainee chained hand and foot in a fetal position to the floor, with no chair, food or water. Most times they had urinated or defecated on themselves and had been left there for 18, 24 hours or more."[83] One prisoner was found unconscious with most of his hair pulled out after one such session. These and other techniques were found tantamount to torture by the International Committee of the Red Cross.[84] Sleep deprivation, long-term solitary confinement, and frightening dogs were also utilized in Guantánamo.[85] Prisoners have reported being beaten while shackled and hooded, left in extreme heat and cold, denied needed medical care, subjected to prolonged and repeated rectal searches, and raped.[86] In one startling report, prisoners told of female interrogators violating Muslim tenets by rubbing against them and flinging what appeared to be menstrual blood in their faces.[87] Not so surprisingly, the CIA also ran a special "prison within a prison" at Guantánamo for high-level detainees. This is off-limits to almost everyone else at the base.[88]

Meanwhile, questions about the now notorious Abu Ghraib photograph of a dead and battered prisoner packed in ice were finally answered. Although the man died at the prison, the MPs were not his abusers. The victim, named "Jamadi," had been captured on November 4, 2003, by Seals Special Operations members working with the CIA. One of the Seals had struck him over the head with a rifle butt, then brought him to a CIA camp, and eventually to Abu Ghraib. There the prisoner was carefully kept from the prison registry, like many other CIA "ghost prisoners." He was hooded and left in a shower stall with two CIA agents, and was later found dead.[89] The agents then carried him out on a hospital gurney with a false IV in his arm, as if still alive.[90] Neither his name nor his death was ever recorded in the prison logs.

Perhaps most disturbing of all are the reports of the CIA's

"ghost prisoners" like Mr. Jamadi. As stated in a *Washington Post* exposé, "Although some of those held in Iraq, Afghanistan, and Guantanamo have had visits by the International Committee of the Red Cross, some of the CIA's detainees have in effect disappeared."[91] At Abu Ghraib, for example, such CIA prisoners were never registered and were intentionally moved around throughout the facility in order to prevent detection by the Red Cross and others. CIA officer Peter Probst insisted to journalists that such captures and secret detentions did not constitute kidnappings: "It has been going on for decades. It's absolutely legal."[92] This, of course, is news to any human rights attorney.[93]

The "ghost prisoner" practice was known and authorized at the very highest levels of the U.S. administration; in some cases the secret detention was even authorized by Secretary Rumsfeld himself.[94] Worse yet, the practice was apparently widespread. The U.S. Army, upon completion of its own investigation, reported eight documented cases of ghost prisoners. However, Gen. Paul J. Kern, who oversaw the inquiry, testified to the Senate Armed Services Committee that the total number was in fact "in the dozens, perhaps up to 100."[95] Senator John McCain, reacting to the news, declared, "The situation with the CIA and the ghost prisoners is beginning to look like a bad movie."[96] The real problem, of course, was that no records were kept on such detainees. Who they were, why they were taken prisoner, how they were treated, or if they are still alive, are questions that have remained unanswered. The CIA refused to cooperate with the army during the probe, announcing instead that it would carry out its own investigation. In short, these prisoners have joined the legions of *"desaparecidos"* in Latin America.

In May 2004 the *New York Times* reported that the U.S. military was investigating the deaths of thirty-seven detainees in U.S. custody, a far higher number than the original estimates. Although basic information, such as death certificates and autopsy reports, was missing in a number of cases, eleven homicides were under investigation: four were undetermined, with no autopsies performed, five were closed as justified homicides, and one, a "heat related" death, was ruled accidental.[97] By August 2004, an internal investigation by the military would note three hundred reported cases of abuse, with sixty-six confirmed at the time the report was published. By March 2005, the army would take initial steps to prosecute twenty-eight cases of suspected or confirmed homicides by U.S. personnel.[98]

HOW DID IT HAPPEN?

Out of the Abu Ghraib and ghost prisoner scandals came yet one more scandal, this time over the now notorious administration memos concerning the use of torture and the applicability of the Geneva Conventions. These were authored by none other than high-level attorneys within the Justice Department, the White House, the CIA, and the Defense Department. As stated by one official, "There are very specific guidelines that are thoroughly vetted. Everyone is on board. It's legal."[99] Many of us within the legal community beg to differ. The executive branch alone does not constitute the entire United States government, thanks to our system of checks and balances. While administration lawyers may certainly issue advisory opinions, when it comes to final judgments on the interrogation methods used, the opera isn't over until the fat lady, specifically the United States Supreme Court, sings.

Although the administration at first balked at handing over the actual memos, they were eventually made public, and the chain of events and key players became painfully clear. Shortly after the attacks on the World Trade Center, the Justice Department had issued certain advisory opinions, broadly interpreting international and domestic bans on torture so as to permit extremely "harsh" treatment of the prisoners. Some of these memos were written by former Justice Department attorney John Yoo and provided arguments for evading the Geneva Conventions altogether in Afghanistan,[100] and thus for dismissing any charges of war crimes which might later arise.[101] The Justice Department, in its own memos, agreed that the Conventions were inapplicable. Secretary of State Colin Powell, together with his attorneys, swiftly protested, urging that such a position would reverse decades of firm U.S. human rights policies and lead to international isolation. However, White House counsel Alberto Gonzales supported the memos, writing that the Geneva Conventions, in the war on terror context, were obsolete and even "quaint," and that the president, as commander in chief, had the power to set them aside on various grounds.[102] Mr. Gonzales, of course, is now attorney general.

Meanwhile, administration lawyers in August 2002 (and again in March 2003) opined that torture could be so narrowly defined as to evade any legal consequences.[103] For example, if an interrogator knows his or her actions will result in severe pain, but the primary goal is not to torture, but rather to obtain intelligence, then he or she would not be guilty of a crime.[104] Moreover, the infliction of moderate or temporary pain would not constitute torture. Instead, the level of pain must be equivalent to the pain "accompanying serious physical injury, such as organ failure, impairment of bodily function, or even death"[105] These guidelines were in stark contrast to Army Field Manual 34–53 ("Intelligence Interrogations"), which prohibit pain induced by drugs or tight bindings, prolonged stressful positions, and the deprivation of food or sleep.[106] Similarly, the memos advised that psychological suffering would only constitute torture if it resulted in significant harm for a prolonged period.[107]

According to *Newsweek*, the military was up in arms. Colin Powell, himself a general, again protested all such changes vociferously, noting that such a course would "reverse over a century of U.S. policy." Military Judge Advocates Generals, or JAGs, also revolted, but to no avail. By January of 2002, the White House decided to apply the Geneva Conventions to the war itself, but to strip the Taliban and al-Qaeda captives of any POW status. As a first step, President Bush issued a secret order granting new powers to the CIA, authorizing them to establish secret prisons abroad and to use extremely harsh interrogation measures.[108] Special "status of forces" agreements were then negotiated with involved foreign governments to grant full immunity from criminal prosecutions to any U.S. personnel or their contractors. At the same time, the extraordinary renditions process was amplified, leading to cases like that of Mahar Arar, discussed above.[109]

These changes in the rules of war had an immediate and predictable effect. Brig. Gen. Rick Baccus, initially in charge of Guantánamo, had provided all incoming prisoners with materials informing them of their rights, and in all other ways complied with the Conventions. In 2002 he was removed, and the camp was placed under the authority of military intelligence.[110] General Miller replaced Baccus and promptly established a "72 point matrix for stress and duress."[111]

Meanwhile, the war shifted to Iraq. In the fall of 2003, Rumsfeld, frustrated by a lack of adequate incoming information, sent Miller to the Abu Ghraib prison to help "improve" the quality of intelligence work there. According to the Taguba report, shortly after General Miller's visit, an order was issued which effectively put Abu Ghraib under the control of military intelligence as well, thereby circumventing the normal lines of army supervision.[112] The MPs and others were told to help "create conditions" for the intelligence interrogators.[113] Slowly, still more rules were "bent," with the army waiving its requirement that military officers monitor CIA interrogations within army bases.[114] Similarly, civilian contractors were permitted to carry out interrogations, despite regulations prohibiting such a delegation of power.[115]

The CIA itself was, of course, already present at the Abu Ghraib base and was using its own severe methods of interrogation.[116] During this same period, Capt. Carolyn Woods and her unit, the 519th Military Intelligence Batallion, arrived from Afghanistan, where harsh techniques were being broadly utilized by the CIA and their partner Special Forces and contractors. Not surprisingly, with the arrival of Miller and Woods, and the ensuing modifications of the chain of command, the treatment of the Abu Ghraib prisoners deteriorated rapidly. Although many of the Guantánamo and Afghanistan interrogation rules and orders were at various times revised and narrowed, creating confusion among the ranks, it is clear that the Pandora's box was wide open and could not be resealed.

In the end, the U.S. military issued an in-depth report on the internal inquiry carried out by Maj. Gen. George R. Fay and Lt. Gen. Anthony R. Jones. The report, *Investigation of Intelligence Activities at Abu Ghraib,* documented forty-four cases of abuse by U.S. forces between July 2003 and February 2004. Significantly, twenty-seven military intelligence agents were implicated in those cases, either by pressuring the MPs or engaging directly in the abuses. Civilian contractors were also cited. Punishment was recommended for Colonel Thomas M. Pappas and Lt. Col. Steven L. Jordan, as well as for three other intelligence officials in charge of interrogations at Abu Ghraib. However, the report concluded that although these officers bore responsibility, they were "not involved" in the abuses that had taken place.[117] On the other hand, the investigations did yield conclusions that CIA and Special Forces practices contributed to the abuses at Abu Ghraib.[118] Specifically, General Fay noted that the CIA, by flouting army rules when carrying out interrogations at Abu Ghraib, had "eroded the necessity in the minds of soldiers and civilians for them to follow army rules."[119]

These basic observations were closely echoed by the Department of Defense investigatory panel headed by James R. Schlesinger.[120] As noted above, the findings included some three hundred reported cases of mistreatment in Iran, Iraq, or Afghanistan, with confirmation of sixty-six at the time of publication of the report. Approximately one third of the cases arose during capture or apprehension. Another third were in the context of interrogation, and in a number of cases the intelligence officials had directed the actions of the MPs.[121] The Schlesinger panel concluded that

"the abuses were not just the failure of some individuals to follow known standards, and they are more than the failure of a few
leaders to enforce proper discipline."[122] Disappointingly, the report criticized leaders at the highest level, including Rumsfeld, but
stopped short of finding an intentional policy or order regarding
the use of torture by such officials. Such a finding would, of course,
create serious legal vulnerabilities for those officials.

The two military reports reflected a growing and deep division
between the army and CIA communities, with General Fay noting
that the agency had refused to make key files and documents available, and the CIA tersely responding that it would carry out its
own investigation. Moreover, as noted by *Newsweek* journalists,
"The uniformed military is in almost open revolt against its civilian masters. . . . The troops resent the Bush administration hard-
liners as dangerously ideological."[123] This anger would seem fair
enough. It is the uniformed servicemen and -women who risk capture and abuse at the hands of Iraqis and others when the administration tosses aside the Geneva Conventions. Justly or not,
both their personal honor as well as the American value system for
which they are sacrificing their lives have been badly tarnished.[124]
Meanwhile, the popular response in Iraq has been clear enough; the
number of attacks and suicide bombings against U.S. troops has
increased dramatically since the revelations of the abuses at Abu
Ghraib and elsewhere. The persons most at risk are, of course, the
men and women in uniform. Hopefully the lesson learned is to refrain from such harmful practices and not simply to better conceal
them.

As the months passed, the young soldiers for the most part continued to stand alone when it came to facing criminal charges.
Higher-level officers were sanctioned, but to date none faces a
court-martial. Given the various eyewitnesses and photographs, a
number of military intelligence and Special Forces agents are under investigation. However, other than the formal charges against
a few private contractors, uniformed servicepersons, and the four

Seals, very few indictments have been brought.[125] The intellectual authors of the illegal practices remain untouched by any legal proceedings. Intriguingly, three Americans, including former Special Forces members John Idema, were sentenced to ten years in prison by an Afghan court for operating a secret prison. The men, plausibly enough, have insisted that they were working for the Pentagon, specifically for General Boykin. Yet they have not been assisted or defended by any of those officials, despite taped conversations offered as evidence.[126] As Idema stated angrily to the press, "This can only have been staged by the U.S. government—we were an embarrassment."[127]

There is little question that the MPs involved in the Abu Ghraib abuses should indeed stand trial and receive punishment. Their conduct was both shocking and unlawful, and they could and should have known better. It is important for both the U.S. forces as well as the Iraqi public to see justice done. However, it seems equally clear that, to use the phrase of many a Vietnam veteran, the MPs are being used, abused, and thrown away. High-level officials from the Bush administration had specifically authorized the flouting of the Geneva Conventions and other U.S. laws and treaties, but they face no consequences of any kind. Meanwhile, the CIA and other intelligence units have long since routinely engaged in torture, either directly or by proxy. When these intelligence agents came to work in close proximity to uniformed and inexperienced servicemen and -women, the inevitable contamination occurred. Yet the MPs still stand alone, sacrificial lambs offered up to mollify an outraged public.

Once again our national leaders seek to lull the U.S. citizenry with a few quick punishments and the promise of many more investigations and reforms to come. Will these ever materialize? The CIA and its partner specialists, caught in the very act of torture, are still evading any responsibility. Well protected by their classified files and by pseudonyms like "John Doe" and "James Bond," the real criminals are sliding into the shadows while their proxies, whether foolish MPs or Guatemalan death squad officers, take the fall alone. Meanwhile, with the passage of time, the public furor is beginning to fade, and the CIA agents and others continue with business as usual. Sister Dianna and I can only shake our heads. Once again, they are getting away with it.

■ ■ ■

In more ways than one, it is important that we evolve and not repeat past abuses. The proverbial skeletons in the closet will always return to haunt us, in this case in the form of continuing U.S. human rights violations and increasing rage against us abroad. This can hardly be expected to increase our national security. Moreover, on moral grounds alone, do we really want the horrors of Abu Ghraib to continue? If not, we need to carefully analyze the roots and causes of U.S. involvement in torture, clarify the issues, and take a long, clear look at our laws and treaties. The time has come to set our house in order.

Although the official investigations have answered some questions, they have also raised many others. Do CIA and related intelligence agents routinely engage in torture, either directly or by proxy, or don't they? If they do, then this is not a question of a "few bad apples" or rogue operators violating the law in the heat of battle. Is there in fact a long-standing albeit unwritten agency practice? Certainly the infamous White House and Justice Department memorandums casting aside the Geneva Conventions and redefining torture opened the door wide to the abuses which occurred in Iraq and Afghanistan. But would a mere change of administration really make a difference? Or do we face a much more serious problem here? If the CIA and other intelligence agencies have been secretly and illegally practicing torture for decades, then a mere electoral change will change nothing at all. Moreover, that secret practice would signal a breakdown of the checks and balances system designed to prevent precisely such an abuse of power. If such intelligence policies exist, how have they evaded legislative super-vision and judicial review? What exactly do our laws and treaties say, and why have the intellectual authors never been brought to justice? Intriguingly, the answers to many of these questions lie in the human rights archives from Latin America's Dirty Wars.

CHAPTER TWO

THE LESSONS OF LATIN AMERICAN HUMAN RIGHTS HISTORY

Today, it remains difficult to obtain all of the necessary information underlying the prisoner abuse which took place in Guantánamo, Iraq, and Afghanistan. Yet without a full understanding of the problem and its roots and origins, needed reforms will remain elusive. This is precisely the situation we now face. Crucial documentary evidence is still classified under broad claims of "national security" and concealed in government files. As discussed above, national leaders still insist that no actual torture ever occurred, or that if it did, such "abuses" were merely the acts of individual soldiers. Anonymous official sources, having made startling admissions on the subject to the press, tend to vanish when the time comes for congressional hearings or court testimonies. Meanwhile, access to many of the prisoners themselves remains limited. Taken together, these obstacles seriously hobble efforts to seek full justice through the courts or genuine reforms through the legislature.

Many of the key questions raised in the preceding chapter can be answered, however, by the human rights documentation slowly emerging from the Dirty Wars of Latin America. Over a period of decades many government files have been declassified, shedding light on the startlingly close relationship between the CIA and the military death squads there. Meanwhile the few survivors of forced disappearances and torture have found the courage and strength to speak out about their experiences. So, too, some of the torturers have experienced a change of heart and have decided to tell the truth about what occurred, including the role played by the United States government.

Taken together, the testimonies and documentary evidence answer the pivotal question raised by the Abu Ghraib scandal. A review of the materials leads relentlessly to just one conclusion: that the CIA and related U.S. intelligence agencies have since their inception engaged in the widespread practice of torture, either directly or through well paid proxies. This policy, or standard operating procedure, has been carried out in a variety of ways, as set forth in detail in this chapter. In short, we are not dealing with any "bad apples" or rogue operators here, but rather something far more dangerous—a rogue agency. Accordingly, legal responsibility goes all the way to the top.

Though disturbing, this clear answer allows us to move forward, evaluate the resulting questions of law and policy, and develop genuine solutions. Averting our eyes from this complex task is no longer a viable option.

THE CENTRAL AMERICAN WARS

There can be little doubt that the internal conflicts of the 1980s in Guatemala, El Salvador, and Honduras involved some of the worst official human rights violations in recent hemispheric history. As the battle for economic and social justice raged between the landed gentry and the landless poor, local military regimes utilized rampant torture and terror to quell the uprisings. Civilian dissidents were dragged from their beds in the middle of the night and left dead and mutilated in public places as warnings to others. Church leaders were shot in their sacristies after crying out for mercy for their parishioners. Entire villages vanished, with hundreds of men, women, and children tossed into unmarked mass graves during army raids. Meanwhile, military death squads combed the streets and countryside, carrying out "disappearances" and torture on a massive scale. Even today, the devastating psychological wounds inflicted on the general populations remain unhealed.

What role, precisely, did the United States play in these hor-rific campaigns? Our intelligence and defense communities pro-vided massive amounts of economic aid, weapons, and military materiel to these regimes, despite their notorious and systematic human rights violations. Our agencies also worked closely with the Guatemalan, Salvadoran, and Honduran intelligence branches, giving extensive advice, support, and training in order to "profes-sionalize" them.

U.S. officials are quick to insist that there is nothing illegal about such support and training, and that in fact the relationship was a benevolent one. This, of course, depends on just how close the working relationship actually was. At some point an innocent business deal crosses the line into criminal conduct, becoming rather much like that of the husband who hires another to shoot his wife. A careful review of the facts in the Central American context suggests precisely this situation. U.S. intelligence officials know-ingly supported the carnage on two different levels: first, by their intimate partnership in and support for the day-to-day activities of intelligence death squads, and second, by their direct participation in cases of torture itself.

With regard to the first aspect, CIA, Special Ops, and other agents worked hand in glove with the deadly local intelligence ser-vices, funding their activities and helping them to plan raids, carry out surveillance, organize interrogations, and infiltrate human rights, religious, and other civilian networks. This was done with full knowledge of the ongoing kidnapping, torture, and murder of all "suspects." Simultaneously, the CIA operated a vast network of paid informants, or "assets," which included numerous local and well-known army torturers. U.S. agents also chose to shield their intelligence contacts instead of reporting their abuses to the U.S. Congress or to local courts or law enforcement agencies. This left the killers free to kill again. In short, when all the facts are mar-shaled, it seems clear that the conduct of our intelligence networks fell within the boundaries of illegal conduct.[1]

With regard to the second aspect, a number of torture survivors have come forward to describe their experiences in Central America and throughout the hemisphere. In the twenty-some individual cases set forth below, an obvious North American was present in their torture cells. In some cases the man simply observed the torture and made recommendations about questions to be asked. In some he actually supervised. In all of the cases the North Americans clearly had authority over the local military officials, but never used it to assist or rescue the victims. Instead, the agents obtained their desired information and left the prisoners to die. This direct participation, when coupled with the sizeable payments made for such brutally extracted intelligence, was unquestionably illegal. For this very reason, the CIA has long denied any such actions.

The substantial evidence and information about these practices, when taken together, make it disturbingly clear that the CIA and other U.S. intelligence agencies fully intended for torture to be routinely utilized in obtaining intelligence. Various methods of physical and mental torture were carefully "refined" and put to use on a broad scale, from Vietnam to Brazil, to Guatemala, and now to Iraq and Afghanistan. Given the realities of the U.S. legal prohibitions and treaties, however, the agencies also developed an extraordinary protective system of secrecy, deniability, and deception. This has permitted the problem to grow and to fester, all the while evading the curative powers of the courts and legislature.

Although the twenty-odd case histories without doubt comprise the most important part of the evidence offered below, the background information as to the CIA's overly close working relationship with repressive foreign intelligence divisions is also key. As in the case of Sister Dianna Ortiz, when the survivors earlier attempted to speak out, they were immediately attacked by U.S. officials as untrustworthy or unstable. Their reports of North Americans in the torture cells were brushed aside as either foolishness or fiction. Since the North American agents, much like the

Special Agents "John Doe" and "James Bond" of Abu Ghraib, never wore name tags and rarely were even in uniform, it has been difficult for the survivors, as individuals, to corroborate their stories. However, when their testimonies are taken together in the context of adequate information about the close U.S. relationship with the army death squads, the conclusions are unavoidable. For this reason, both the overall relationship as well as the individual cases will be set forth here.

THE HISTORICAL CONTEXT: HOW MUCH SUPPORT AND HOW MUCH AID?

In the early 1980s the Reagan administration, still in the mindset of the Cold War era, became deeply concerned about the new Sandinista government in Nicaragua. Fearing the spread of Communism in "our own back yard," U.S. officials took strong measures not only to topple the Sandinistas by funding and arming the Contras, but also to take firm control over the entire region. Fledgling insurgencies in Guatemala, El Salvador, and Honduras were to be crushed and a closer partnership established with the various military regimes. As the Dirty Wars in these three nations progressed, human rights violations reached extraordinary levels. Yet U.S. military aid continued, as did the close working relationship between CIA agents and local army death squads.

The following background information is set forth to answer certain key questions. Specifically, how serious and systematic were the human rights abuses? Were they really carried out by the local armies and intelligence units? Were U.S. intelligence agents fully aware of all this at the time? How closely did our agents collaborate in human rights violations? Did our actions in fact contribute to the ongoing repression? These questions must be answered before a meaningful evaluation of the legal and policy issues raised is possible.

GUATEMALA: A VERY SPECIAL RELATIONSHIP

The CIA's intervention in Guatemalan affairs is as well documented as it is chilling. The country is in many ways reminiscent of the old South Africa, with the indigenous Mayans composing some 80 percent of the population, yet utterly disenfranchised in their own homeland. The direct descendants of the conquistadors and other European immigrants form the tiny lighter-skinned and upper-class minority, which owns virtually all of the rich agricultural lands. Little alternative industry exists, so a lack of land spells starvation. As a result, the Mayans suffer an 80 percent severe malnutrition level and an 80 percent illiteracy rate. They also bear the highest infant mortality level in the Western Hemisphere, second only to Haiti.

Not surprisingly, the Mayans have not meekly submitted to their subjugation. Refusing to assimilate, every generation since the arrival of the conquistadors has risen up to fight, only to be crushed by a well-fed and well-armed military famous for its brutality.

In 1944 the Guatemalans elected their first reformist president. Juan José Arévalo worked tirelessly to modernize his country, creating a social security system, financing education improvements, extending the vote to illiterate persons, and initiating health programs and literacy campaigns. He also ended the forced conscription of villagers and passed legislation providing for basic labor rights. When his term ended, he was succeeded by Col. Jacobo Arbenz, who continued to press for urgently needed changes. Most importantly, Arbenz began a modest land reform program, recognizing that the concentration of 70 percent of the land in the hands of 2 percent of the population was stunting economic growth and causing widespread starvation.[2] The program applied only to the largest landholders in Guatemala, and only to unused acreage. Moreover, the land was purchased, not confiscated, by the Guatemalan government, then sold at low monthly rates to peasant cooperatives. President Arbenz began this new effort by relinquishing his own lands.

The program worked quite well until 1954, when land belonging to the United Fruit Company (UFC), one of the largest landowners in the country, was forcibly purchased by the government.[3] As it turned out, the UFC had greatly understated its property value on the company's tax returns, resulting in a low sales price. The furious company officers returned to Washington at the height of the McCarthy era and complained of Communism. The response was swift and predictable. The CIA armed a ragtag group of military dissidents and organized a violent coup against Arbenz, who was driven into exile.[4] Virtually all of the Arévalo-Arbenz reforms were abruptly canceled, the peasant co-ops were stripped of their newly acquired lands, and a bloodbath ensued. Thousands of Arbenz supporters—unionists, peasant leaders, and civil rights workers—were either killed or driven from their homeland. There was never again such a progressive government in Guatemala. To this day the people wistfully refer to the 1944–1954 period of creativity and reform as the "Ten Years of Spring."

From 1954 until 1986 the Guatemalan presidency was occupied by one military leader after another, and even today all civilian governmental institutions, including the presidency and the judiciary, remain firmly under the control of the army. Determined to demonstrate the superiority of the capitalist model, the United States raised aid from $600,000 to $45 million annually. Rather like our efforts today in Iraq, Guatemala was to become a "showcase of democracy."[5] These efforts failed miserably. Civil war broke out and lasted for thirty-five years. The Guatemalan economy remains a shambles to this day.

The civil war was one of the most brutal in the hemisphere, ending only with the signing of the final Peace Accords in December of 1996. Throughout the 1980s and 1990s the Guatemalan military engaged in a deadly counterinsurgency campaign, systematically carrying out acts of terror against both civilians and members of the largely Mayan resistance forces, the URNG.[6] The use of torture and forced "disappearances" became routine, and all civilian reform efforts were crushed. Church leaders were killed, peasant cooperatives were burned, rural health networks were destroyed, and unions suffered staggering losses. The fledgling Mayan rights movement was decimated. As stated by the United Nations Truth

Commission (officially known as the Commission for Historical Clarification of Guatemala, or CEHG) in 1999, the government campaign was "designed and implemented . . . to provoke terror in the population."[7]

Given the current official tendency to use sanitized language in order to evade public outcry over U.S. tactics in Iraq and Afghanistan, it is important for us to understand the realities behind these statistics. When, for example, the Mayan Campesino Unity Committee or "CUC" members peacefully occupied the Spanish Embassy in 1980, seeking help and explaining their grievances, the security forces burned the building over their heads. Thirty-nine people died in the fire, including twenty-two Mayan protesters and most of the embassy staff.[8] One badly burned CUC member survived but was dragged from his hospital bed and murdered. In 1982, three hundred people died in a single day in San Francisco Nentón, one of hundreds of Mayan villages massacred by the army. The women were raped and shot, the children disemboweled. The despairing men, packed into the small meeting house, died when a soldier tossed in a hand grenade. Only one old man was able to flee through a rear window and reach Mexico alive.[9] During Easter week of 1984, young Rosario Godoy de Cuevas, desperately searching for her missing husband, was murdered by members of the security forces together with her nineteen-year-old brother and her two-year-old son Augustín. Her body showed bite marks and cigarette burns across her breasts and her child's fingernails had been pulled out.[10] Such was daily life in Guatemala for thirty-five years.

For good cause, the Guatemalan army swiftly earned the title of worst human rights violator in the Western Hemisphere. Throughout the 1980s massacres were carried out in some 660 Mayan villages. By the war's end 200,000 people had been either forcibly "disappeared" or murdered. According to the U.N. Truth Commission report, the Guatemalan military was responsible for 93 percent of the atrocities, and their counterinsurgency practices constituted genocide.[11] The army intelligence division, or G-2, was singled out for particular responsibility.[12] The guerrilla movement, or URNG, was deemed responsible for only 3 percent of the human rights violations. Significantly, the report also sharply criticized the United States for having continued its support for and collaboration with the army's intelligence division, despite its notorious human rights record:

> The CEHG recognizes that the movement towards polarization, militarization, and civil war were not just the result of national history. . . . Whilst anti-communism, promoted by the United States within the framework of its foreign policy, received firm support from right-wing political parties and from various other powerful actors in Guatemala, the United States demonstrated that it was willing to provide support for strong military regimes in its strategic backyard. In the case of Guatemala, military assistance was directed towards reinforcing the national intelligence apparatus and for training the officer corps in counterinsurgency techniques, key factors which had significant bearing on human rights violations during the armed confrontation.[13]

President Clinton, upon reading the report, issued an apology to the people of Guatemala in 1999. "For the United States it is important that I state clearly that support for military forces and intelligence units which engaged in violence and widespread repression was wrong and the United States must not repeat that mistake."[14]

Just how closely did the United States intelligence agents work with the Guatemalan intelligence death squads throughout the war? As noted in the Introduction, Everardo was tortured and killed on the orders of Col. Julio Roberto Alpirez, an intelligence officer and also a paid CIA informant, or "asset." As I later learned, Alpirez received $44,000 from the CIA in June of 1992, the same month that he supervised Everardo's torture.[15] Evidently this financial relationship was not at all unusual. According to Colonel Hooker, a former Defense Intelligence Agency (DIA) chief for Guatemala, "It would be an embarrassing situation if you ever had a roll call for everybody in the Guatemalan army who ever collected a CIA paycheck."[16] The 1996 Intelligence Oversight Board (IOB) report confirmed that between 1984 and 1986, the CIA used numerous "assets" in Guatemala, and was often aware that those assets were "credibly alleged" to be involved in serious human rights abuses such as torture.[17] Nevertheless, the CIA's periodic evaluation of its assets included no human rights information.[18] Evidently, the issue was of little importance to the agency.

Moreover, throughout the 1980s the U.S. government continued to provide crucial economic support as well as badly needed helicopter and tank parts and other military supplies and training opportunities. Civilian economic aid from the United States was used to cover budget deficits resulting from the costs of the military counterinsurgency efforts, and under the Reagan administration aid rose from $26.6 million to $82.5 million.[19] The private sale of weapons, including handguns popular with death squads but forbidden to civilians, as well as shackles, stun guns, and other similar items, was routinely authorized.[20] Despite the slaughter that had ensued under General Ríos Montt in 1982, Reagan not only resumed economic aid but also lifted the arms embargo and sent $6.3 million worth of helicopter parts.[21]

Even when military aid was curtailed for human rights reasons under President Carter, and again in 1990 when U.S. citizen Michael Devine was murdered, money, support, and supplies continued to reach the deadly intelligence division. High-level military officers continued to be trained by the United States at the School of the Americas, including Colonel Alpirez and many other known human rights violators. More than 114 sales of handguns and rifles were authorized by the government even after Devine's murder.[22] Most importantly for officers like Alpirez, "the CIA established a liaison relationship with the Guatemalan security services widely known to have a reprehensible human rights record, and it continued covert aid after the cutoff of military aid in 1990."[23] Such covert aid, which went to assets and liaisons, was considered "vital." The results were clear enough. Although Alpirez was implicated in the 1990 murder of Michael Devine, and was known to have "excelled" in the liquidation campaigns of the 1980s, he continued to receive CIA payments even as he tortured Everardo and others.

The partnership between the CIA and the Guatemalan intelligence and security forces included far more than money, supplies, and training, however. Their long-term joint activities, planning sessions, and full knowledge and acceptance of the ongoing repression are starkly illustrated by the following declassified documents obtained by the National Security Archives:

1. A January 4, 1966, cable reports that a U.S. "safety advisor" named John Logan would assist in establishing a counterterror task force and advises on how to establish covert and overt operations. This document reflects the extraordinarily close, if not dominant, relationship between the U.S. intelligence services and their Guatemalan partners.[24]

2. A secret 1968–69 USAID report recommends that U.S. security assistance to Guatemala focus on the insurgency crisis, and that a Joint Operations Center, or "JOC," be established in the Presidential Palace to collect and maintain intelligence.[25] Once again, we see the U.S. planning and control over Guatemalan security matters.

3. A 1966 USAID report references certain victims of the mass abduction, torture, and execution of more than thirty members of the Guatemalan Workers Party.[26] This reflects full awareness of the ongoing official repression of civilians from the earliest years.

4. A March 29, 1968, State Department document contains a moving plea from an official named Vyron Vaky, who urges that the Guatemalan government's use of counterterror was indiscriminate and brutal and was impeding national development. He wrote, in addition, that the U.S. was condoning such conduct "not because we have concluded we cannot do anything about

it but because we never really tried. Rather, we suspected that maybe it is a good tactic.... Murder, torture and mutilation are alright if it is our side that is doing it and the victims are communists."[27]

5. A DCI Watch Committee Report of February 5, 1982, reports that the army was planning a sweep through the Ixil area and that there were plans to destroy a number of villages.[28]

6. Apparently no warning was issued. A CIA document of February 1982 reports that the "sweep" is ongoing, but the successes have been limited to destroying villages and killing Indians. No major guerrilla forces have been found.[29]

7. A March 1986 State Department document reports that the security forces were behind the majority of the abductions from 1977 to 1985 and that the victims were peasants, Mayan farmers, students, and teachers. Such victims were routinely taken to army interrogations centers, tortured, and killed.[30] This frank assessment was not shared with the U.S. Congress.

8. A 1988 DIA cable indicates that the army intelligence division was behind the bombings of the headquarters of the Peace Brigades International, an international human rights group, and the GAM (a Guatemalan support group for the "disappeared").[31] This was not shared with the victims or local police.

9. In May 1991, U.S. Ambassador Strook reported that the modus operandi behind a recent wave of violence against activists would indicate that the perpetrators were almost certainly members of the security forces.[32]

10. In 1994 a DIA report indicates that prisoners at the military base of Retalhuleu were kept in pits of water so deep they had to hold onto overhead bars to keep from drowning, and that after "interrogation" sessions, they were loaded dead or alive onto helicopters and thrown into the sea.[33] None of this was shared with Congress.

11. A March 18, 1992 CIA report to the White House and to the State Department notes that Everardo had been captured six days earlier, and that the army would probably falsify his death in or-

der to take advantage of his intelligence value.[34] This information was withheld from concerned congressional members and human rights networks until well after his death.

EL SALVADOR: ONE MILLION DOLLARS A DAY

The role of the United States in El Salvador throughout the 1980s was equally devastating. Despite the congressional intent to halt assistance to known and systematic human rights violators, including the notorious military regimes of Central America, the CIA and related intelligence officials were able to continue a vast, sometimes clandestine campaign of support and assistance. The results speak for themselves.

El Salvador's history is not unlike that of Guatemala. Pedro de Alvarado and his men arrived in El Salvador in 1524, waging war and seizing land. The effects of the conquest were all too predictable. After the first fifty years of war, slavery, starvation, and disease, the indigenous population dropped from 500,000 inhabitants to 75,000.[35] The lands were divided up among the Europeans, and agriculture became the main industry. Although the British were the dominant trade partners throughout the 1800s, they were replaced in the twentieth century by U.S. entrepreneurs investing heavily in banana and coffee exports.[36]

As in Guatemala, the distribution of wealth and land remained vastly disproportionate, with the small upper class, called the Fourteen Families or *"Catorce Grande,"* retaining most of the national wealth and resources. As stated by one U.S. observer in 1931, "Thirty or forty families own nearly everything. . . . They live in almost regal style. The rest of the population has practically nothing."[37] During the Depression coffee prices declined, and as a result wages dropped and jobs vanished. The desperate conditions gave rise to a revolt of the indigenous Pipil peoples in the Izalco region. Augustín Farabundo Martí organized a similar workers' revolt in the city. The urban leaders, including Martí, were seized and shot, and the Pipil revolt was brutally crushed in a military sweep now remembered as the *"Matanza"* ("The Killing"). As many as 30,000 indigenous rebels were lined up and executed. Throughout the slaughter, U.S. military ships hovered off the Salvadoran coast, and U.S. Marines in Nicaragua were on alert.[38]

In the 1980s, the per capita GDP in El Salvador was less than $1,000 per year, 74 percent of the rural population lived in absolute poverty, and the average life expectancy was sixty-five years. Between 1961 and 1975, the landless peasant population increased to 40 percent of the population.[39] For many years Salvadoran workers had sought employment in Honduras, only to be violently expelled during the "Soccer Wars" of 1969.[40] As a result, the internal pressures for basic socioeconomic reforms began to rise dramatically. Church leaders worked to organize Christian base communities, and popular organizations of peasants, workers, students, and others seeking social justice began to make themselves heard.

In 1980, the Farabundo Martí National Liberation Front (FMLN) was formed, uniting four separate guerrilla groups.[41] Much as in Guatemala, a brutal civil war raged through El Salvador until 1992. The Salvadoran military responded with predictable ferocity, using torture, terror, forced disappearances, and murder as routine counterinsurgency techniques. The human rights violations that occurred were thoroughly documented by both Salvadoran human rights organizations and the United Nations Truth Commission in its report, *From Madness to Hope*.[42]

As the political polarization between reformists and right-wing military leaders rose in the early 1980s, death squad activities surged dramatically. Despite this, the United States began to greatly increase military aid, supplies, and assistance, especially to the intelligence units. Was this due to a lack of accurate information about the true human rights situation? Sadly, no. The realities of daily life in El Salvador were open and notorious, and were quite well known to all U.S. agents and officials there.

How obvious was the official campaign of terror within El Salvador at the time? Monsignor Oscar Arnulfo Romero himself, in one of his last sermons, gave the most articulate description of daily life during this period:

We have lived through a tremendously tragic week.... Last Saturday, on 15 March, one of the largest and most distressing military operations was carried out in the countryside.... In La Laguna, the attackers killed a married couple, Ernesto Navas and Audelia Mejía de Navas, their little children, Martín and Hilda, thirteen and seven years old, and eleven more peasants. Other deaths have been reported, but we do not know the names of the dead. In Plan de Ocotes, two children and four peasants were killed, including two women. In El Rosario, three more peasants were killed. That was last Saturday....

Last Monday, 17 March, was a tremendously violent day.... The campus of the national university was under armed siege from dawn until 7 P.M. Throughout the day, constant bursts of machine gun fire were heard in the university area....

As I entered the church, I was given a cable that says, "Amnesty International confirmed today... that in El Salvador human rights are violated to extremes that have not been seen in other countries."... Amnesty International recently condemned the government of El Salvador, alleging that it was responsible for six hundred political assassinations.... [Mr.] Fuentes said that during his stay in El Salvador, he could see that the victims had been tortured before their deaths and mutilated afterward.... The victims' bodies characteristically appeared with the thumbs tied behind their backs. Corrosive liquids had been applied to the corpses to prevent identification of the victims by their relatives and to prevent international condemnation, the spokesman added.

I would like to make a special appeal to the men of the army.... In the name of God, in the name of this suffering people whose cries rise to heaven more loudly each day, I implore you, I beg you, I order you in the name of God: stop the repression.[43]

Despite this moving plea for sanity, Archbishop Romero was shot dead by a sniper as he gave mass on March 24, 1980. An estimated 50,000 mourners attended his funeral, but while they gathered at the Cathedral, a bomb was set off. As people tried to run, they were met with machine gun fire. Between twenty-seven and forty victims died on the steps of the church and another two hundred were wounded.[44]

These events were only a beginning. Later that year, four American churchwomen were raped and murdered by the Salvadoran National Guard. Although U.S. military aid was briefly suspended in response, it was fully restored by President Reagan the following January. There were also great increases in training and funding for the army.[45]

Meanwhile, the extraordinary repression continued against the civilian population throughout the country. As in Guatemala and Honduras, the military turned its fury against religious and labor leaders, peasant organizers, political dissidents, and academic critics alike. All those opposing current government policies lived in fear, and many of the rural poor were simply presumed by the army to be subversives.

By way of illustration, in March 1981 thousands of refugees tried to flee the violence in El Salvador by crossing the Lempa River into Honduras. They were attacked by the military both from the air and on land. Some 20 to 30 people were killed, and 189 left missing. The tragedy was repeated that fall, when 147 more were killed, including 44 minors.[46] Over 50 villagers, mostly women and children, were slaughtered in the town of El Junquillo, with similar massacres occurring in remote rural cooperatives and hamlets. In December 1981 the Atlacatl Batallion massacred the entire village of El Mozote, killing hundreds of unarmed civilians, a large percentage of whom were children.[47] The slaughter continued, and among the countless deaths were four Dutch journalists shot by the army in 1982. In 1989, bombs went off in both the offices of COMADRES, the committee for the "disappeared", and FENASTRAS, a union, in a single day, wounding more than forty people and killing nine. Six Jesuit priests, their cook, and her young daughter were assassinated by soldiers in San Salvador in 1989. Once again the Atlacatl Battallion was responsible for ordering and carrying out the murders.

By the end of the war, human rights organizations estimated that between 40,000 and 50,000 persons had died as a result of the political violence.[48] Eighty-five percent of the cases were attributed to the state, paramilitary groups, and related death squads. The FMLN was implicated in 5 percent of the cases.[49]

Thus the United States was hardly "unaware" of the ongoing slaughter. Yet our intelligence services knowingly contributed to the repression. President Reagan, alarmed by events in Nicaragua, was determined to prevent any similar changes in El Salvador. Toward that end, he greatly increased U.S. economic and military aid, military training, and covert involvement throughout the war; creating a close working partnership between the U.S. and Salvadoran intelligence divisions. By 1985 the United States was pumping an extraordinary one million dollars a day into El Salvador. A total of 1.8 billion dollars was sent between 1980 and 1985, the years of peak repression. It is estimated that the U.S. also provided billions of dollars worth of equipment and hardware between 1980 and 1990.[50] As stated by author William Blum, "One telling result of this massive provision of weapons and training, as well as money to pay higher salaries, was the sizeable expansion of the Salvadoran armed forces. From an estimated seven to twelve thousand men in 1979, the army alone jumped to more than 22,000 by 1983, with an additional 11,000 civilian security forces; three years later, the total of these two forces had spiraled to 53,000."[51]

The United States also provided intensive training to many Salvadoran military officials. Roberto D'Aubuisson and others clearly linked to the worst repression in El Salvador, including the murder of Archbishop Romero, were trained at the School of the Americas (SOA) and at other U.S. training centers.[52] The infamous Atlacatl Brigade also benefited from the SOA and U.S. trainers.[53] Significantly, a former SOA instructor has admitted that manuals teaching torture were used at the school,[54] and some congressional members have indicated that the school also serves as a CIA recruitment center.[55] Moreover, U.S. training manuals used in the

Central American region during this time period confirm that U.S. counterinsurgency training included the teaching of human rights violations.[56] This was again confirmed by a former Treasury Police officer, who stated that in 1980 U.S. instructors openly discussed interrogation methods such as beatings and the administration of electrical shocks to prisoners.[57]

Funding, supplies, and training, however, were not the only form of support provided by the United States to the Salvadoran army. U.S. military "advisors" were also sent in large numbers to assist the army. Intriguingly, Greg Walker of the U.S. Special Operations forces, has reported that despite the congressionally imposed limit on Special Operations advisors in El Salvador to fifty-five, the Pentagon easily found ways to circumvent this rule:

> Positions allotted to the Embassy-based U.S. MilGrp could be stocked with Special Forces operators who would not be counted under the formal fifty-five limitations. In this fashion, the actual number... stood at between eighty-five and one hundred at any given time. Those advisers were supplemented by an additional fifty to seventy-five CIA contract personnel.[58]

Although officially in El Salvador for advisory purposes only, there are many reports that U.S. military agents also played a role in the combat areas as well.[59] After the war in El Salvador drew to a close, a number of U.S. "trainers," whom officials had insisted were never in combat situations, began to come forward and speak of their experiences under fire and demand recognition.[60] Nidia Díaz, a high-ranking officer of the FMLN, confirms that as she lay wounded during a battle, a man jumped from a military helicopter and took her prisoner, thinking that she might be Nicaraguan or Cuban. He was blond, bearded, athletic, and wore Ray-Ban sunglasses—in her words, "A Yankee!"[61]

Meanwhile, the CIA itself had agents working very closely with members of the Salvadoran army's death squads. Although most of the CIA's paid informants remain secret, Col. Nicholas Carranza, who was Vice Minister of Defense during the years 1979–81, and later head of the dreaded Treasury Police, was identified as just such a paid CIA informant by *New York Times* columnist Philip Taubman. Taubman based his report on statements by a U.S. official familiar with CIA activities in El Salvador.[62] General José Alberto Medrano, the organizer of the rural paramilitary and intelligence network ORDEN, also received CIA payments and was sent by the U.S. government on a tour of Vietnam, where he traveled with Green Berets and CIA operatives.[63] According to Medrano, the Green Berets in fact helped him establish ORDEN, and the CIA regularly provided the army with intelligence about various "suspects." Many of these people were later "disappeared" or assassinated. In return, intelligence gathered by the Salvadorans was routinely passed on to the CIA.

Mr. César Vielman Joya Martínez, himself a former intelligence officer and death squad member, gave perhaps the most startling testimony linking U.S. intelligence agents to his unit's activities.[64] He had served in the Intelligence Department of the First Infantry Brigade in El Salvador during the late 1980s. He later risked his life by publicly admitting that his department was responsible for recruiting and maintaining a network of informants in the community, and for the capture, torture, and extrajudicial execution of all persons believed to be subversives or their sympathizers. Down the hall from Mr. Joya Martínez's office were a number of cells where "disappeared" suspects were secretly held and "interrogated" through the use of torture. Most were later taken away in the night and murdered.

Mr. Joya Martínez also stated that two U.S. advisors, both U.S. military officers, had offices in his department, at one point even sharing an office space with him. They gave daily advice as to how to carry out surveillance operations, including methods for following victims, analyzing information, and questioning the prisoners. They also advised on the types of questions to be asked during interrogations. They provided all funds for the salaries of the informants, as well as gasoline, equipment, and vehicles for the department's activities. They knew all of the Salvadoran officials by name and were in a clear position of authority over them, on one occasion even countermanding a high-level officer in front of Mr. Joya Martínez. The advisors worked not far from the interrogation cells where people were tortured and would certainly have heard what was going on and noted the prisoners' conditions.

Moreover, the U.S. officers received all intelligence reports from the department. As congressional pressure mounted in the United States with regards to human rights violations in Central America, the two advisors repeatedly ordered Joya Martínez and others to refrain from actually telling them the details of such violations, and would hurriedly leave the room when the others discussed an execution or kidnapping, giving rise to quite a few jokes. It was obvious that the Americans were fully aware of what was happening, yet continued their funding, advice, and technical support of the Department. In short, they engaged in the "wink and nod" approach, sending clear signals to the Salvadoran team that the abductions, tortures, and kidnappings were to continue.

THE "U.S.S. HONDURAS": BUYING OUT A COUNTRY

The Reagan administration, bent on destroying the Sandinista government in Nicaragua, launched an intensive clandestine drive to assist the Contras. As special needs, especially for military bases and intelligence centers, grew, so did U.S. interest in Honduras. As discussed below, the country was virtually rented out by the United States for a number of years. Predictably, the CIA and other intelligence branches worked closely with the most ruthless of Honduran military officials, resulting in a virulent human rights crisis.

Honduras has long been one of the most impoverished nations in the Western Hemisphere. Conquered by the Spaniards in the 1500s, the country quickly settled into the usual Central American pattern of large landowners and impoverished landless workers.

Even the agricultural exports business was swiftly dominated by foreign interests, with the Vaccaro brothers and the United Fruit Company soon controlling two-thirds of the Honduran banana and coffee exports and owning more than a million acres of the best farmlands.[65] In the 1980s, rural Hondurans made up 60 percent of the population, and of these, 70 percent lived in desperate poverty, 40 percent were landless, and 80 percent suffered from malnutrition.[66]

Not surprisingly, a powerful land reform and labor rights movement took hold, especially in the rural areas. As usual, this met with strong opposition from large landowners as well as the U.S. investment community. A successful strike by banana workers in 1954 resulted in President Villeda Morales's 1962 agrarian reform act. Although a very moderate program, the fruit companies shut down Honduran jobs in order to force the government to dilute the measures.[67] The program was revived in 1972 by General Oswaldo López Arellano, who also initiated a National Development Plan. However, he was forced from office and replaced by a military clique that swiftly moved to repress the workers and activists. Two foreign priests and a number of peasant leaders were massacred by the army at Los Horcones in 1975, and the Las Isletas banana cooperative was destroyed in 1977.[68] Father James "Guadalupe" Carney, a U.S.-born priest serving in Honduras, wrote movingly of these turbulent and dangerous years in his autobiography, *To Be a Christian Is to Be a Revolutionary*.[69] Father Carney was himself tortured to death in Honduras by U.S.-backed security forces in 1983.

Ironically, it was under the civilian president Roberto Suazo Córdova that the worst of the repression began. The ever weakening economy was subjected to stringent austerity measures by the IMF, which in turn led to higher risks of a crippling general strike. Responding to Washington's call for a stable base of military operations for the Contras, President Suazo Córdova agreed to permit the CIA to use Honduran national territory. In exchange, the U.S. sent $572 million in aid between 1980 and 1985.[70] The CIA station in Honduras became one of the largest in the region. In this context Gen. Gustavo Álvarez Martínez, trained by the leaders of the Dirty War in Argentina, rose to power and initiated an Argentine-style wave of terror and "disappearances."

Were U.S. officials aware of the growing military repression in Honduras? The National Commissioner for the Protection of Human Rights in Honduras, Dr. Leo Valladares Lanza, documented over 140 reports of persons who were violently "disappeared" by Honduran death squads between 1981 and 1984.[71] Significantly, a number of these persons were Salvadoran or Nicaraguan, or were suspected of having links to these two countries. In short, they were of great interest to the U.S. and Contra intelligence agents. According to the Committee in Defense of Human Rights in Honduras (CODEH), 138 people vanished between 1981 and 1984 alone, and 85 labor and campesino leaders were murdered outright. After General Álvarez was forced out of Honduras in 1984, CODEH reports that the executions decreased, but that illegal detentions and torture of Honduran dissidents in fact increased.[72]

Although the numbers of death squad victims is lower for Honduras than for Guatemala and El Salvador, the stories of the "disappeared" are equally grim, and had the desired result of instilling terror and paralysis throughout the civilian population. The following cases are but examples. Taken together, this history gives a bleak view of what our CIA considered appropriate investments for U.S. tax dollars.

■ Milton Jiménez was a twenty-nine-year-old law student in 1982, and a student activist. He was living with Rafael Rivas Torres, an assistant attorney general, and several others. They were dragged out of bed by armed men in the early dawn hours and taken to a clandestine center where they were severely tortured. One prisoner was subjected to "hoodings" to provoke asphyxiation some fifteen times, requiring artificial respiration to revive him. Jiménez himself was interrogated constantly about university politics. At one point, he was taken past a man lying on the floor wrapped in newspaper: "As a result of the torture, this person was reduced to a bloody mass that could only groan in pain."[73] Jiménez was one of the lucky few to survive.

- German Pérez Alemán, a union leader, was abducted and tortured to death by members of the notorious Batallion 316, apparently because of his numerous trips to El Salvador. Although his family desperately explained that he was merely collecting payments on his father's life insurance policy, he was never released.[74]

- Oscar Reyes, a journalist critical of these practices, was abducted and tortured with his wife, Gloria. He was strung up naked and beaten "like a piñata" and she was given electrical shocks to the genitals that damaged her internal organs.[75]

- Nelson Mackay, a lawyer, was abducted and found dead with a rope around his neck and his mouth filled with a thick black pesticide.[76]

As in Guatemala and El Salvador, the tortures and killings were open and notorious. The goal of the death squads was to terrorize the public into submission. Certainly all U.S. intelligence agents were fully aware of these actions. Yet despite the systematic repression, the U.S. increased aid and support. During the Contra war era, military aid to Honduras jumped from $3.9 million in 1980 to $77.4 million in 1984.[77] As reported by Gary Cohn, "The tiny country was eventually so crowded with so much U.S. military equipment and personnel that some people started referring to it as the "U.S.S. Honduras."[78] President Reagan, determined to overthrow the Sandinistas in Nicaragua, ordered the expansion of covert operations in 1981 to include all forms of training equipment and support to countries like Honduras. He also ordered the CIA to work through non-Americans, such as the Argentines, who would in turn be paid by the agency.[79]

More disturbingly, U.S. officials backed and protected General Álvarez throughout these years of extreme repression. Trained in Argentina, as he rose to power he openly declared to U.S. Ambassador Binns that he admired the Argentine methods used during the murderous Dirty Wars there and planned to use the same techniques in Honduras. The ambassador immediately cabled a warning to Washington. As the "disappearances" began to spread, Binns continued to urge that the situation be "nipped in the bud," and eventually recommended that Washington bring a halt to the violence by cutting off military aid. His advice was coldly ignored, and he was soon replaced by John Negroponte.[80]

General Álvarez established the now notorious Batallion 316, inviting both Argentine and U.S. military officials to give the new group its training in interrogation and counterintelligence techniques. In 1982, Col. Leonidas Torres Arias, a former head of intelligence, informed journalists at a Mexico City press conference that Álvarez was heading this new de facto death squad, and he named several of its victims, including Mackay. Although the U.S. Embassy was flooded with reports and appeals for help from desperate relatives of the "disappeared," nothing was done. As noted by Honduran Congressman Efraín Díaz Arrivillaga, "Their attitude was one of tolerance and silence. . . . They needed Honduras to loan its territory more than they were concerned about the killing of innocent people."[81] Despite the clear evidence of systematic and serious human rights abuses, Álvarez remained the darling of the U.S. Embassy. When CIA station chief Don Winters adopted a child, Álvarez was asked to be the godfather. In 1983 the Reagan administration awarded him the Legion of Merit for encouraging the democratic process in Honduras.[82] Honduran military officials were more realistic and forced Álvarez out of Honduras in 1984. Becoming a religious fanatic in Miami, he eventually returned to preach in Honduras, where he was shot to death in the streets.

Disturbingly, the United States not only trained many of the responsible Honduran military officials at the School of the Americas, but the CIA and other intelligence agents directly trained Batallion 316 members themselves. Florencio Caballero, a former Batallion 316 member, described in detail his training in the United States. He and others were flown to an undisclosed location, apparently in the Southwest, to an isolated training center. There they were taught to use a number of interrogation methods, including sleep deprivation, placing rats on the person, or threatening to kill a loved one. He also received training from a U.S. advisor named "Mr. Bill" and from various Argentine advisors in Honduras.[83]

Although it has been reported that the U.S. advisors did not teach extreme measures of physical torture on the grounds that it was counterproductive, it was the United States that paid the Argentines, despite their abysmal human rights record, to carry out the training as well.[84] The Argentines, of course, did not hesitate on the issue of torture. In fact, the Argentines and the CIA worked very closely indeed in Honduras, with Argentine officials acting as surrogates for the CIA's Contra actions. In short, the CIA contracted out torture in Honduras just as it often does today in Iraq and Afghanistan. As stated by Prof. Ariel Armony:

> The CIA's decision to prop up an exiled indigenous army trained by a third country provided an effective solution. . . . The CIA left day-to-day military management to the Argentine advisors. Aid to the Nicaraguan Contras was concealed in assistance monies for Argentina. Given the ample prerogatives enjoyed by Casey, it was possible for the CIA to set up the covert program in Central America without major interference from Congress.[85]

As indicated by Florencio Caballero, the CIA's relationship with the Batallion 316 death squad was all too close. Mr. Caballero, José Valle, and José Barrera were all one- time members of the Battalion, but they eventually fled Honduras and dared to speak out. In a lengthy interview with the *Baltimore Sun*,[86] they detailed their personal involvement in the kidnapping, torture, and extrajudicial execution of numerous suspected "subversives." Their methods routinely included rape, beatings, electrical shocks to the genitals, drownings, and asphyxiations.

According to Mr. Caballaro, CIA officials had full access to secret detention centers where not even the Honduran police or court officials were permitted to search for the "disappeared." There, the CIA operatives could see for themselves that the detainees had been tortured. As stated by Caballero, "The Americans knew everything we were doing. They saw the condition the victims were in, their marks and bruises. They did not do anything."[87] In the case of Inés Murillo, discussed below, an American called "Mr. Mike" frequently visited the INDUMIL center where she was secretly detained and tortured. He observed her condition, but merely helped her tormentors frame additional questions for her.[88] Chillingly, a U.S. official later confirmed that a CIA agent did in fact have access to INDUMIL during the time of Ms. Murillo's detention.[89]

Sadly, the Department of State and Ambassador Negroponte were also complicit in the violence, in that they consistently failed to share information that might have saved lives, and they continued to underreport and to outright conceal the true human rights situation in Honduras from the U.S. Congress. Despite the widely publicized abduction and torture of journalist Oscar Reyes and his wife, for example, the 1982 U.S. human rights report on Honduras stated that "No incident of official interference with the media has been recorded for years."[90] Similarly, the 1982 report indicated that workers, students, and others were free to organize and hold frequent demonstrations, yet no mention was made of the numerous disappeared students and other activists. The 1983 country report, remarkably, stated that "There are no political prisoners in Honduras. Individuals are prosecuted not for their political beliefs but rather for criminal acts."[91]

A former aide, Rick Chidester, attempted to include information about the ongoing abuses in the 1982 report, only to be taken aside by a supervisor and pressed to remove them.[92] Family members meeting with embassy officials to beg for help were brushed aside. Ms. Oliva, who sought help for her husband, says of one official, "He was cold, very cold. Any kindness was gone. He did not even smile at us." [93]

Ambassador Negroponte, so notorious in Honduras for concealing the truth, was sent by President Bush to Iraq and will now become chief of U.S. intelligence.

CONCLUSIONS

As the above historical information reflects, Guatemala, Honduras, and El Salvador were in the throes of deep-rooted internal conflicts throughout the 1980s. These de facto civil wars were extraordinary in terms of the routine use of torture, terror, and "disappearances" by the government forces. Indeed, in Guatemala the army counterinsurgency campaign reached genocidal levels, according to the United Nations findings. There was no effort to conceal the atrocities from the local population. To the contrary, abductions commonly occurred in broad daylight, and the mutilated victims were often abandoned in public places as a warning to others.

Many members of the United States Congress were keenly aware of the systematic human rights violations taking place, and tried again and again to help curb the abuses and to keep U.S. tax dollars out of death squad hands. They were circumvented, however, by the very intelligence agencies supposedly under congressional oversight. In short, our elected policymakers were not permitted to enforce their collective wisdom. The CIA and other clandestine operatives simply made an end run around them.

U.S. officials on the ground in Central America were fully aware of the grim levels of human rights violations taking place on a daily basis. They knew, as well, that their own local military intelligence partners were fully responsible. This key information, however, was routinely withheld or vastly understated to the appropriate congressional committees. The contents, or lack thereof, of many such reports veer into criminal misrepresentation.

Meanwhile, enormous levels of U.S. funding were poured into these three countries in order to halt the spread of any Sandinista-like governments. Much of it went directly or indirectly to funding the deadly security forces, despite legal prohibitions on sending U.S. military support to systematic human rights violators. The U.S. also provided much-needed weaponry, tank and helicopter parts, and other equipment either through donations or through authorized sales. The SOA, the CIA, and other intelligence agents gave extensive training to many of the most notorious military abusers, including Julio Roberto Alpirez in Guatemala, Batallion 316 members in Honduras, and the Atlacatl Brigade members in El Salvador. Recently disclosed manuals have confirmed that torture techniques and other human rights violations were taught. Meanwhile, known torturers were placed on CIA payroll as paid informants ("assets") or as liaisons.

Worse yet, our own intelligence agents were working as full partners with the local military death squad members. Although it was Guatemalan, Salvadoran, and Honduran "especialistas" who physically carried out the torture itself, U.S. agencies were closely involved in many aspects of the operations, from planning counterinsurgency campaigns and establishing joint operations centers, to teaching surveillance and interrogation methods, to reviewing intelligence "obtained" from secret prisoners, to paying informants. Victims were never warned in advance, even when entire civilian villages were at risk, as in Guatemala. Once kidnapped and secretly detained, the "suspect" was simply left to his or her fate. The families and courts were never notified. The death squads were carefully shielded from any adverse legal or political consequences for their actions.

All of the above certainly points to aiding and abetting and conspiracy to commit torture, and torture "by proxy" as seen in the current practice of extraordinary renditions, discussed above. But did CIA and other U.S. intelligence agents go even further? Did they in fact cross the line and participate in the torture itself, as has been documented in Iraq and Afghanistan? It is time to review the testimonies of the survivors themselves.

FROM THE LATIN AMERICAN TORTURE CELLS

The following testimonies have much to teach us about the direct participation in torture by U.S. intelligence agents during the past many decades in Latin America. Taken together, they leave little doubt that such involvement was the official practice, or standard operating procedure, of the CIA and similar agencies. Moreover, the refined torture methods reported were clearly carried on to Guantánamo, Afghanistan, and eventually to Abu Ghraib, with disastrous results.

The testimonies and case histories vary in many respects. In some cases, a great deal of evidence exists and has been confirmed by government sources. In others, the victim was able to obtain only scraps of information, which were nevertheless particularly damning.

EVERARDO: TORTURE BY PROXY IN GUATEMALA
The personal story of my relationship with my husband is set forth in detail in my earlier book, *Searching for Everardo*.[1] However, the voluminous official information later disclosed in his case sheds much light on the CIA's practice of hiring notorious torturers as "assets" or paid informants. This gave the public one of its first clear views of U.S. torture by proxy. The information also provided a framework for better understanding the other case histories, which follow below. For this reason, although the facts of Everardo's case are summarized at the beginning of this book, additional evidence and details are set forth here.

Suffice it to say that I met Everardo after monitoring human rights abuses in Guatemala for many years. I was outraged by the lack of adequate reporting on the rampant violations, and was working on an anthology of oral histories. That, in turn, took me to the battlefront in 1990 to interview indigenous women combatants in the resistance forces. Everardo[2] was the commanding officer for the region.

During my thirty days in the mountains we spoke from time to time when his crushing responsibilities permitted. I found his life story very moving. He was born in a remote community of laborers on a southwestern coffee plantation near El Tumbador, and began working the fields at a very young age with his father, a Mam speaker. Everardo's clearest childhood memories were of the endless hunger and his deep frustration at being unable to go to the distant schoolhouse. He wanted to learn, but an education was out of the question. He had to work. They were starving.

At the age of eighteen he left home for good and joined the URNG forces. In the mountains, he learned to read and write and swiftly rose to the high rank of Comandante. When we met I was impressed by his voracious mind and the time he carefully set aside each night to read by the campfire. His life had been difficult, spanning as it did the peak years of the army's ruthless counterinsurgency campaign. His first *compañera* was shot to death at his side; the second was "disappeared." Despite the hardships, he remained in the mountains for seventeen years. When he came to Mexico in 1991 to help prepare for the peace negotiations, he wrote and invited me to visit. We quickly became inseparable, and married that September.

By early January 1992 the war was taking a difficult turn, and Everardo returned to his embattled front. On March 12 he vanished during a brief skirmish with army soldiers not far from the town of Retalhuleu. His fellow combatants found no boots, no backpack, no rifle, and no body. Local villagers reported that the soldiers had left with what seemed to be a person in a burlap bag, but whether a corpse or a living being they did not know. The next day the army reported that they had found a cadaver in olive green at the combat site. We asked the G-2 intelligence division for forensic information and received a highly detailed written description of the body, which matched Everardo feature by feature. For a long time, we believed he was dead.

In early 1993 Santiago Cabrera López managed to escape from a military base in Guatemala. He had fought for years under my husband's command and knew him well. Throughout the thirty-five-year civil war, the army had never presented a single prisoner of war alive, so Santiago's return seemed quite miraculous. He explained that the military continued to torture and kill most prisoners, but that a new program from Argentina was being utilized. Prisoners with special intelligence value were subjected to long-term torture under medical supervision. The goal was not to kill but to break.

Santiago's own "softening up" period consisted of hanging him from a hook and beating him with blocks until he hemorrhaged, beating his feet until his toenails fell out, applying electrical shocks to his testicles, burying him in a pit under an officer's desk, and chaining him to a bed with no blanket for many months. In order to survive, he pretended to be "broken," sharing out-of-date information and identifying the dead.[3]

On March 12, 1992, Santiago saw Everardo dragged into the Santa Ana Berlín military base. The officers were laughing among themselves about faking his combat death. They interrogated and abused him constantly. After some weeks he was abruptly taken away in a helicopter and the prisoners were told he was dead. However, in June 1992, Santiago was sent to the San Marcos military base where he was startled to again see Everardo, who was very much alive. This time the conditions were even worse. As described earlier, Everardo had apparently been injected with a toxic substance. He was bound, stripped, blindfolded, and raving. His entire body was terribly swollen, one arm and leg heavily bandaged. Col. Julio Roberto Alpirez was presiding.

On hearing this from Santiago, I flew to Washington, D.C., to marshal support from the human rights networks, the O.A.S., and U.S. congressional members. All were deeply concerned and carried out urgent actions on our behalf. I also met with a number of State Department officials, including Marilyn McAffee, the newly named ambassador to Guatemala. They told me that there was no information about Everardo in their files. Form letters with this response were sent to all inquiring members of Congress until 1995.

The Guatemalan army indignantly responded that Santiago was a drunk and a Communist, and that my husband was buried in Retalhuleu, as they had stated before. To settle the matter, I opened the grave. There we found the body of a young man, perhaps eighteen years old, and of very slight build, and with gold crowns on his teeth that Everardo did not have. An autopsy report dated the day after the gun battle showed that the youth also had different scars, coloring, and features. He had not died in combat, but had been tied, fingerprinted, shot, stabbed, beaten, and strangled. His head had been crushed by rifle butt blows. We later learned from a defecting intelligence officer that the man in the grave had been a young soldier dragged from the barracks and "sacrificed" as a human decoy.[4]

After the exhumation, I visited once again with the U.S. ambassador, who repeated that she had no information. I spoke with the Minister of Defense and asked that Everardo either be turned over to the courts of law, or processed as a prisoner of war under the Geneva Conventions. He only laughed. Meanwhile, in Washington, support for the case grew. State Department officials continued to send out the same form letter, claiming that they had no information about the fate of Mr. Bámaca, and that there was no independent evidence that any secret prisoners existed in Guatemala.

By late 1994 it was predicted that the final Peace Accords would soon be signed, so I sat down in front of the Guatemalan National Palace and declared a hunger strike to the death. I stayed there for thirty-two days, as congressional inquiries mounted, death squad cars circled the square, and I grew steadily weaker. Embassy officials daily expressed their concerns about my health, but insisted that they had no information. After nearly four weeks a *60 Minutes* program aired, reporting a CIA memo to the embassy which confirmed Everardo's capture. In the ensuing outcry I was abruptly invited to meet with the White House National Security Council.

Hoping that something would at last be done, I returned to a whirlwind of meetings. The official story was different, yet maddeningly the same. It was admitted that Everardo had indeed been captured alive and that he was not seriously wounded. There was "no evidence that he was still alive," yet I was to presume him dead. Untrusting, I filed a Freedom of Information Act demand for all additional records, but received nothing. On the March 12 anniversary of Everardo's capture I resumed my hunger strike, this time in front of the White House. After twelve days, then U.S. representative Robert Torricelli publicly stated that U.S. intelligence files (all of which had been routed to the White House and State Department) confirmed Everardo's murder. Torricelli also denounced the startling "asset" relationship between the CIA and Colonel Alpirez.

In the political uproar that followed, Congress demanded an explanation, President Clinton ordered an investigation, and I went to court to request all FOIA-eligible documents. An army intelligence defector and a second escaped prisoner of war gave us additional details. The many documents and disclosures received give a grim, albeit enlightening portrayal of Everardo's fate and the role played by the CIA.

As we learned, a team of high-level Guatemalan intelligence officials, including Alpirez, had been responsible for Everardo's torture and extrajudicial execution. Some team members, like Alpirez, were locally based. Others were part of an intelligence death squad called "The Comando," which was headquartered in the capital but carried out its deadly missions throughout the country and even in Mexico. From the list of full or partial names I have received, between eight and twelve Comando members were trained at the

School of the Americas. A number of them were paid CIA assets.[5] Colonel Alpirez was also a suspected drug trafficker,[6] and was described as a violent and dangerous man who "excelled" at the liquidation campaigns in the Mayan highlands during the 1980s.[7] In June of 1992, the same month that Alpirez was seen bending over my husband's swollen body, a CIA agent drove to a remote area and paid the colonel $44,000,[8] a startling sum in a land of such abject poverty.

The Comando unit was frightening in its own right, often using such names as the "Jaguar Justicieros" (Jaguar Avengers) and other notorious death squad names. An escaped prisoner of war, John Doe, was once their captive and later identified many of its victims, including Everardo. According to Doe, the Comando's sole mission was to watch and infiltrate not only URNG networks, but also all human rights, labor, academic, religious, and other civil organizations. The targeted person was later either "disappeared" and tortured, or murdered outright in the streets. In the capital, one of the Comando leaders frequently announced that it was "time to visit Uncle Sam," and would order his driver to take him to a high-rise building just down the street from the United States Embassy.[9]

According to John Doe, one of the leading Comando officials, Maj. Alberto Gomes Guillermo ("Don Rolando"), participated in Everardo's capture and the decision to fake his death. He also ordered Everardo's transfer to the capital for further "interrogation." An obvious North American[10] flew the helicopter that took them away. All of these facts, when taken together, certainly suggest an "asset" relationship between many of the Comando leaders and the CIA.

As for Everardo, we know that he was repeatedly tortured and drugged by army physicians. We know that he tried so often to escape, and was considered to be so highly intelligent, that he was placed in a full body cast to immobilize him. We know that he was held at the Santa Ana Berlín base for a month or so, then taken to Guatemala City; that he was later briefly in an army base in Quetzaltenango; and that by June of 1992, he was once again in the southwest. That fall he was taken away and never seen again in the area. According to one report, he was taken to the nearby army outpost of Las Montañitas, where between five hundred and two thousand death squad victims lie buried beneath the ramshackle buildings. There he was tortured yet again, then presumably executed. Others assume he was thrown into the sea from a helicopter, since that was a frequent practice in the region. However, the most probably account, supported by several insiders, is that he was taken back to Guatemala City, where he survived in captivity well into the spring of 1994. He was then taken to a sugar cane field near Escuintla and dismembered to prevent my identification of his remains.

What did U.S. officials know and when did they know it? Within six days of Everardo's capture, the CIA had confirmed to the State Department that he was alive in army hands, and that his death was being faked in order to torture him for his information. In 1993, after Santiago escaped and I began my endless rounds in Washington, D.C., yet another CIA bulletin was released, noting that three high-level Guatemalan officers had confirmed that Everardo was still alive, and that 350 other secret detainees were in the same situation. For more than a year, the CIA continued to receive and share information about the routine torture and execution of the prisoners, including Everardo. By the time the truth was revealed, all were dead. Those lives could have been saved.

U.S. government documents released either in response to my FOIA litigation or by the Intelligence Oversight Board, reveal the extraordinary degree of U.S. involvement. This, in turn, sheds crucial light on the CIA practice of torture by proxy, an issue highly relevant today in the war against terror.

1. On March 18, 1992, the CIA sent a report to both the White House and the State Department, confirming that Everardo had

been captured alive, that he was a very important prisoner, and that the army would fake his death in order to better take advantage of his intelligence.[11]

2. Because of Everardo's intelligence value, his captors had decided to keep his capture top secret, even from other military leaders. Thus the CIA could not have obtained this information from anyone other than its own paid assets who were directly involved in Everardo's detention and torture. Non-assets would not have shared the highly sensitive information with outsiders, and those who were not involved did not have the information. The CIA certainly was aware of the human rights records of their own assets,[12] and knew that Everardo's torture and execution at their hands were inevitable. Payments were continued nonetheless.

3. The local CIA officials were enthusiastic about Everardo's capture, reporting that he was a very valuable prisoner. The tone of such reports indicates a very high level of U.S. interest in receiving more information.

4. In 1992 the CIA was indeed requesting additional information, as reflected by the fact that four more CIA documents about him were compiled during that time period.[13] These continue to be withheld by the agency. In 1992 I did not yet know that Everardo was alive and had not requested help from the U.S. government. These reports were the results of the CIA's own interests.

5. Standard operating procedures of the CIA would have required a handsome payment for this information about Everardo. Requests for further intelligence, coupled with large payments, would certainly have encouraged Alpirez and the others to further torture Everardo. This was obvious and acceptable to the CIA.

6. Several of the CIA branch managers and others involved during this time period were later fired or disciplined in the wake of the Torricelli disclosures and the IOB investigation.[14]

7. There is no evidence that prior to 1995 the local CIA officials attempted to discipline, instruct, or control any of the assets involved in Everardo's torture.

8. Shortly after my first contacts with the State Department in 1993, the CIA issued another report, disseminated yet again to the White House and the State Department. It states that three high-level military officers were interviewed. Two responded that Everardo was still alive, while the third remained silent. It was also reported that between 300 and 350 persons were being secretly detained by the army at that time. This information was concealed for years.[15]

9. Throughout 1993 and 1994 the CIA and DOD continued to inform the State Department and White House of ongoing abuses of prisoners in Guatemala, including Everardo. One document, for example, reports that prisoners at the Retalhuleu military base were often kept in pits of water so deep that they had to hang onto overhead bars to keep from drowning, and that many prisoners, dead or alive after "interrogation," were thrown from helicopters into the sea.[16] Another indicates that the army routinely tortured and killed all prisoners of war.[17] None of this was shared us.

10. Throughout this time period, numerous "ARA guidelines" were issued, instructing State Department personnel on press communications. For example, after a clear report that Everardo might have been thrown from a helicopter, staffers were instructed, if asked about that report, to say they knew of no such thing, and had tried in every way to be of assistance to me.

In short, this case confirms the U.S. practice of torture by proxy. The CIA was operating an enormous network of paid informants, most of them well known for their involvement in torture and other war crimes. The CIA and related intelligence officials knew which prisoners had been kidnapped, where they were being held, and the fact that their torturers were the CIA's own paid informants. Instead of disciplining the assets and insisting on compliance with human rights requirements, the CIA simply requested and paid for more information, knowing that this would result in further torture. Although required to report human rights violations to the Congressional oversight committees, crucial information was instead concealed. Worse yet, the torturers were shielded from any legal or political consequences. The cost in Everardo's case alone was 350 lives. The cost to the hemisphere over the last many decades is difficult to imagine.

SISTER DIANNA ORTIZ: THE U.S. AGENT IN THE TORTURE CELL

Sister Dianna Ortiz grew up in a large, tightly knit family in the town of Grants, New Mexico. A home video shows a jumble of laughing children and adults crowding around the kitchen table while her father plays the accordion. It is an image that one remembers, full of gaiety, warmth, and affection, and utterly impossible to reconcile with the brutality she suffered in Guatemala.[18]

As a young woman, Dianna grew to be ethereally beautiful, her life rooted in a deep faith in God and the teachings of Christ. Very early in life she decided to become a nun, joining the Ursuline Sisters and living briefly in Kentucky until she was sent to rural Guatemala to serve. There she resided with several other Sisters in a small convent, teaching the local schoolchildren to read and write. She quickly fell in love with the Mayans, and with her own gentle ways soon won their trust and affection in return, no small feat in a land where outsiders have always brought disaster. Life in Guatemala was tumultuous, and troubles with the army constantly rocked the town. Yet for the most part Dianna's own existence was a quiet one, and she was absorbed by her small charges at the school.

When death threats against her began to arrive in 1989, people were baffled. Why was she the target? What possible motives could there be? Yet the messages were grim and very explicit; "Rape Dianna" and "Decapitate Dianna" were but a few of the notes left at the convent doorstep. A frightening man stopped her in the street and warned her to leave Guatemala.

Alarmed, the Sisters sought advice, and many friends urged Dianna to leave the country at once. That, in the end, proved impossible. Her bonds with the children were too strong. She felt that if God had placed her in this town, then it was for her to continue to serve the people, not to run from the hardships they too were suffering. She and her Sisters went to a retreat in Antigua, and it was there that she knelt in the small garden to pray for guidance and discernment. It was there that the strange man appeared once again. He pulled her through a hole in the surrounding hedge, threatening to kill her friends if she cried out. Then he and several other men took her to Guatemala City, to the infamous basement of the Politécnica. Sister Dianna Ortiz had just become one of the "disappeared" of Guatemala.

The men dragged her roughly into a small cell and beat her, then began her interrogation. For every question she answered, they would burn her back with a cigarette. Her answers made no difference to them. If she said "yes" she was burned, and if she then said "no" to the same question, she was burned. They showed her a photo of a woman who looked nothing like her and asked who it was. She did not know, and was burned. Asked if the photo was of herself, she replied "no," and was burned again. They accused her of guerrilla connections and continued to burn her no matter what response she gave. In the end, she was left with more than 111 burns on her body. Then the gang rape began, the men laughing and pulling off her blindfold, one revealing his hideously marked face.

Dianna remembers, too, a terrifying dog, and the whirring and flashing of cameras. As the tortures progressed, she was briefly left alone with a woman who was battered beyond any recognition. They tried to comfort one another and prepare for what was yet to come. When the men returned they wrapped Dianna's hands around a machete and then used it to stab the woman to death. To this day she is haunted by the screams and the blood. To this day she remembers hanging in a pit filled with cadavers and rats.

After some time, her captors threw her to the floor to rape her once again. This time, though, something was different. There was a new person in the room. The others were clearly familiar and at ease with him. "Come on, Alejandro," called one. "Come on and join the fun." It was then that Sister Dianna heard him respond with the familiar American English expletive "Shit!" The man was angry, and snapped that she was an American citizen and that there was already an uproar over her disappearance.

He then demanded that she be dressed and handed over to him. The newcomer clearly had full authority, because the torturers obeyed without protest. They helped her to dress and released her to the man, who took her to his jeep and drove off through the city.

Sister Dianna looked at him carefully. He was clearly wearing an odd wig of frizzy dark curls and large sunglasses, but he looked and sounded American. He was tall and light-skinned, with a long straight nose, thin lips, and a long narrow jaw. His beard was light-colored. As he drove through the streets, he began telling her to forgive her torturers, as they were merely trying to fight Communism, and he said he would take her to his "friend" at the U.S. Embassy. Although he insisted on speaking Spanish with her, he spoke with a heavy American accent, and he certainly understood her English. When she asked him outright if he was from the United States, he was evasive. Convinced he was taking her somewhere to be killed, she leaped from the vehicle and ran for her life.

Fleeing desperately through the streets, Sister Dianna came upon an older woman in simple dress and begged for help. Given the media alerts, the woman at once knew who she must be, and pulled her into her small home, giving her towels and water to cleanse her wounds. Within hours Dianna was reunited with the other Sisters, who had been searching frantically for her since she vanished from the garden. After a brief recovery period, they took her to the U.S. Embassy where, still horrified and in pain, she told her story and asked that the American "friend" be sent to save the others who were dying in the Politéchnica. For the next many years, State Department officials quietly insisted that Sister Dianna seemed rather deranged, that somehow her story was confused or contradictory. When church leaders visited the embassy on her behalf, staffers scoffed and mentioned their troubles with unstable nuns. Rumors flew that Sister Dianna had perhaps been injured during a tryst with a lover, or was in fact mentally unstable. Nothing was ever done.

Recovery for Dianna took many years. Her faith had been shaken to its foundation, and she was wracked with horrific memories of the dying woman and the screams of the others in the basement. Her torturers seemed to stay with her, haunting her every move. The smell of cigarettes or the sight of a rat or a dog brought unbearable flashbacks. Worse yet, with her trauma came the double betrayal of her own government leaders. They were part of it. They said she had imagined it, despite the telling burn scars on her back. They said she did not know herself what had happened and hinted loudly at dishonor. She had tried to save the others but no one had listened. And yet, step by step, Sister Dianna pulled herself through. She worked tirelessly at the Guatemalan Human Rights Commission, trying to help other survivors, and pressing for the abolition of torture. She and a number of Guatemalans brought a civil rights suit against General Gramajo in the United States, charging him with violations of international law. When I began my search for Everardo, she was with me every step of the way no matter how much pain the story brought her.

Cruelly, the U.S. government still refused to provide Sister Dianna with any basic answers. Yet the wheels of justice did grind onwards. With the disclosures in Everardo's case, the official claims that there could have been no such North American in her torture cell began to sound ridiculous. Moreover, as Sister Dianna began to tell her story, her credibility became obvious to the public.

Working closely with a renowned police artist, she also produced three sketches; one of the American they called "Alejandro," and two of her torturers. More than a year later I sat in an audience watching a slide show. One of the pictures showed him with an arm around a tall, fair American whom he identified as the local CIA agent on the ground in Guatemala. Though it had been a long time since I had looked at the sketches, the familiarity of this face shocked me. The man had such a long jaw, coming to a narrow point from two sharp cheekbones. The face had a wolflike quality, accentuated by the long straight nose and the thin, slightly snarling lips. Sitting in the audience, I felt cold. We later had an artist draw up a curly brown wig and sunglasses on sheer tracing paper, making an over-lay for the photograph. With the wig and glasses, the man in the photo looked even more like the man in the sketch. We then called in Sister Dianna, and she looked at the photo, with and without the wig, for the first time. "That's him," she said, and wept.

She has never looked at the photograph again. Instead, she has healed herself and channeled all of her extraordinary powers into healing others, founding and directing the Torture Abolition Survivors' Support Committee, or TASSC, in Washington, D.C. Today she works tirelessly to assure that what happened to her, and to so many others, will never happen again.

And the photograph? In the end we have Dianna's sketch of a man with a disguise, and a photograph of a man who certainly bears a very strong resemblance to the sketch. When Sister Dianna was dragged through the convent hedge, her Sisters raised an all-out alarm within minutes, and calls and cables were soon flying between church members, Washington, D.C., and the United States Embassy. It would have been logical enough for the U.S. ambassador or other official within the embassy to place an urgent call to the local CIA station. Indeed, they would have been remiss had they not done so. Who else would have the high level military connections to find out what had become of her, and where she might be?

Would U.S. officials also have defamed her in order to conceal those unsavory connections with the death squads? Perhaps. After all, both the State Department and CIA had been willing to deceive congressional members about Everardo's situation. While he and 350 other prisoners were still alive, they insisted they had no information. After they learned of his death, they still left me to starve. Could they also have intentionally sacrificed a tortured nun in order to keep their secrets? Probably.

"Miguel," Citizen of Guatemala

Miguel is a young physician today, and could lead a safe and prosperous life if he chose to do so. He has nothing to gain by rocking the political boat in his ever dangerous homeland. He is, however, fiercely idealistic and committed to the promotion of social justice and human rights. This is less surprising when he stoically recounts his own experiences.[19]

In 1982 Miguel was fourteen years old, growing up in Guatemala City as a member of a middle-class Ladino family. That year marked the peak of military repression, with village-by-village massacres in the Mayan highlands and massive army sweeps and "disappearances" within the cities. Everyone lived in fear of being the next to vanish. Miguel and his two young friends were seized in the streets and dragged to a local police station where they were shackled and tortured. Miguel's sisters and several other friends were quickly rounded up as well. During one session, the torturers pulled a rubber hood over Miguel's head to cause asphyxiation. He was beaten again and again and was denied food for long periods. At one point he and the others saw a man lying on the floor, near death, with blood seeping from his bandaged eyes.

After two days, Miguel and his friends were taken one by one for questioning to a special room of the feared Department of Technical Investigations, or "DIT." There his blindfold was removed and he was startled to find himself face to face with a North American flanked by two Guatemalan guards. The gringo was tall, perhaps in his forties, with short, light hair and an athletic, military build and bearing. He spoke Spanish well, but with an obvious American accent and syntax.[20] He questioned Miguel at length about every detail of the lives and actions of his friends and family. Worried that he would cause the capture and abuse of yet more people, Miguel tried not to involve others in his answers. The man was clearly experienced in interrogation, however, and already knew a great deal about him. Angered at one point, the gringo threatened to "burn Miguel's ass" with hot coals if he didn't start cooperating. Miguel's friend was questioned next, and the strange man told him not to try any tricks, then bragged about his experiences in Vietnam and Africa.

Given their unusually young ages, Miguel and his sisters and friends were eventually released, and they fled the country. Two friends, however, remain "disappeared" to this day. This is but one of 200,000 cases in Guatemala. It is unusual because Miguel survived and was willing to speak about the American directly involved in his torture.

John ("Juan") Doe, Citizen of Guatemala

Much of John Doe's experiences are set forth above in the section on Everardo's case.[21] The details of his own torture, however, shed additional light on important aspects of the U.S./death squad relationship in Guatemala. "Juan" was born and raised in an impoverished Ladino peasant family in rural Guatemala. He had little education but was highly intelligent and, like the rest of his family, keenly aware of the social injustices he observed around him. In the early 1980s he and his brothers joined the resistance forces, or the URNG, and left home to serve in a combat unit. His father, a URNG civilian sympathizer, was "disappeared" by the Guatemalan military, his name and picture later appearing in the notorious "registro," the army's record of its own death squad victims. Not long afterwards, Juan's mother, wife, and sister were also abducted by the army during a violent raid on their home; they were never seen again. His two toddlers were left with his in-laws, who immediately went into hiding.

Juan himself was captured by the army and turned over to the intelligence division in 1988. As with all prisoners of war, he was brutally tortured. He was beaten with a bat, given electrical shocks to the testicles and underarms, and drowned repeatedly in a deep vat of water. He was also "hooded," or asphyxiated with a rubber hood filled with pesticides, and held in a tiny cell where he could barely move. To further pressure him, the soldiers forced their way into a church sanctuary and seized his two small children. They told Juan that if he did not give better information, his children would be dragged to death behind a car.

During one torture session, Juan was tied and blindfolded, and seated on a chair. He had heard commotion outside as a new person arrived and was ushered down the hall. Most of his captors then left the room, with one Guatemalan officer returning with the newcomer. They approached and stood over him. The Guatemalan spoke in regular Guatemalan Spanish, and from his relatively short height seemed to be a Guatemalan. The other man was far taller and spoke with a heavy American accent. Noting that Juan had been very badly beaten, he promised better treatment, but said that Juan would "have to work with them." He then asked a number of questions about Cuba. Were the URNG members training there? What about medical care in Cuba? What role were the Cubans playing in the civil war in Guatemala? What about weapons from Cuba? At last the man was finished, and as he left, he told the Guatemalan officer that he wanted photographs of Juan. He spoke with authority and was treated with deference. He then left the room and never returned or checked in any way on Juan's continuing abuse.

"David," Citizen of Guatemala

David was a young man in Guatemala when he was abducted by the army in 1969, together with his friend.[22] They were leaving a small pharmacy in the capital when they were surrounded, beaten, and forced into a vehicle by several men in civilian clothes. They were blindfolded and bound, so he could not see where they were going, but after about a half an hour the car stopped and they were dragged into a building and placed in a small cold cell, which he estimates to have been six feet long. Shortly afterwards, they were taken out for questioning and the torture began.

David was stripped and beaten severely, then burned with lighted cigarettes. He was "hooded" with a plastic bag filled with pesticide to cause his asphyxiation. He also remembers the psychological abuse, the men attempting to fondle him, threatening him with rape. After several days, he was taken to a different room and placed in a metal chair. To his surprise, he heard a man giving the orders and speaking with the obvious accent of a North American. This "gringo" was in charge of the session that day, and David was subjected to repeated electrical shocks to the most sensitive parts of his body. He was again badly beaten, his captors insisting that he admit he was a guerrilla and was fighting against the government of Guatemala and the United States.

Two days later his blindfold was removed and he was taken to another room, where he was presented to two men, perhaps fifty years old and, again, "gringos." The two claimed that they were from the Red Cross, and were dressed in blue, with a Red Cross insignia. They told David that if he confessed to being a member of the guerrillas and fighting against the government, they would protect him and take him to another country. When David and the others refused to confess, the men grew angry and walked out. He never saw them again.

María Guardado, Citizen of El Salvador

María Lorenza Guardado was living in San Miguel, El Salvador, when she was abducted in 1980.[23] Tough, pretty, and exceedingly bright, she was working with a local peasant union and, despite the risks, was involved in a number of political activities. When the threats began, she was hardly surprised, but she kept on with her efforts nonetheless. She had already been badly beaten by the local police once before, and she knew that she was being followed by members of the security forces.

In January she was dragged from an ice cream parlor in broad daylight by a group of masked and armed men, one of whom she was nonetheless able to recognize as a member of the security forces. They blindfolded her and threw her into a vehicle, driving off at high speed and eventually stopping at an unknown location. There she was beaten, raped, and given electrical shocks to her breasts and genitals. The men insisted that she give the names and addresses of her colleagues, but she refused. Certain that she would be killed, she was unwilling to cause the torture and death of yet another person. When she yielded no information, they impaled her through the rectum with a stake, causing her to hemorrhage so severely that she lost consciousness.

When she awoke, the vehicle had stopped again and the men were dragging her inside a building. There she heard the same voices of the men who had abducted her, but also a new and startling voice. In it, she heard the unmistakable accent of a North American. She was familiar with the accent not only from the radio and television programs, but also from working with the many international human rights workers who had accompanied the popular marches and protests. The American was apparently in charge, asking who would be the first to torture her, for example, then asking who would go next, and what would be tried, throughout the entire session. The Salvadorans responded with respect and obedience. They took turns stamping on her kneecaps, broke her wrist and ribs, burned her arms and legs repeatedly, and jumped on her back, fracturing the discs in her spine. She screamed, but gave no information. Finally the American said, "She's dead, get rid of her." She felt herself being carried back to the van. Once again they drove and drove, then stopped and threw her onto a grassy patch of land. She has no idea where they were. Again she was beaten, this time so severely that her pelvis broke, and she was left for dead.

Miraculously, she survived, and was able to crawl to a nearby roadway. There a taxi driver spotted her and drove her home, leaving her on the steps of her front door at dawn. Her terrified relatives moved her from safe house to safe house until she was strong enough to travel, then hurried her into exile. Despite everything, she has spoken out about her experiences since the day of her escape.[24]

José Rubén Carrillo Cubas and Oscar Alexander Ortiz, Citizens of El Salvador

For many years my friend Lisa Brodyaga, a fellow lawyer from Texas, served as a volunteer human rights worker in El Salvador. She became fast friends with Herbert Anaya, who was the coordinator of the Salvadoran Human Rights Commission and a long-time human rights hero. Anaya worked tirelessly to expose the repression despite the near certainty of his own assassination. When several colleagues at the Commission were arrested and detained at the Mariona prison, he had them interview fellow inmates who had survived torture at the hands of the security forces. Lisa herself met with many of the survivors and helped smuggle out their sworn statements. As noted in chapter 1, the testimonies were accompanied by careful sketches depicting the forms of torture utilized. These bear an uncanny likeness to the photographs taken at Abu Ghraib. One shows a North American inflicting electrical shocks to a prisoner's ears. The team's remarkable findings were published in "Torture in El Salvador" in 1986, by the Human Rights Commission of El Salvador.

On October 26, 1987, Herbert Anaya was shot dead in front of his home at 6:45 A.M. when he stepped outside to take his children to school. He remains a popular hero to this day among the people of El Salvador. Certain aspects of his own remarkable story must be noted here. On May 26, 1986, over a year before his murder, he had been abducted and tortured by the feared Policía de Hacienda. His wife Mirna and their small children were present when he was dragged away by heavily armed men. Mirna had relatives working at the Policía headquarters and was thus able to confirm his whereabouts almost immediately. He was being held in the main offices, where Colonel Golcher was the chief and Victor Cartagena headed intelligence. Mirna's various connections also confirmed that two North American advisors were permanently working there at that time. When Herbert's lawyer went to visit, he was first denied permission by the Salvadoran officer in charge. When the lawyer persisted, the officer called one of the North Americans, who finally authorized a five-minute visit. Herbert was quickly pulled from his torture cell and dressed, then seated behind a desk so that his feet were not visible. His feet were so badly swollen he could no longer put on his shoes. He had been standing for three days with no sleep, no food, and no toilet privileges. Was a North American present during his questioning? Most likely, but Herbert was hooded at all times and could not say for sure. Did the Yankee advisors know he was there and enduring torture? Of course. Did they assist or intervene in any way? Of course not.

The following two accounts come from Herbert Anaya's remarkable documentation at Mariona prison.

José Rubén Carrillo Cubas was a twenty-three-year-old student from Soyopango when he was interviewed at the La Esperanza prison in 1986. He and his brother-in-law, Juan Argueta, had been visiting a local engineer who was trying to assist Juan in getting a job. Unfortunately for them both, the house was close to the army barracks of San Carlos. As they left, six members of the PRAL, or Long-Distance Reconnaissance Patrol, stopped them, checked their papers, and threw them into a truck, covering them with a tarpaulin so that they would not be visible to persons on the street.

They were taken to the army barracks, where José was forced to stand with his feet one meter apart, as the men beat him on the chest and across his body. After that he was hung by his handcuffed hands from a pole running between the toilets in a bathroom. He was left in that painful position, with a hood over his head, for the entire night. At one point, soldiers swung him back and forth. The next morning he was interrogated at length, but could not answer any questions because he did not know anything. This infuriated the soldiers, who beat him badly, then stripped him naked and flung him into a room filled with ants. There were so many swarming over him that he could not open his eyes.

When he was taken out later, a North American military advisor walked by. José could see him quite well as the blindfold had been removed. The man was about six feet tall and thin, with corrective glasses on. He was also dressed in an olive green camouflage uniform, with a knife, canteen, and a small apparatus at his belt. The advisor and another soldier took José to a small room with a desk and washbasins around the wall. They placed him in front of the wall and the advisor touched the apparatus to Jose's back and his ears, giving him painful electrical shocks. José estimated that the shocks were about 200 volts. This torture lasted for about fifteen minutes.

José was then taken away for more interrogations and beatings. At one point the soldiers fired a gun to his head, but it had no bullets. They also forced him to watch the torture of other prisoners, including the beatings of his own brother. He went for long periods without food. Eventually, it was decided that he really knew nothing and he was allowed to live. First, however, he was forced to falsely confess to his "crimes" on video, which he accepted to avoid more torture. Based on this confession, he was serving time in prison. The American advisor never returned or interceded in any way.

Oscar Alexander Ortiz Hernández, a sixteen-year-old worker from Morazán, gave his testimony in the la Esperanza prison in August 1986. He was a young member of the FMLN forces and was captured by the Salvadoran army after a brief combat on February 23, 1986. He stated that his unit had attacked the military post of the Police of Hacienda El Martillo. Oscar had approached the radio post to requisition the equipment, when a soldier launched a grenade at them, killing the government radio operator and also blasting shrapnel through Oscar's legs. He was bleeding heavily when the soldiers captured him, but they nevertheless beat him severely before taking him to an army base. He was placed in a room all alone, beaten regularly for days, and given no medical care at all. His wounds festered and began to stink, and he coughed up coagulated blood.

After three days a medical worker arrived and said that he was going to give Oscar a shot that would kill him. The injection caused Oscar to feel very hot and groggy, and eventually he did lose consciousness. When he awoke, the interrogation began again, and he was kicked and beaten. This hurt his wounds, but they mocked him when he wept in pain. At one point a sergeant brought back a strange device, like a pistol with a wire attachment. The wire was very hot, and he inserted it again and again into Oscar's wounds. Sometimes they stood on his stomach. He was given no food, only water, and denied bathroom privileges.

After about eight days, they took Oscar on a stretcher into the courtyard and left him there. He could not walk, and was not blindfolded. A North American came to him and began asking questions. He spoke in poor Spanish. His skin was light, a bit reddened, with blond hair, blue eyes, a long thin nose, and freckles. He was tall and slim, with hairy arms. He couldn't understand Spanish that well either, and a Salvadoran sergeant called "Tiger" was with him. After asking Oscar many questions, the man said, "Use your balls, it will be better soon," then walked off.

Shortly afterwards, Tiger and another official called the press and forced Oscar to make a public call to his comrades and confirm that he had been treated well, fed, bathed, and given medical attention. When Oscar at first declined, the sergeant put a gun to his head and threatened to kill him. At the press meeting, he sat nearby with the gun while Oscar spoke. There were only three journalists there, all from the Press Committee of the Armed Forces. After that the beatings stopped but he was still not taken to a hospital. He remained in this place for fifty-two days. Eventually he was forced to sign papers, and was placed in the prison at Mariona.

"Marco," Citizen of El Salvador

Marco was an idealistic young doctor in El Salvador in the 1980s, and was devoted to serving the poor. To this day he still provides medical service in impoverished areas, but his idealism was shattered long ago.[25]

Like so many others working with rural communities, Marco was abducted by the Salvadoran military in 1982, accused of assisting the guerrillas, and severely tortured. Even today, some twenty years later, he can barely speak of what was done to him. Despite his clear distress, he tells of two particular torture sessions because he understands their significance, and because he knows that only if survivors like himself speak out, will the suffering ever end. He wants to help, but as he tells me about his experiences the tears roll down his gentle face.

During one session he lay bound on the floor, seriously injured. He had not been given medical care, and his wounds were festering. That particular day his captors said they would "treat" him, and scraped his wounds so roughly it caused him great pain. He was blindfolded, but clearly heard a North American speaking to the others in the room. The man kept telling the others what questions to ask and how to press for more information. He had authority and was making many suggestions, none of them helpful to Marco. The man's accent was easy enough to recognize. Well educated, Marcos had met many North Americans in El Salvador, and he had listened to them on radio and television. After living in the United States for many years, he still remembers the man's voice and remains certain of the accent.

At one point during the session, the Salvadoran torturer pulled a maggot out of Marcos' shoulder wound and placed it on his chest, ordering him to eat the maggot. When Marcos did not comply, he was kicked and given electrical jolts. In the end, he tried to obey but because he was so tightly bound he could not reach the maggot with his mouth. The men continued to beat him. What he remembers most is the North American's laughter.

The North American was present on a second occasion as well. That time Marcos was hanging from his wrists, his feet not able to quite touch the ground. His hands pained him terribly, and the damage to his tendons would trouble him long afterwards. A sharp instrument had been inserted into his rectum, so that if he tried to shift the weight from his hands to his feet, he would be impaled. The gringo made no effort to help, instead continuing to discuss questions and strategies with the torturers.

Josephine Beecher, U.S. Citizen in El Salvador

Josephine Beecher was a thirty-seven-year-old American serving as a church volunteer in El Salvador during the civil war. Her disturbing story was reported by the *Washington Post* on November 30, 1989.[26] One week earlier, the Salvadoran military had raided a refugee sanctuary in the Saint John the Evangelist Episcopal Church where she was working. She and another American were arrested, as were six others who were released the same day. Some fourteen Salvadoran workers were still being detained when the story was published. The arrests came shortly after the murders of the six Jesuit priests, and many religious workers had been receiving death threats. The detentions were fiercely condemned by leaders of the Episcopal Church.

Josephine herself reported that U.S. Vice Consul David Ramos was nearby and merely watched as police removed her watch and glasses and led her away. He made no effort to assist her, and was on the premises while she was being abused. According to her, he was drinking coffee with the colonel. Meanwhile, she was struck, threatened, and had a hood filled with talcum pulled over her head. The officers threatened to give her electrical shocks and ran an object over her throat, threatening to kill her. Before she was released, she was told to sign a form saying she had not been mistreated. She crossed out that portion, but Ramos himself insisted that it be retyped with the clause intact. She later complained to the embassy, where she was told that she had received normal treatment for a prisoner of war and that there was no problem with what had occurred. When *Washington Post* journalist Laurie Goodman contacted the embassy she was told they were too busy trying to protect Americans to respond.[27]

Andrés Pavón Murillo, Citizen of Honduras

Andrés Pavón Murillo sits upright behind his desk.[28] He is neatly dressed and professional in manner. He has long been a human rights leader in Honduras, helping to take testimonies from the survivors and working to end the official violations. Yes, he himself was abducted and tortured in Honduras, he says. Yes, there was an American present.

In 1983 he was a young man of twenty in Tegucigalpa. He was walking down the street when a group of heavily armed men in civilian dress accosted him and forced him into a car. As they drove him toward a clandestine center, they were singing "Where is the tomb of the guerrilla member?" and threatening to put a bullet through his head.

At the torture center, they stripped him naked and began interrogating him, asking again and again about Cuba, Nicaragua, and the Honduran guerrilla forces. They choked him, beat his hands until his fingernails broke open, and hung him by the arms until the pain was terrible. He was always handcuffed and they never turned off the lights. It was always very cold in his cell. For a week he was denied food, then it was thrown in his face as if he were an animal. He was told that if he did not talk, they would drag in his mother and torture her as well. At times he thought he heard her screaming nearby. They threatened to kill him by running a stake through his rectum to his brain, as the Spaniards had with the indigenous leader Atlacatl so long ago.

Andrés suffered for thirty-five days. He was then taken to a new place. They removed his blindfold and he found himself in the presence of two men. One was clearly Honduran and wore a military uniform. The other was a North American, a "gringo." He was about forty years old, taller than most Hondurans, with the fitness of a military person. He had light greenish eyes and sandy hair. Andrés noted that he had no indigenous or African features, unlike most Hondurans. He wore civilian clothing.

The Honduran official told Andrés that if he wanted to live he would have to present himself to the press and declare that he had voluntarily turned himself in, had been staying in a hotel, and had been well treated. He was also to admit that certain weapons to be produced at the event were in fact his. Andrés nodded, knowing that he had no choice. When he nodded, the gringo would also nod, as if to signal approval. The man clearly understood what was happening but chose not to speak. As the damage to Andrés's hands and fingernails was still very evident, it was clear that a hoax was being carried out. Yet the North American was in full agreement with it all. He did nothing to intercede or protect Andrés in any way.

"Elena," Citizen of Costa Rica

"Elena" is a strong, feisty feminist, full of hilarity and bigger than life to those who know her.[29] She works in the field of communications, reads voraciously, and has opinions and witty comments about everything. She does not like to discuss her 1982 abduction and torture in Honduras, but she is willing to do so if it might help end the abuses.

Elena is a citizen of Costa Rica. As a young adult she moved to New York, where she lived for eight years, spending four of them in a convent. Utterly independent and full of ideas about working for the poor and for societal reforms, she believed that joining the Sisterhood was her best option. She became highly educated and fluent in English before she decided to return to the life of a layperson, going home to Costa Rica as a teacher and a wife.

She was affiliated with the university and with popular literacy campaigns throughout Costa Rica for many years. In the early 1980s, as war spread across Central America, she also volunteered to work with various refugee populations, assisting them in establishing literacy projects of their own. For a long time she worked with the Salvadorans. In 1982, under U.N. auspices, she also traveled to the Mesa Grande refugee camp in Honduras. The fear and repression there was palpable. The Honduran social workers warned her again and again to be careful, that the security forces considered them to be as much of a political target as the refugees themselves.

Elena was grateful when a Honduran woman named "Alicia" offered her the key to her own apartment, advising her against staying alone in a hotel. Arriving in Tegucigalpa, Elena went straight to the address, feeling weary and tense. She put the key in the lock and entered. As she placed her suitcases on the floor, she felt two gun barrels on her neck and saw a row of bound feet in front of her. She had arrived just as the house was being raided by the Honduran death squads. She was bound, blindfolded, and tossed in a vehicle with the others. They were taken to a clandestine center, where she learned that her friend Alicia had already been taken prisoner and was there as well.

Alicia suffered from the worst torture; she was stripped, battered, sexually molested, and given electrical shocks to the breasts and genitals until blood flowed from her vagina from the burns. Elena endured less severe abuse, because her captors were worried about her Costa Rican citizenship and her U.N. papers. They clearly wished to avoid an international incident and were uncertain as to what to do with her. She was however, bound, blindfolded, beaten repeatedly, denied food, sexually molested, and left to sleep on the floor without a blanket or mattress. She vividly remembers the threats to kill her and the screams of the others throughout the building.

Elena also remembers lying bound on the floor with some other women when their captors entered the room with a newcomer. She was taken aback by the voice. He was speaking with a very heavy American accent, which she promptly recognized from her years in the United States. The "gringo" asked what information the officers had got out of the prisoners, chatted for a while, then simply left the women on the floor. He never returned or reported their whereabouts, never assisted or protected them in any way. Elena later learned that the group had come very close to extrajudicial execution, but had been released instead, most probably because of her U.N. connections.

Father James "Guadalupe" Carney of Honduras

As a child Father James Carney did not plan to become a priest, but as an adult he became a much loved one.[30] He grew up in a large Catholic family in the Midwest, and was an avid sports fan and an athlete himself. He enlisted in World War II and served in Europe for several years before returning home and attending college. Only then, after much reflection, did he decide to join the seminary.

Once ordained, Father Carney enthusiastically pressed to be sent to Honduras as a missionary. Arriving there in 1961, his life changed rapidly. Known by all as Father Guadalupe, or just "Lupe," he quickly came to love his impoverished parishioners, and he committed his every moment to serving them. He was shocked and angered by the needless suffering he witnessed and by the great disparities between the small, wealthy upper class and the masses of landless poor. As his brother-in-law and friend, Joseph Connolly, writes:

> Lupe saw the real world not from a distance but from inside it. He saw the children bloated with hunger...the peasant families living in the gullies between the roads and fences while landowners and corporations left huge pastures idle and undeveloped....Many of us see the increasing chasm between haves and have-nots...but Lupe's problem was that he saw with total certainty that this was not the plan of God.[31]

Resolved to live in accordance with Christ's teachings, Father Guadalupe moved into a tiny house in the countryside, where he lived and worked along side the campesino members of his community. The more he learned of their struggle to survive, the more deeply involved he became in the movement for basic labor rights and socioeconomic justice. He spoke out again and again against the extreme government repression he was witnessing. Soon enough he came under constant death threats himself.

In 1979 the Honduran government expelled Father Guadalupe

once and for all, canceling his Honduran citizenship. Heartbroken, he worked in Nicaragua for a number of years, while desperately trying to arrange for his return home. In 1983 he agreed to accompany a small band of guerrillas back into his beloved Honduras, serving as their chaplain. The group, led by José María Reyes Mata, was ill-fated from the very beginning. Supplies soon ran low and the terrain turned difficult.

On August 1, 1983, two members deserted and reported the presence of the guerrilla column to the Honduran military. The reaction was swift and brutal. By September 20, the army reported to the press that after four firefights the guerrillas were all dead. Father Guadalupe was said to have perished of starvation in the jungle.[32] Given his knowledge of the terrain this seemed unlikely, and there were discrepancies in the official stories. His family tried for years to obtain answers to their many questions about his death, both from the U.S. Embassy and the Honduran government, but they received no adequate explanations.

Even at the time of the September press conference, soldiers were reporting that Reyes Mata had in fact been taken alive, as had other prisoners. Workmen at the local El Aguacate air base said that on September 5, General Álvarez himself had arrived, and that later a number of prisoners were brought to the base under heavy guard, including Reyes Mata, whom they recognized from photographs. The workers were warned to discuss this matter no further.[33] Meanwhile, the prisoners were "interrogated" and their information then led to several more skirmishes, during which sixteen guerrillas were killed and four more were taken prisoner. These four were also interrogated at El Aguacate.

The El Aguacate base was being used at the time for U.S.-Contra activities and had a very large U.S. presence, including troops, Black Hawk helicopters, and an array of CIA agents.[34] The Department of State, moreover, has admitted that a U.S. attaché had helped to "debrief" the prisoners since August 1.[35]

One of the prisoners, later shot to death, was able to get word out

85

that two U.S. advisors, a Lt. West Blank and Maj. Mark Kelvi, were involved in the torture of various prisoners, including James Carney. Much of this was later confirmed by a Honduran National Guardsman.[36]

In 1987 Florencio Caballero of Batallion 316 reported that Father Lupe had indeed been captured alive, tortured, then thrown from a helicopter. He also confirmed that El Aguacate had a very heavy CIA presence for Contra activities. According to Caballero, General Álvarez had held a meeting prior to the capture of the priest and others. Caballero himself was present, as was "Mr. Mike," a CIA agent, and other U.S. officials. During the discussion it was revealed that Father Lupe was with the insurgent group. Álvarez ordered that he and the others be killed upon capture. The Americans made no protest.[37] "Mr. Mike" was also involved in the torture of Inés Murillo (see below).[38]

The Carney family members continue to seek the truth to this day. On an early visit to El Aguacate they saw, scratched onto a brick wall, the words "Mario was here"—Mario being the pseudonym used by Father Lupe. When they returned, the words had been removed. Eventually a Bible used by Lupe was found at the base and returned to them. Words scrawled in the margin of the story of Jeremiah in the cistern read "People suffered here for speaking the truth."[39]

The campesinos of Honduras have never forgotten their beloved Father Lupe. Rural cooperatives and even a human rights center have been named in his honor. But no answers about his death have ever been provided.

The CIA has acknowledged that during the time period in question, their operatives in Honduras did not properly disclose to Congress the ongoing human rights violations taking place.[40] This matter was the subject of an Inspector General investigation. Despite disturbing findings, the CIA attempted to close the investigation down with no further action in 1996, only to have the Senate Intelligence Committee demand that it be reopened. This was vexing to some agents. "How long do you have to reexamine the past?" asked one.[41]

In the end, nothing was done. Dr. Leo Valladares, the Honduran Human Rights Ombudsman, long sought the declassification of U.S. files pertaining to Honduran cases. He received very little. The truth remains concealed, and the dead remain "disappeared."

Inés Murillo, Citizen of Honduras

Inés Murillo was a tough, brilliant, and quite beautiful young attorney in Honduras when she and a friend were dragged off the streets by members of the notorious Batallion 316 in March 1983. She was secretly detained for seventy-eight days and subjected to tortures which included drowning in a vat of water, beatings, and electrical shocks. After the first few weeks, she was moved to a second location, a military center called INDUMIL, where not even the Honduran police or courts were permitted to enter or search for the *desaparecidos*. There her torture continued. She was again submerged in water, deprived of food, tied in excruciating positions, kept naked, denied toilet privileges, and terrorized with a ferocious dog. Sleep deprivation was extreme. She was left on the floor with no mattress or blankets, and ice cold water was thrown into her face every ten minutes. Her torturers constantly beat her and threatened to kill her family.[42]

As with Father Carney, an American called "Mr. Mike" came often to the INDUMIL center. She would hear her torturers call out "Here comes Mr. Mike!" as he arrived. He knew of Ms. Murillo's situation and could see her visible injuries. He also was present during one interrogation session and helped to draft additional questions to ask her. She could hear him writing, then passing the sheet of paper to her captors. The Honduran interrogator then asked the new questions as written, complete with the grammatical and syntax errors of a foreigner.[43]

Florencio Caballero, a former member of Batallion 316 and himself one of Ms. Murillo's torturers, confirmed her story, including the presence of the North American.[44] U.S. officials have also admitted that a CIA operative was in fact stationed in Honduras and had access to INDUMIL during the time period of Ms. Murillo's imprisonment there.[45]

Mr. Mike apparently did more than simply suggest questions, however. Although Florencio Caballero died abruptly in Canada at a young age, raising a flurry of questions about murder or suicide, he had spoken further with journalist Anne Marie O'Connor of the *Atlanta Journal*. According to Caballero, it was Mr. Mike who urged them to keep prisoners awake by dousing them with cold water or letting rats into their cells. He also, informally, recommended electrical shocks as the best way to get a prisoner to speak.[46] Once again, the "wink and nod" approach was used.

Ms. Murillo survived because her father was a high-level military officer in the Honduran army. Some U.S. officials claim that they themselves helped to better her treatment and obtain her release. Inés Murillo begs to differ. Her treatment can hardly be said to have "improved." Moreover, the CIA agents never disclosed her name or whereabouts to her family, the courts, or the police during her torture. She was, after all, a victim of an illegal kidnapping, subjected to violent and criminal acts on a daily basis. If the CIA agents had the power to obtain her release, they also had the power to halt her torture. They apparently chose not to do so until her interrogation was complete.

■ ■ ■

We do not, of course, know who the real "Mr. Mike" is, other than that he was a CIA agent who assisted in the interrogations of clandestine prisoners in Honduras. However, an autobiographical book called *SEAL!*,[47] by Lt. Cmdr. Michael Walsh, certainly offers us insight as to the kind of person this "Mr. Mike" may have been.

Mr. Walsh was a Navy Seal and a member of Operation Phoenix, a de facto death squad in Vietnam, where he excelled in

planning the interrogation of prisoners. He certainly did not dis-
approve when captives were tortured by his Vietnamese partners,
and he made no effort to stop them. He did, however, believe that
prisoners were far more valuable alive than dead for intelligence
purposes. He had a close working relationship with the CIA.

Like many other Vietnam vets, he was sent to Central America during the 1980s and became involved in the "dirty little wars"
there. He was in Honduras, Panama, and Venezuela in 1980. Was he
still in the region when Inés Murillo or James Carney were tortured
in 1983? His book suggests that he was not—he states that he was in
Norway in early 1983, then in training back in the U.S. in October,
and eventually in Grenada. In the late 1980s he was in Panama, and
he refers to his continuing intelligence work in El Salvador and
Honduras, "where we were fighting some very dirty little wars."[48]
He also boasts of the high number of Phoenix agents from the Vietnam era teaching in Latin America.[49]

Significantly, Walsh utterly despised priests and nuns engaged
in liberation theology, such as Father James Carney. He expressed
these feelings as follows:

> People tend to believe catholic priests and nuns are above such activ-
> ities. Hogwash! Some are clean and some aren't. . . . My own experi-
> ence . . . shows me the Jesuits and Maryknollers are the worst. . . . To
> this day I will not address a priest as Father. . . . In Central and South
> America we knew for a fact that many of the nuns and priests were up
> to their ears in direct support of guerrilla operations. . . . When they
> end up dead I consider it the price of playing a very dirty game with
> some very tough customers on both sides. God bless the good ones,
> the ones who really care and seek to do the Lord's will. As for the oth-
> ers . . . Wear the name, play the game.[50]

Thus with a flourish he dismisses the countless attacks on brave
and selfless church leaders in Central America, from Bishop Romero and the four churchwomen in El Salvador to Sister Dianna
Ortiz in Guatemala.

Intriguingly, Walsh states in the book that his nickname in Vietnam, where his Vietnamese partners had difficulty pronouncing his name, was "Mr. Mike."[51]

Charles Horman and Frank Teruggi, U.S. Citizens in Chile

Charles Horman was a gifted young American journalist with a Harvard education and a promising career. The turbulent era of the 1960s had left him with many questions, and in 1971 he and his wife Joyce set off to travel through Latin America. They arrived in Chile after the election of President Allende, staying on to study and learn about the new government and its social and economic programs.

They made many friends, both Chilean and American. Creative and artistic, Charles became involved in a number of activities, including *FIN*, a magazine devoted to reporting on U.S. activities in Chile as well as the antiwar movement.[52] He was also researching the recent assassination of the Chilean general René Schneider. The general had been stopped in broad daylight by two vehicles, whose occupants then opened fire with automatic weapons. At the time such political murders were unheard of in Chile, and the news had rocked the nation. It later became known that Schneider had rebuffed early CIA proposals for a coup d'etat.[53] Questions about this murder remain to this day.

On September 11, 1973, General Pinochet, with much assistance from the CIA,[54] carried out a violent coup against President Allende. La Moneda, the presidential palace, was bombed, and Allende was shot to death. On the day of the coup, Charles Horman and a friend were in the resort town of Viña del Mar and spoke with several U.S. officials who were there celebrating the "victory." With some difficulty Charles was able to return to Santiago and find his wife Joyce. Given the growing military violence against civilians, they both made urgent preparations to leave the country.

Charles was home alone on the evening of September 17, 1973, when neighbors saw a large truck filled with soldiers arrive and park in front of his house. The soldiers hurried inside, later emerging with boxes of books and papers and dragging Horman with them. A local woman followed the army vehicle and watched it pull into the National Stadium.[55] During the early days of the coup, the Chilean military had arrested 75,000 Allende supporters as well as suspected "leftists" and detained them in the stadium and similar locations. There they were intensively interrogated and tortured, and many were killed without trial.[56]

Joyce Horman and her father-in-law made repeated and desperate efforts to obtain help from the United States Embassy, only to be told again and again that there was no information. It was later learned that embassy officials had in fact received several reports of Charles's arrest and, later, of his death.[57] Yet none of this was shared; if anything, the embassy played an obstructive role. Eventually it was confirmed that Charles had been shot to death and "buried in a wall."

Years later a 1976 State Department document was declassified. The report states that the Horman case "remains bothersome" and that there was evidence to suggest that "U.S. intelligence may have played an unfortunate part in Horman's death. At best it was limited to providing or confirming information that helped motivate his murder by the GOC [Government of Chile]. At worst, U.S. intelligence was aware that the GOC saw Horman in a rather serious light and U.S. officials did nothing to discourage the logical outcome of GOC paranoia."[58] Another document confirms that the U.S. deputy consul at the time of Horman's murder was a CIA officer.[59] According to Philip Agee, a former CIA agent who worked throughout Latin America, such CIA infiltration of U.S. embassies was not unusual.[60]

■ ■ ■

Frank Teruggi was a young American who was also living in Chile at the time of the coup.[61] After attending the California Institute of Technology, he enrolled in the University of Chile School of Political Economy. He became a friend of Charles Horman, and also an active member of the *FIN* network.

On the evening of September 20, 1973, a number of Chilean soldiers forced their way into Teruggi's apartment, which he was sharing with his close friend David Hathaway. The troops searched the apartment, seized certain books, then took the two Americans to Carabinero station, where they were severely beaten. They were later driven to the National Stadium. Frank Teruggi was taken away the following evening and never returned to his cell. David Hathaway was released after further questioning.

Although the State Department had released a report that Teruggi had left the country, Hathaway remained deeply concerned and joined forces with the Hormans. On October 1, Frank Teruggi was found dead in the Santiago morgue, one of hundreds of battered corpses in endless rows. It was later learned that the morgue had notified the U.S. Embassy on September 25 that they had a body of a person tentatively identified as Frank Teruggi, yet U.S. officials there told Horman's father on September 28 that Teruggi had been released alive.[62]

Recent disclosures raise serious questions about the U.S. contribution to Frank Teruggi's murder as well. These indicate that U.S. intelligence sources may have provided information about Teruggi's political life and background to the Chilean security forces, which may in turn have motivated them to detain and kill him.[63]

Peter Wohlstetter, U.S. Citizen in Chile

Peter Wohlstetter was a young U.S. citizen traveling through Latin America and writing about his experiences and observations. He was in Chile when the coup began and was arrested, with two friends, by the Carabineros. They were taken to a local station and forced to lie face down on the floor with their hands on their heads. A soldier with a machine gun stood over them, questioning them about their activities in Chile and asking if they had ever been to Cuba. Wohlstetter was able to turn his head slightly and saw a short man with blond hair, wire rims, and a blue suit enter the room with two soldiers. He spoke with one of the officers for a while and then left.

When Wohlstetter was released and sought help at the U.S. Embassy, he was shocked when he came face to face with Vice Consul Shaffer. This was the same blond man who had entered the station as they were being questioned, yet who had done nothing to help them or to even ascertain their identities.[64]

■ ■ ■

Brazil is yet another nation where United States intervention played a key role in a coup d'etat. As in so many other countries, the 1964 overthrow of civilian president João Goulart was followed by years of military repression.[65] Throughout this period U.S. advisor Dan Mitrione, under the auspices of the U.S. Office of Public Safety, initiated and carried out a controversial police training program in Brazil that many insist brought systematic torture to the country.[66] He was later transferred to Uruguay, where he carried out similar duties. He was eventually kidnapped and executed by the Tupamaros, a Uruguayan revolutionary organization.

The coup, the activities of Mitrione, and the ensuing wave of torture in both Brazil and Uruguay were carefully researched and documented by A. J. Langguth, long-time *New York Times* reporter and professor of journalism at USC. The following cases, documented by Langguth, certainly corroborate the testimonies described above with regard to U.S. involvement in torture.

Jean Marc Van Der Weid, Citizen of Brazil
In 1965 Jean Marc Van Der Weid was an upper-class Brazilian university student, pursuing a degree in engineering.[67] His father was a Swiss engineer and his mother came from a prominent local family. Initially quiet and conservative, Jean Marc became more and more involved in student politics and was eventually forced to go into hiding. During a military dragnet in 1969 he was captured by

the Brazilian police and taken first to the DOPS (Department of Political and Social Order), where he was beaten severely before the questioning even began. He was then detained at the CENIMAR prison, in the basement of the Ministry of the Navy. U.S. Naval officials based there sometimes could hear the screams of the prisoners. They also occasionally saw North Americans in civilian dress near the intelligence offices.[68]

Jean Marc was eventually shipped to the Ilha das Flores, where he suffered long-term and extreme torture, which included prolonged beatings and electrical shocks to the genitals, nipples, ears, and mouth. The shocks were given from battery-operated field telephones similar to those provided by the United States to Jean Marc's own marine reserve unit. He was beaten across the kidneys and ears until he believed his eardrums would burst. On the seventh day of torture he heard a Brazilian officer present translating the questions into English for a foreigner in the room. The man was responding in English with an American accent. [69]

Marcos Arruda, Citizen of Brazil

Langguth's extensive research also brought him to Marcos Arruda, a Brazilian geology student. Once a campus leader, Arruda had difficulty finding even menial jobs and ended up working in a factory in 1970. There he met Marlene Soccas, a resistance member who was struggling to find a safe place to live and some means to support herself. He tried to help her, but in the end both were abducted and tortured. He was beaten with paddles until he bled, then given electrical shocks to his toes, testicles, belly, mouth, and ears. He went into convulsions and was hospitalized.

When he recovered somewhat, they tortured Marlene in a cell nearby, forcing him to listen to her screams. Then they beat him again and withheld his medications. The convulsions returned and he was sent to the medical unit, where he spoke with other patients and learned that two other prisoners had been tortured in the presence of men who spoke only English.[70]

Uruguay: A Young Woman Protests

Professor Langguth also documented Mitrione's later work in Uruguay. With Dan Mitrione there arrived smaller and thinner wires that the police could use to more adeptly inflict electrical shocks. Some of the wires could even fit between a man's teeth. These and other similar equipment were apparently brought into the country in the U.S. Embassy's diplomatic pouch.[71] As in Brazil, torture, as opposed to vigorous beatings, became routine at the police stations.[72]

A retired Uruguayan police officer, still frightened and insisting on anonymity years later, admitted to Langguth that during one session Mitrione entered a torture cell as a prisoner was receiving electrical jolts under his fingernails. Mitrione made no effort to halt the session or instruct the police against such tactics.[73] A double agent named Manuel Hevia Cosculluela insisted that Mitrione himself presided over the torture training sessions in Uruguay and frequently visited the torture cells as part of his supervisory duties. Manuel had attended these sessions and knew and spoke with Mitrione personally.[74]

In the end the protest came, ironically, from Alejandro Otero, a Uruguayan policeman and CIA liaison chosen to run a special office of police intelligence. In 1969 a young woman who was both a Tupamaro sympathizer as well as a personal friend of Otero's was seized and tortured.[75] She complained to Otero after her release, insisting that Mitrione had watched and assisted in her torture. Otero, opposed to the use of torture, complained bitterly and was replaced.

■ ■ ■

In his book *Pasaporte 11333: Ocho Años con la CIA* ("Passport 11333: Eight Years with the CIA"), Manuel Hevia Cosculluela made even more startling accusations against Mitrione. According to Cosculluela, a former CIA agent, Mitrione had personally organized and carried out a training session for interrogators in Uruguay. The session began with lectures on anatomy and related matters, but quickly turned sinister. Four street people were brought in as human guinea pigs and were tortured as part of the "class." All four died.[76]

Could such an extraordinary allegation possibly be true? Very similar statements were made by a confidential source to Father Roy Bourgeois about interrogation classes given at the School of the America when it was in Panama. According to that source as well, street people were brought in for use during torture demonstrations.[77]

The two claims are given uncomfortable support by the well-documented MKULTRA program carried out by the CIA during the 1960s. In search of a drug that would provide an effective interrogation tool, CIA scientists and physicians experimented on unwitting patients and strangers. The selected persons were given powerful drugs, including LSD, without their knowledge or consent. This caused enormous psychological trauma and long-term suffering and resulted in the suicide of Dr. Olson, one of their own scientists.[78]

Back to Vietnam

Professor Langguth also served as the Saigon bureau chief for the *New York Times* in 1965 and is the author of the renowned book *Our Vietnam*. He cites two cases from Vietnam which shed additional light on the matter of U.S. involvement in torture.

The first is the case of Ms. Nguyen Thi Nhan, who was arrested in 1969 in Saigon and taken to police headquarters. There she was given electrical shocks and an iron rod was forced up her vagina. Three Westerners in U.S. uniforms watched, and a police officer told her they were CIA agents. One of the three Westerners ordered needles to be driven under her fingernails.[79]

Mrs. Nguyen Thi Bo was also arrested in 1969 and taken to the police station in Danang. A stick was forced into her vagina and her face was held down in a toilet bowl filled with excrement. She was then moved to the Nan Muoc station, where she was questioned by five U.S. agents in green fatigues who beat her.[80]

These reports are hardly unique. Don Dzagulones, an American veteran of the Vietnam War, was a specialist in interrogation. Although all interrogators were required to carry pocket cards reminding them to respect the Geneva Conventions, Dzagulones admitted that their use of basic torture techniques was rampant throughout the war. Although this was well known to other officials, nothing was done to prevent or curb the abuses.[81] According to one former CIA officer, few Operation Phoenix detainees ever survived their interrogations: most died of torture or were thrown from helicopters.[82] Although the South Vietnamese actually carried out the torture, the CIA and Special Forces clearly played a supervisory role.

Similarly, Anthony Poshepny, a CIA agent working in Southeast Asia, was notorious for collecting human ears and dropping human heads into enemy villages. According to one Washington analyst, "In the post–September 11 security environment, fearless men like Tony . . . are what America needs to combat . . . the new unconventional threat that America faces from abroad in exotic and uncharted lands."[83]

CONCLUSIONS

These case histories, when taken together with the background information provided above, lead inexorably to a number of grim conclusions about the parameters of U.S. intelligence involvement in torture.

A key question is who, precisely, were the North Americans in the torture cells? When the survivors first tried to report their experiences, U.S. officials brushed them aside, insisting that the claims were fictional, or that the Yankee in question must have been a mercenary or perhaps of some other nationality. Definitive answers, of course, lie concealed in long-classified government files. Nonetheless, the evidence we already have tells us a great deal.

There can be little doubt that the men in question were from the United States. Central Americans are quite familiar with the many tourists, human rights observers, and businesspeople from our country, and even more so with our radio, television, and cinema productions. They know our accents. Some of prisoners had even lived in the United States. Although many of them were blindfolded, others saw the foreigners at close range, commenting on the hairy arms, light or reddened (sunburned) coloring, tall rangy builds, and narrow Caucasian features. Unlike the vast majority of Central Americans, these men showed no sign of a blended indigenous or African heritage. Could they have been some of the few locals with northern European looks? Perhaps. Could they have been blond Guatemalans, Salvadorans, or Hondurans who somehow spoke their own native language, Spanish, with Yankee syntax and accents? Impossible.

Could the foreign interrogators have been Canadians? Hardly. The Canadians had no military or intelligence presence in Central America during the Dirty Wars there. Moreover, the interrogators were without exception very anxious to learn more about Cuba and the Sandinistas, a U.S. obsession not shared by Canada or other nations.

U.S. officials have also argued that the men described were surely mercenaries, soldier of fortune types, but this too is belied by the details. Mercenaries are hired guns. They work for foreign armies. They are employees. The Yankees in the torture cells were not working for local military officials at all. To the contrary, they were very much in charge, and had clear authority over the torturers themselves. The Americans were not taking orders, they were giving them. At times they were even supervising the entire torture session. Moreover, it was the local intelligence officials, many of them known torturers, who worked as "assets" for the United States, specifically for the CIA, or were otherwise largely dependent on the U.S. for vital funding, equipment, and protection.

Were all of the Yankees in the torture cells, as described by the survivors, in fact CIA agents? Or were they perhaps from military intelligence units, or from the Defense Intelligence Agency, or from the Special Forces? This question is more complex. The men were dressed in civilian clothing with no nametags or other identifying military insignia of any kind. They tended, moreover, to use pseudonyms like "Mr. Mike." This certainly suggests the CIA's modus operandi, as the above information suggests. Moreover, in some of the cases there is confirmation that the "guest" interrogator was indeed a CIA agent.

Some of the Yankees, however, were in army uniforms, as in the cases of José Rubén Carrillo Cubas and Oscar Alexander Ortiz. These men were working closely with army personnel. It is thus quite possible that they were Special Forces operatives or military intelligence agents. Perhaps we will never know for certain.

In the Guatemalan cases in general, however, the CIA is by far the most probable suspect. The U.S. was not involved as intensively in combat activities there, and it would thus be less likely that the Special Forces or military intelligence agents were the Yankee interrogators. Moreover, we know that the CIA had a large number of high-level Guatemalan intelligence officers on its payroll. The agency thus had the necessary connections to enter top-secret cells that were off-limits even to other Guatemalan military leaders, let alone to the civilian courts or law enforcement officers. In the cases of Everardo and Sister Dianna Ortiz, CIA involvement is confirmed.

In other Guatemalan situations, as in the case of Miguel, the interrogator is described as very much an intelligence specialist—a man well trained in analyzing information, developing questions and contradictions, and inflicting psychological pressure. He was clearly a professional, and he bragged about Vietnam. Was he one of the many former Phoenix operators working with the CIA in Guatemala? Quite likely. David's story is also intriguing, because he reports the North American supervising an electrical shock session. This was more or less during the time frame that Dan Mitrione had been teaching just such techniques in Brazil and Uruguay. Once again, the CIA would seem the likely culprit.

In Honduras the Special Forces and various U.S. military operatives were active, together with the CIA, which had an enormous presence there during the Contra war. In the cases of both Inés Murillo and Father Carney, the involvement of a CIA interrogation specialist has been documented. Moreover, it was the CIA which had been primarily charged with planning and carrying out the Contra activities.

In El Salvador, as discussed above, there was extensive U.S. military and CIA involvement. In the cases of prisoners tortured in army bases in the presence of uniformed gringos, it would seem likely that the foreigner was military and not CIA. However, when the prisoner was a civilian tortured in a safe house, especially with a Yankee supervising the session, as in the case of María Guardado, suspicion must shift back to the CIA. It was the CIA that was working closely with the death squads, and it was the CIA that for decades had been "perfecting" ways to extract information through torture. The MKULTRA experiments are but an example.

It should be noted, of course, that any given U.S. interrogator might well have had multiple relationships. Michael Walsh, for example, had been a Seal and an Operation Phoenix leader who worked closely with the CIA and later carried out CIA functions in Central America, although he was by then in the Navy. However, in the interrogation context, any involved Special Forces or other operatives in Central America would have been working very closely with the CIA.

In Brazil and Uruguay the cases are straightforward enough. The Yankees in the torture cells arrived with Dan Mitrione and were working for the Office of Public Safety, and thus de facto linked to the CIA.

The CIA, of course, has no monopoly over torture. Different U.S. agencies have doubtless been involved at different times, perhaps acting independently, perhaps in tandem. However, when working together, it would seem clear that the CIA, given its special expertise in intelligence and interrogation, would have been in the driver's seat. A Special Forces member, for example, will possess extraordinary combat and survival skills. However, when it comes to questioning an important prisoner during a joint effort, such soldiers would be under the authority of the Central Intelligence Agency and not the other way around. A skilled CIA interrogator would hardly have been taking orders from someone in the Delta Forces.

In what way did the CIA participate in torture? The above described evidence suggests that its agents not only kept known torturers on agency payroll, but were often physically present in the torture cells as well. Sometimes the agents merely observed, sometimes they did the questioning, sometimes they advised, and sometimes they supervised. But they were there. Often.

Did U.S. agents actually lay hands on the prisoners and personally torture them? Not often, at least in Central America.[04] This was the gory task of much lower-level "specialists" from the local armies. Florencio Caballero and César Vielman Joya Martínez are but two examples. But the CIA did develop very specialized torture techniques over the decades, and they taught these techniques to their partners in the death squads.[85] The CIA and others knowingly helped to fund the torture, prepare interrogation questions, and deal with problem prisoners, as reflected by the above accounts. The agency kept many local officers responsible for torture, such as Col. Julio Roberto Alpirez, on the U.S. payroll as spies and liaisons. The agency received intelligence brutally extracted from the secret prisoners, paid handsomely, and asked for more. This is clearly torture "by proxy" or torture "for hire."

By contrast, in Afghanistan and Iraq it appears that CIA agents were quite willing to physically engage in torture so long as they were given legal protections by the Bush administration, which they received. However, torture by proxy remains the preferred approach, as illustrated by the current increase in extraordinary renditions, and the CIA tendency to utilize civilian contractors, or even gullible young MPs, for the "dirty work."

The Latin American case histories lead to still further grim conclusions. The highly sophisticated torture methods used on most of the survivors, as described above, all too closely mirror the abuses of the prisoners in Iraq and Afghanistan. Hence the much insisted upon "bad apple" story falls apart.

Could the overlap of torture techniques used in Latin America with those used in Afghanistan and Iraq be merely coincidental? Not a chance. They are far too sophisticated for low-level MPs to have dreamed up alone on a Saturday night. These methods took years to develop and refine. The use of excruciating positions, including the "Vietnam" (portrayed in the now iconic photograph of the prisoner dangling wires at Abu Ghraib), were routinely used across Latin America. Chillingly, sketches of the "stress and duress" positions, compiled by survivors in El Salvador and described by Florencio Caballaro of Honduras, are indistinguishable from the photographs of the Iraqi prisoners. Stripping the prisoners and leaving them hooded or blindfolded for long periods was routine. So, too, was the denial of basic sanitary needs and the long-term deprivation of food and sleep. Both Inés Murillo and Sister Dianna remember the ferocious dogs and the rats. Many remember the threats against their families, and being forced to listen as the other prisoners screamed. John Doe remembers his two small children, their mother already dead, being dragged into the army base during his own torture session.

The survivors remember worse than that. They remember the rapes, the sexual assaults, and the methodical, excruciating electrical shocks. These happened in Iraq and Afghanistan. The Latin Americans also remember what the CIA blithely refers to as "water-boarding," a method put to use in Afghanistan. The victim is submerged in water until he or she begins to drown and loses consciousness, only to be revived, then drowned once again. Intelligence agents have also vaguely mentioned "cutting off air" to prisoners in the Middle East. Might this include the "hooding" practiced so widely in Central America, which means holding a plastic bag over the prisoner's head until he or she collapsed? The "water pit" discussed as a possible CIA technique in Afghanistan, was certainly used in Guatemala. The prisoners there were left in pits of water so deep they had to hang onto overhead bars to keep from drowning. Everardo may have been held in just such a pit in Retalhuelu.[86]

This continuity of techniques is also reflected in the harsh KUBARK manual used in Vietnam, later recycled into the *Human Resource Exploitation Training Manual of 1983* used in Central America.[87] Although the KUBARK manual was far more explicit about torture, the 1983 document recommended stripping and blindfolding the prisoners and interrogating them in dark rooms with no toilets, depriving them of food and sleep and the use of painful positions for long periods. It also recommended "arrests" at early morning hours, which of course translated into middle-of-the-night death squad raids and kidnappings. The KUBARK manual openly recommended the use of electrical shocks. Clearly, these methods were not dreamed up by the young Abu Ghraib MPs. To the contrary, the torture methods have been around for a very long time.

The most frightening parallel is perhaps the CIA's creation of ghost prisoners in Afghanistan and Iraq, refusing to report their identities, treatment, or whereabouts and concealing them from the Red Cross and other appropriate international authorities. Latin America knows all about ghost prisoners. They are called *desaparecidos*—"the disappeared"—and their relatives still search for them. This practice had long been considered a grim phenomenon of the Dirty Wars of Latin America. Apparently the roots lead back to Washington, D.C. Even today, the CIA is refusing to respond to ACLU requests for information relating to a number of secret and high-level prisoners from the Middle East. [88]

In short, it seems that the CIA and related agencies brought a nasty repertoire of well-honed torture methods from Central America to Afghanistan and Iraq, eventually contaminating uniformed U.S. servicemen and -women over there. Did it all begin in

Central America? Certainly not. Many of the practices go at least back to Vietnam, where they were developed in the Phoenix and similar intelligence programs. The CIA and others then brought their "pros" to Latin America to share.

If nothing is done, if only a few "bad apples" are forced to pay for the sins of our intelligence leadership, then the deadly structures responsible for the human suffering described above will remain intact. Soon enough the grim practices depicted in the Abu Ghraib photographs, so shocking to the American public, will be repeated. Others will die or "disappear" if we allow ourselves to look away, to tell ourselves that all is well, to return to our comfortable private lives.

CHAPTER FOUR
WHAT CAN BE DONE: THE LAW

Torture has never been legal in the United States. Indeed, it is difficult to imagine any prohibition more fundamental to American jurisprudence. Many of the first colonists in the Western Hemisphere were in fact refugees fleeing the rack, the screw, and the Star Chamber of Europe. The collective memories of those horrors remained vivid in the minds of our early government leaders and the framers of the Constitution. When some members of Congress debated the issues of torture and national security, Patrick Henry's response was both fierce and eloquent:

> What has distinguished our ancestors?—That they would not admit of tortures or cruel and barbarous punishment. But...Congress... may introduce the practice of France, Spain and Germany—of torturing...and they will tell you there is a necessity of strengthening the arm of government.... We are then lost and undone.[1]

If this is our legal heritage, then what can our courts of law do to protect the detainees from torture by U.S. personnel and contractors? It is, after all, the role of the judiciary to enforce our laws and treaties and to preserve the balance of powers between our three branches of government. In answering this question, the fields of civil, criminal, and international law must be analyzed separately, as each has distinct requirements and possibilities.

CIVIL LAW

The courts of the United States have articulated and enforced the fundamental constitutional prohibition against torture again and again, and in many different contexts. The most common is that of coerced confessions, with the U.S. Supreme Court insisting that "neither the body nor the mind may be twisted until it breaks."[2] Thus in *Culombe v. Connecticut*,[3] the Supreme Court ruled that the prolonged detention and frightening interrogation of a mentally retarded man in order to compel a "confession," violated due process. Similarly, when police physically tackled a man suspected of drug possession, and forcibly pumped his stomach, the court again found that constitutional limits had been transgressed:

> This is conduct that shocks the conscience. Illegally breaking into the privacy of the petitioner, the struggle to open his mouth and remove what was there, the forcible extraction of his stomach contents.... They are methods too close to the rack and the screw to permit of constitutional differentiation. *Rochin v. California*, 342 U.S. 165 (1951)

The infliction of physical and mental cruelty by government officials has been prohibited in numerous other situations as well. The Eighth Amendment, for example, forbids the cruel and unusual punishment of prisoners. Ironically, though the death penalty itself has been held constitutional in the United States, the executions must be carried out through humane methods and not involve excessive pain or suffering.[4] Similarly, prison conditions need not be comfortable, but they cannot be cruel.[5] For this reason, the entire Texas prison system was for many years monitored by the federal courts.[6] Prison authorities cannot deliberately leave weaker or effeminate inmates exposed to obvious dangers,[7] or deliberately ignore basic medical needs.[8]

Nor may prisoners be sadistically disciplined. In *Hudson v. McMillian*,[9] for example, a prisoner was beaten by a guard after an argument. Although handcuffed and thus helpless, the man suffered a cracked dental plate, loosened teeth, and facial bruises. The Court found that the constitution had been violated. In *Hope v. Pelzer*, an inmate had twice been handcuffed to a hitching post in the sun for seven hours, with little drinking water and no toilet privileges. The court found the punishment unconstitutional, as it reflected the "wanton and unnecessary infliction of pain" and exposed the prisoner to circumstances that were "both degrading and dangerous." One can only imagine what the Court would have said about the practices at Abu Ghraib.

Police brutality cases are yet another example of constitutional prohibitions against unnecessary cruelty on the part of government officials. When excessive force is used in making an arrest, such police actions are unconstitutional under the Fourth Amendment. Thus in *Tennessee v. Garner*[10] the Supreme Court struck down a Tennessee statute authorizing the use of deadly force in arresting a fleeing suspect. In that case, the police had shot an unarmed seventeen-year-old of slight build, simply because he ran from the scene of a burglary.

These constitutional protections from official cruelty are not limited to the criminal arena but also apply in civil contexts. When government officials detain or take custody of a person for other reasons, they once again take on a measure of responsibility for fair and humane treatment. For example, when a severely retarded young man was institutionalized, his mother was distraught to find that he had been battered by other patients, had harmed himself, and had been placed in physical restraints. The Supreme Court found that the situation violated the due process clause of the Constitution, and that the state hospital was required to provide safe conditions as well as reasonably adequate training and rehabilitation.[11]

Does the Constitution prohibit the brutal "interrogation techniques" developed and utilized by the CIA in Vietnam, Central America, and now in Iraq and Afghanistan? As the above discussion makes clear, our long-standing intelligence methods fall far beyond even the outermost limits of our Constitution. The nudity, denial of toilet privileges, and painful positions have already been struck down in the penal context. The water-boardings, electrical shocks, suffocations, and severe beatings are unthinkable. These kinds of official conduct have always been held abhorrent. In short, the CIA has been making a mockery of traditional American values and legal principles.

How do they get away with it? The FBI and state police must daily deal with frightening psychopaths, dangerous drug lords, "unsavory" informants, and even terrorists like those responsible for the bombing of the Federal Building in Oklahoma City. Yet these law enforcement agents (with some notorious exceptions) have managed to work within the confines of our Constitution. Hence, when the CIA began using draconian measures in its interrogation efforts in Afghanistan and Iraq, the FBI ordered its own agents to stay away.

Why the difference? Because the FBI and other federal agents who violate constitutional limits are subject to suit by their victims. This has long had the very healthy effect of requiring powerful law enforcement officials to utilize physical force with care and reason. Are CIA agents not subject to similar discipline? Surprisingly, they are not. This is because their actions take place outside of the United States.

Under the doctrine of sovereign immunity, neither the U.S. government nor any federal officers or agencies can normally be sued. Certain very limited exceptions exist, and constitutional violations are one of those exceptions. If a federal officer, even a high-level agency chief like Mr. Rumsfeld, acts in a way that clearly violates constitutional restrictions, then although the U.S. government itself still cannot be sued, the officer may be personally subject to suit. Any resulting monetary award would be paid out of his or her own pocket. This clearly has a strong deterrent effect. The Supreme Court, however, has made it clear that most constitutional prohibitions will not apply outside of the territories of the

United States, unless U.S. citizens are involved. See, for example, *U.S. v. Verdugo-Urquidez.*[12] The CIA, which operates almost exclusively outside of our borders, has thus escaped the moral and legal confines of the constitution altogether.

In *Rasul v. Bush,*[13] the Court did find that certain detainees in Guantánamo had some basic rights to habeas corpus; however, this was based on the finding that Guantánamo is de facto under the full control of the United States. Thus the question of the constitutional prohibitions against torture reaching beyond Guantánamo or U.S. citizen detainees has not been expressly resolved. Certainly the ruling suggests that this would be judicially frowned upon. Moreover, as the prisoners in Iraq and Afghanistan were fully in U.S. custody and control, our own officials should indeed be responsible for any tortures they authorized or ordered. Many such suits are being initiated at this time. However, our government officials continue to argue that extraterritorial acts are beyond the reach of the Constitution.

This situation has led to strange but predictable results. The CIA, long free of any legal worries and well shielded from public scrutiny, has run wild in Iraq and Afghanistan, confident that there will be no consequences for any of its agents and officers. (As stated by one Special Operations official, "I had to deal with CIA guys in El Salvador; they were on their own wavelength."[14]) The FBI, in contrast, was well trained to work effectively without such barbaric practices, and chose, even when working abroad, not to contaminate its agents or its evidence.[15]

Are there other exemptions to sovereign immunity when it comes to actions as heinous as torture? Certainly. The Federal Tort Claims Act[16] offers a broad waiver of sovereign immunity for most torts carried out by federal officials. Under this waiver, the U.S. government itself becomes liable. These include the negligent failure to properly supervise any independent contractors. Obviously this waiver of immunity would be of great help in dealing with the CIA's tendency to hire known torturers as "assets," utilize brutal civilian contractors, and engage in the extraordinary renditions described above. To the extent that the CIA pays a third party to carry out interrogations, works closely with that third party, and knows that torture is being applied, the tort of negligent supervision is clearly committed. However, the Supreme Court has recently ruled, in *Sosa v. Alvarez-Machain*,[17] that actions carried out beyond the borders of the United States also are not subject to the Federal Tort Claims Act waiver of immunity. This is true even when the decisions, orders, and funding originate in Washington, D.C. Once again, the CIA goes scot-free for actions which would result in the most severe of penalties if carried out by FBI and other officers.

The Administrative Procedure Act offers a waiver of immunity, but only in cases seeking injunctive relief only against the federal agency. This also raises complications. If a prisoner has access to an attorney and is able to speak out, it is unlikely that he or she is still under torture, and the government will no doubt urge that the case be dismissed on the grounds that it has become "moot."

A very promising civil avenue of redress and protection may be found in two specific statutes. Their viability in the context of U.S.-sponsored torture will greatly depend on future court decisions about agency powers and limitations.

The two statutes were clearly designed to deal with these human rights situations. The first, the *Alien Tort Claims Act* ("ATCA"), is more than two centuries old; it simply states that "The district courts shall have original jurisdiction of any civil action by an alien for a tort only, committed in violation of the laws of nations or a treaty of the United States" (28 U.S.C. § 1350). The second is the *Torture Victim Protection Act of 1991* (28 U.S.C. § 1350 n.). This statute imposes liability on any individual who "under real or apparent authority or color of law of any foreign nation subjects an individual to torture." Both statutes should permit suit against U.S. officials here in the United States courts. Yet at the time of this writing, the Department of Justice is fiercely opposing such claims. I report this somewhat wryly, having spent a number of weeks in legal battles on precisely these issues in Everardo's case. We are awaiting the court's decision.

It would seem clear enough that the ATCA was written with the intent to give any alien a right to sue in federal court for a tort, such as assault and battery or wrongful death, which would violate U.S. treaties or international law. Nevertheless, for a number of years the courts were in disagreement as to whether or not the statute provided an actual right to sue, or merely proffered jurisdiction. This was favorably resolved in the recent case of *Sosa v. Alvarez-Machain,* 159 L.Ed.2d 718 (2004). The Supreme Court specifically held that the statute provided a right to sue for violations of international law, so long as such violations were of a sufficient clarity and importance. In turn, there can be little doubt that the matter of torture is one of the most universal and clearly defined legal prohibitions in international law today.

The difficulty arises, once again, with regard to the Federal Tort Claims Act. Since the ATCA gives a cause of action for common law torts, the Justice Department is now arguing that the FTCA is required to release sovereign immunity, and that hence the same FTCA exemptions for foreign torts apply, as discussed above. As a result, lawsuits against Guatemalan and Salvadoran military officials may proceed; but cases against U.S. officials for torture abroad are still barred by sovereign immunity. This is perhaps an ironic result, but government lawyers, in fact, are now raising precisely this issue in Everardo's case and many others.[18]

It is certainly true that there must be a waiver of sovereign immunity in order to sue for acts taken on behalf of the U.S. government by its officials. It is equally true that certain individual actions can never be deemed acts of the sovereign. As with constitutional violations, in such "ultra vires" situations the individual official may be sued directly, and must pay any damages award out of his or her own pocket. Because the United States is not considered a defendant in such cases, there is no need for a waiver of immunity.

Obviously a postal worker, for example, who beats his neighbor while he is off duty, cannot claim sovereign immunity. He will instead be sued as an individual.

There are various categories of actions which are defined as ultra vires—acts automatically considered to be those of the individual and not the government. One such category consists of constitutional violations, as discussed above. Yet another is composed of actions that lie beyond the congressional delegation of authority to the agency in question. In short, if our high-level national leaders have acted outside of the scope of their congressionally defined powers by ordering torture, they may be sued.

This second category is important in the context of the Alien Tort Claims Act and other suits based on claims of torture abroad. The CIA has only those powers that were specifically provided by Congress at the time of the agency's establishment in 1947. Any actions which fall outside of that legislative grant of power will be treated as the unprotected acts of individuals.

The question of an agency's proper scope of authority has been given strict scrutiny by the courts, in light of the impact on the separation of powers. An agency will not be permitted to award additional powers to itself, and rogue agencies are disfavored in the extreme, as they should be. In *Larson v. Domestic and Foreign Commerce Corporation*, 337 U.S. 682 (1948), the Supreme Court discussed these matters in a case involving the breach of a contract by a government official. The Court held that if the official was acting within the scope of his authority, albeit erroneously or even unlawfully, then sovereign immunity applies and no orders could be issued to require the government to act or to cease a given action. However, where the official's actions are so outrageous as to actually exceed his *statutory authority*, then his actions must be deemed those of an individual: "The action of an officer of the sovereign . . . can be regarded as so illegal as to permit a suit for injunctive relief against the officer as an individual . . . if it is not within the officer's statutory powers or, if within those powers, . . . constitutionally void" (*Larson*, id. at 701–702). In short, actions which violate the constitution or which exceed the limits of the agency's statutory delegation of power, can never be immunized as government acts. The individual offending officers are on their own.

The initial question is thus whether or not torture lies within the congressional grant of powers of the agency. If torture violates the congressional authorization limits, then the FTCA waiver is not needed and the defendants may be sued in their individual capacities.[19]

In evaluating the appropriate boundaries set by the congressional delegation of authority, the activities in question need not be expressly prohibited: "Were courts to presume a delegation of power absent an express withholding of such power, agencies would enjoy limitless hegemony, a result plainly out of keeping with Chevron and quite likely with the Constitution as well" (*Ry. Labor Executives' Ass'n v. Nat'l Mediation Bd.*, 29 F.3rd 655, 671 [D.C. Cir. 1994], cited with approval by *Ass'n for Lutherans*, id. at 1175). In short, common sense must be applied in deciding what Congress intended.

In examining the legislation establishing the CIA, it is clear that the agency was established to properly gather intelligence abroad for purposes of national defense.[20] Not one of the statutory provisions grants any authority of any kind to order, participate, collaborate, or conspire in direct acts of torture. Indeed, a review of the historical and judicial context both before and after the establishment of the CIA makes such an interpretation unthinkable. The numerous legislative actions and statements of the time make clear that its intent and understanding was that torture was, as always, flatly prohibited.

The CIA was first established in 1947. At that time the horrors of World War II, in particular the torture of civilians and prisoners of war alike, were fresh in the minds of all lawmakers. The Fourth Hague Convention, Annex, Art. 4 (36 Stat. 2277, 2296, 2306, and 2307) of 1907 already prohibited the torture of captured combatants or civilians. The Geneva Conventions[21] were being developed and were finalized on August 12, 1949. The Japanese general Yamashita was already standing trial for war crimes, including torture and the abuse of prisoners of war (see *In Re Yamashita*, 327 U.S. 1 [1945]). The Nuremberg trials were imminent for similar acts. Clearly Congress did not intend to grant the CIA the authority to carry out the very acts, including torture, that were currently the subject of war crimes trials and protective and extensive new human rights treaties.

The obvious intent to proscribe torture as a method of intelligence gathering is underscored by the fact that torture has been firmly repudiated in the United States since the days of the founding fathers. Moreover, as stated in *Filartiga v. Pena-Irala*, "Turning to the act of torture, we have little difficulty discerning its universal renunciation in the modern practice and usage of nations."[22] This special history and fixed repudiation were certainly in the minds of the legislature when it established the CIA and authorized intelligence gathering activities. Yet Congress made no effort to specify or grant such extraordinary or long prohibited powers to the agency.

Finally, it is clear that the legislature has firmly continued to withhold authorization for the use of torture ever since its establishment of the CIA. This is reflected in part by the ongoing acceptance and promotion of the numerous treaties and U.N. resolutions discussed at length above.

Moreover, the Executive branch has repeatedly indicated its own understanding that it has no such powers. For example, the CIA's General Counsel opined in 1947[23] that the CIA had not been granted legislative authority for subversion and sabotage—two actions far less egregious. Executive Orders 12036 (1978) and 12333 (1981) both prohibited any actions by the CIA either directly or through proxy, that would be unlawful in the United States or violate civil liberties; and the CIA's own internal directives also prohibited torture and similar abuses again and again.[24]

Given that torture clearly lies beyond the congressional delegation of power to the CIA, acts of torture can never be shielded by sovereign immunity.[25] As a result, an ATCA suit by any detainee against the CIA or others should be possible. In fact, it is mandated by the Convention against Torture, which requires the United States, like any other party states, to ensure an enforceable right to compensation.[26] But will the courts permit this? Or will legal technicalities or claims of "political questions" continue to give de facto impunity to these officials? In light of the long-term refusal of the courts to hold the CIA and other intelligence agencies responsible for acts of torture abroad, the future is cloudy at best.

Suits based on the Torture Victims Protection Act, or TVPA, face fewer obstacles. The statute provides a direct cause of action, and it does not require a showing that the claims are based on federal or international common law, as in the ATCA situation. Such an expressly created statutory cause of action is independent of the FTCA and thus not subject to its foreign tort exemption clause. The only real question, then, is whether or not U.S. intelligence agents acting abroad may be said to be acting "under real or apparent authority or color of law of any foreign nation."

These words are legal terms of art. They were explained by the Second Circuit in *Kadic v. Karadzic,* 70 F.3d 232, 245 (2nd Cir. 1995), which held that the same "color of state law" jurisprudence utilized in the old civil rights cases is applicable here, and simply requires that the individual acted together with government officials or with significant government aid. See also *Lugar v. Edmondson Oil Co.,* 457 U.S. 922, 937 (1982).

In the cases out of Latin America, there can be little doubt that the CIA and other intelligence officials were working quite closely with the government, and had its full support as well as its special privileges and powers. The U.S. agents received top-secret information on a regular basis and had access to all military and law enforcement centers at any time. They were even able to enter clandestine prisons and speak with and question the "disappeared," a power not even granted to the local courts or police. The local governments also permitted them a share of overall decision-making and strategy authority with regard to all counterinsurgency efforts. In short, the U.S. agents were fully cloaked with the authority and power of the local governments when they acted in Latin America.

The same is true in Iraq and Afghanistan. To the extent that our officials are acting with the permission, authority, powers, and collaboration of the local governments, they are acting under the color of state law.

Once again, however, it remains to be seen how the courts will rule in these cases. The Department of Justice is opposing TVPA claims brought by Latin American survivors against U.S. intelligence agents with great vigor. To date the many decades of CIA criminal activity abroad have not resulted in a single judicial victory for the plaintiffs. Hence the abuses and violations continue.

CRIMINAL LAW

As discussed above, it remains difficult for the detainees to successfully bring a civil rights claim for torture against any of the "intellectual authors," the high-level U.S. government officials who ordered and authorized the practices, or even against the offending agency itself. This leaves only the criminal law branch of our justice system, discussed below.

Intriguingly, international law is increasingly vehement that no sovereign immunity can exist when crimes against humanity, including torture, are at stake. This was emphasized in the Nuremberg Charter, which stated at Article 7 that "The official position of defendants, whether as heads of state or responsible officials in government departments, shall not be considered as freeing them from responsibility or mitigating punishment."[27] Both the federal War Crimes Act and the federal anti-torture statute, discussed below, offer criminal sanctions for all implicated officials. Unlike the civil law context, any and all persons in the United States, including government officials, can be brought to trial for a criminal act. In theory at least, no one is above the law.

Turning first to basic criminal law principles, if it is a crime for an irate husband to hire someone to kill his wife, then some rather obvious questions are raised here as well. Criminal conspiracies exist when two or more persons agree to carry out a crime, and take concrete action upon that agreement. All parties to the agreement are responsible for the crime that occurs, whether or not they serve as the actual "triggerman," as it were. So long as the person takes an actual step, legal or illegal, toward furthering the criminal objective, then he or she will bear responsibility.

The CIA practice of torture by proxy, as set forth above,[28] more than meets the requirements of criminal conspiracy. "Extraordinary renditions," whereby detainees are sent to third nations where they will be tortured, are a good example. There is certainly an agreement to torture prisoners. The CIA begins with de facto custody of a detainee, then sends him or her to a carefully selected third country where the routine use of torture is well known. Moreover, many steps are taken to further the goal of torture. The prisoner is transported to the third nation by U.S. officials, using U.S. tax dollars.[29] The CIA usually provides the questions it wants answered, and often has an agent standing by during the interrogation to give advice and to assist. The pipelines to the police and intelligence services in these third countries are "well lubricated" with U.S. cash.[30] Similarly, the hiring of "civilian contractors" to carry out torture falls well within the definition of a criminal conspiracy. So, too, is ordering an MP to abuse the prisoners in order to "soften them up" for interrogations, or to hide them from the Red Cross. There is an obvious agreement that the abuses should be carried out, and often explicit instructions have been given.

Faced with growing congressional outrage during the Dirty Wars in Central America, the CIA was a bit more cautious there. Intelligence officials have insisted again and again that they had no part in torture during those wars. Rather, they simply purchased important information from "unsavory characters," a basic practice necessary to any reasonable intelligence work. Yet as noted earlier, concealed behind these bland assertions are the devastating practices described by the survivors.

Turning to the preliminary question, would the CIA practices in Central America normally constitute a criminal conspiracy? There certainly was agreement that torture should be used as a tool for intelligence gathering. The "wink and nod" approach is discussed at length above. The CIA clearly knew and accepted that its local intelligence partners were active death squad members. CIA agents, moreover, taught more "refined" torture techniques to the local interrogators, helped them plan to stalk and kidnap civilians, facilitated and provided funding and equipment, and often were present and assisting in the torture sessions themselves. Known abusers were kept on CIA payroll as assets, and payments were continued despite contemporaneous abuse. Obviously, the CIA officials knew and intended that the detainees would be tortured, and took active steps to promote and support the illegal practice.

The "unsavory character" argument raises yet a second, and very important, policy question as well for the current war against terror.[31] The CIA today does not just innocently purchase useful information from such "unsavory characters," as it has claimed throughout the war in Iraq and Afghanistan. To be precise, the agency is using and paying for torture in order to obtain desired intelligence in day-to-day cases. There is a vast difference between these two scenarios. As discussed earlier, if an al-Qaeda member offered to sell information about a terrorist plan he had recently heard about, few would argue that the CIA should not pay up. In that situation, the CIA would not be supporting any act of torture. Quite a different situation is presented, however, when a well-known torturer is given cash, a cattle prod, and a list of questions, and then asked to interrogate a specific prisoner down the hall. This obviously supports and even promotes torture, as the Latin American cases make painfully clear. These two issues must thus be evaluated separately.

At the outset, it is interesting to compare CIA informant practices with those of the FBI, which must also deal with extremely dangerous and well-armed criminals. As we learned in Oklahoma, these agents may well face a devastating bomb situation. While certainly the FBI, like any other law enforcement agency, may utilize paid informants, there are clear and well-thought-out legal limits. To begin with, secrecy and confidentiality with regard to informants and their testimony are not absolute, and those protections must reasonably yield to the need for a fair trial. Fabrication of evidence and other abuses seen during the COINTELPRO era are prohibited. These restrictions have not destroyed the agency's realistic ability to recruit and work with informants. Moreover, the rules have been slowly refined over the years, and represent collective public wisdom on balancing the needs of law enforcement with public safeguards against corruption and abuse.

More importantly, although an FBI or other domestic agent may use and protect a known criminal informant, the agent may not de facto become a partner in crime. Precisely these limitations were showcased in the notorious Boston FBI–Mafia case. Certain officers had assisted collaborating Mafia operatives in evading detection and prosecution, and even allowed an innocent man to stand trial and spend years in prison for a murder committed by one of their own informants. The shrieks of judicial rage still echo through the hallways of the Boston courthouse today. There is no reason why the same tried-and-true limits should not apply to the CIA. Absolute power, as observed in Iraq and Afghanistan, corrupts absolutely. In the long term, this can and will endanger us.

Many people have urged that torture might still be justified in the context of the "ticking bomb," an extreme and hypothetical situation which is analyzed in detail in chapter 5. In that "what if" situation, law enforcement officials face the imminent explosion of a nuclear weapon in a large city, or a similar catastrophic event, and believe that they must torture a prisoner in order to locate and disable the device. To date this has never actually occurred. Hopefully it never will, so long as U.S. intelligence agencies correct the errors of the past and take early and well coordinated actions to prevent such situations from arising in the first place. However, a close look at our legal system shows us that if such a horrific situation ever did occur, full protections for any officer are already in place.

What does the law actually say? It says that torture is flat out illegal, as discussed above, even in the ticking bomb scenario. Despite some doomsday prophets, there is no need to change this. If a law enforcement or CIA agent really prevented the destruction of the entire city of New York by reluctantly torturing a prisoner, it is rather improbable that he or she would ever be indicted. If indicted, the judge would still have a great deal of leeway in determining a "just" sentence. If sentenced to any prison time, a presidential pardon or grant of clemency would be virtually guaranteed. There is simply no need to legalize torture. The ticking bomb, in short, is a red herring in this debate. Worse yet, it is offered in order to frighten us into accepting the practice of torture.

More crucially, as discussed at length in chapter 5, the use of torture will not increase our national security but rather will greatly endanger us. Although the "tough guy" approach is all too human a response to the frightening realities of the war against terror, history and current events indicate that this strategy is mistaken indeed.

Altering our legal system and authorizing torture for the first time in our history would open a dangerous Pandora's box. Once torture is formally permitted, it becomes nearly impossible to draw the line or enforce any limitations. There was, of course, no ticking bomb in Latin America, where the U.S. faced no national security risks of any kind. Nor was such an imminent crisis generally presented at Abu Ghraib. There was no imminent terrorist attack against the United States being planned in Iraq. In Afghanistan, many of the prisoners were simply foot soldiers or sympathizers on the wrong side of the war, like the persons captured with John Walker Lindh. Others were reportedly neighbors of al-Qaeda members, possibly knowledgeable about a cache of weapons, or simply opposed to the presence of the United States in their homeland. No one seriously thought these detainees had information about a devastating bomb about to explode within the next few hours. This illustrates all too well the problem. The true ticking bomb hypothetical, which is based on the imminent loss of hundreds of thousands of lives, becomes blurred with the everyday interrogation of all prisoners and all suspects during wartime. This leads to precisely the human rights disasters we have witnessed in Central America, Guantánamo, Iraq, and Afghanistan. As discussed below, in the end we are not protected by such practices, but rather endangered.

Quite apart from general conspiracy issues, federal law now makes it a felony punishable for up to twenty years of imprisonment for any U.S. official to torture, or conspire to torture, a person abroad. If the victim dies, the death penalty or a life term may be imposed. The anti-torture statute, 18 U.S.C. § 2340 et seq., was enacted after the U.S. ratification of the Convention against Torture and gives a very precise definitions of the prohibited actions.

Under this statute, torture means any act by an official intended to inflict severe physical or mental pain or suffering on a person within his or her custody or control. Severe mental pain and suffering means prolonged mental harm caused by 1) the infliction or threatened infliction of severe physical pain, 2) the administration or application, or threatened administration or application, of mind-altering substances or procedures calculated to profoundly disrupt the senses or personality, 3) the threat of imminent death, or 4) the threat to imminently torture, mentally or physically, or to kill another person.

Almost all of the abuses carried out in Iraq and Afghanistan, especially the harsher methods utilized by the CIA and its intelligence partners, fit within this definition of torture. The prisoners who were hung from their arms until their hands turned black, held in scorching hot containers, repeatedly thrown into walls headfirst, or hung upside down and beaten with rubber mallets, obviously suffered severe pain. So, too, did the prisoner with the bullet in his groin who was selectively denied medication, the general who suffocated in the sleeping bag during interrogations, or the detainees who were subjected to water-boardings. Many prisoners suffered prolonged and painful sleep deprivation. Excruciating positions, moreover, were exactly that—excruciating.

Other "refined" methods were equally illegal. FBI officers described a punishment frequently used on the prisoners. The detainee was stripped naked and seated in a chair, hands and feet shackled to a bolt in the floor. He was then subjected for up to fourteen hours of flashing strobe lights, shrieking music from close-up loudspeakers, and very cold temperatures. "It fried them," said one official. Another confirmed that the prisoners were quite "wobbly" after such punishments, and "completely out of it."[32] Obviously both severe mental and physical pain were inflicted.

The long-term and extreme sensory deprivations, such as the constant hoods and blindfolds combined with solitary confinement and immobilization in duct tape, would certainly be "calculated to disrupt profoundly the senses and personality." So would the extended deprivation of sleep, which has long been declared a form of torture by many sources, including the United States.[33] Threatening the prisoners with ferocious dogs, or threatening to rape or kill them, also qualifies as mental torture. The Iraqi general who watched his son shivering desperately in the cold, helpless to rescue him from the Americans, also understood all to well the meaning of mental torture. These deep wounds will be slow indeed to heal. Many survivors never recover.

In May of 1997, the U.N. Committee against Torture expressly ruled that such practices constitute torture. In reviewing very similar Israeli GSS interrogation tactics, the committee wrote as follows:

> These methods include 1) restraining in very painful positions, 2) hooding under special conditions, 3) sounding of loud music for prolonged periods, 4) sleep deprivation for prolonged periods, 5) threats, including death threats, 6) violent shaking, and 7) using cold air to chill; and are in the Committee's view breaches of Art. 16 and also constitute torture as defined in Art. 1. . . . This conclusion is particularly evident where such methods of interrogation are used in combination, which appears to be the standard case.[34]

It should also be remembered, too, that many of the "humiliations" were designed to be of particular degradation to traditional Islamic men. Many such techniques went well beyond humiliation and constituted mental torture, such as forcing one man to curse Islam, or others to violate their beliefs through simulated homosexual actions. As intended, this caused far more than mere embarrassment. The person's religious beliefs and culture must be taken into account in evaluating the degree of mental suffering inflicted.

The criminal statute also makes the CIA and other federal agents criminally liable for any torture resulting from their extraordinary renditions, as in the case of Maher Arar, or from their employment of civilian contractors. This is because conspiracy to commit torture is specifically included in the statute. The same goes, of course, for hiring known torturers as "assets."

Once again, the conspiracy clause of the statute would make the high-level government officials who developed, authorized, and ordered these practices also responsible for the crime of torture. It would not just be the seven young MPs from Abu Ghraib who would face trials, but the intellectual authors as well. This is as it should be. For good reason, the Nuremberg trials focused not on every German foot soldier, but rather on the Nazi leadership. The same calls for justice still echo across Latin America.

Another applicable statute is the U.S. War Crimes Act of 1996.[35] This applies to any member of the armed forces or to any national of the United Stated who commits a war crime. War crimes, in turn, are strictly defined as any grave breach of the Geneva Conventions, including Common Article 3, the Annex to the Hague Conventions, or the Protocol on Prohibitions and Restrictions on the Use of Mines, Booby Traps and Other Devices. The specifics of these treaties are discussed below. Suffice it to say here that egregious violations have taken place in Iraq and Afghanistan.

Given these ample criminal provisions, one might well assume that formal indictments would soon issue against many CIA and other intelligence officials. Yet this has not occurred. The decision as to whether or not to prosecute a federal crime is the exclusive prerogative of the U.S. prosecutor, in this case Mr. Alberto Gonzales, who wrote the notorious White House memo authorizing torture. All prosecutors enjoy complete discretion in their decision-making process and cannot be compelled to initiate charges in any given criminal case. Their discretion is virtually absolute. Although, under extraordinary circumstances, a "writ of mandamus" or direct court order, might be possible, in real life this will not occur.

Under future administrations, a new attorney general might decide to prosecute as long as the statutes of limitations have not lapsed. This is a long shot, but apparently the possibility has been of great concern to a number of CIA officials since the prisoner scandal broke.

This refusal to prosecute is a direct violation of the terms of the Convention against Torture. Article 7 of the convention *requires* all party states to either extradite or prosecute. Article 12 requires all party states to ensure that their authorities proceed with a prompt and impartial investigation whenever there is reasonable ground to believe that torture has been committed. Clearly these provisions are being ignored with regard to the high-level officials who authorized the abuses. Article 9 requires each such state to ensure that anyone suffering from violations within a territory under its jurisdiction will have the right to complain and be heard. What does this say about the agreements worked out by Paul Bremer, as U.S. administrator of postwar Iraq, providing full immunity to U.S. personnel for just such violations?

The CIA, their contractors, and the Pentagon did well in obtaining the needed "pre-clearance" memos from the Justice Department and special executive orders from the president, at the outset of the wars in Afghanistan and Iraq. They were, in effect, given full immunity before they engaged in illegal methods of interrogation. This highlights yet another weakness in our system of checks and balances. The executive branch has been able to act simultaneously as legislator, perpetrator, and judge. Administration officials acted to redefine torture and the applicability of the Geneva Conventions and other laws and treaties without so much as a nod to our elected representatives on Capitol Hill. Federal agencies from the same government branch then carried out the intolerable abuses on the detainees in Guantánamo, Iraq, and Afghanistan. These matters will not be brought to court because executive officials have decided not to prosecute. Clearly, some housekeeping efforts are in order here.

INTERNATIONAL LAW AND TREATIES

What about international humanitarian law and the many treaties ratified by the United States? It must be remembered, at the outset, that President Bush has taken care to reject the jurisdiction of the International Criminal Court, even though President Clinton had already signed in during the last weeks of his presidency.[36] Moreover, the United States has never accepted the jurisdiction of the Inter-American Court on Human Rights of the Organization of American States (OAS), despite our OAS membership. The United States is, of course, subject to civil suit in the World Court, and was in fact sued by the Sandinista government in that forum over the illegal mining of Nicaraguan harbors. The World Court ruled against the United States, but the Reagan administration simply laughed it off. Worse yet, as noted above, Paul Bremer and other executive officials have worked through broad grants of immunity to all agents and contractors in Iraq and other areas, thus preventing any local prosecutions.[37] As a result of this experience, our intelligence officials know that they can commit criminal actions such as torture with guaranteed impunity. This has led, inevitably, to corruption and the abuse of power.

Numerous international treaties, of course, prohibit the torture of any person under any circumstances. These include, but are not limited to, the following:

1. The Universal Declaration of Human Rights was adopted by the General Assembly of the United Nations in 1948, with U.S. approval, and states that "No one shall be subjected to torture or cruel, inhuman or degrading treatment or punishment." Art. 5, G.A. Res. 217A (III), U.N. GAOR, 3rd Sess., U.N. Doc. A/810 (1948).

2. The Declaration on the Protection of All Persons from Being Subjected to Torture was passed without dissent by the U.N. General Assembly in 1975, and forbids torture as well as cruel and degrading or inhuman punishment. G.A. Res. 3452, 30 GAOR, Supp. (no. 34) 91, U.N. Doc. A/1034 (1975).

3. The American Declaration of the Rights and Duties of Man protects human life and personal security.[38] OAS Res. XXX, adopted by the Ninth International Conference of American States (1948), reprinted in Basic Documents Pertaining to Human Rights in the Inter-American System, OEA/Ser.L.V/II.82 doc.6 rev.1 at 17 (1992).

4. The International Covenant on Civil and Political Rights prohibits torture and cruel, inhuman, or degrading treatment or punishment, at Article 7. This provision is non-derogable (that is, it cannot be suspended), even "during time of public emergency which threatens the life of the nation."[39] The covenant entered into force in the United States in 1992. Dec. 19, 1996, 999 U.N.T.S. 171, reprinted in 6 I.L.M. 368 (1967).

5. Most on point, of course, is the Convention against Torture, which defines torture as any infliction of severe mental or physical pain for the purposes of punishment or of obtaining information or a confession. Significantly, the prohibitions apply to abuses inflicted or instigated by, or with the acquiescence of, any public official or other person acting in an official capacity.[40] Torture cannot be justified by the state of war or a public emergency.[41] Sending a person to a third country where torture might occur is prohibited.[42] All parties must ensure that acts of torture are an offense under its criminal laws.[43] The

convention also prohibits any form of cruel, inhuman, or degrading treatment or punishment.[44] Moreover, training and information about the convention must be given to all personnel.[45] November 1994. Dec. 10, 1984, G.A. Res. 39/46, 39 U.N. GAOR, Supp. No. 51 at 197, U.N. Doc. A/39/51 (1984), reprinted in 23 I.L.M. 535.

6. The Geneva Conventions, signed in 1949 and discussed in detail below, prohibit the torture of any prisoner, whether a formal prisoner of war, a saboteur, or a resistance leader in an internal conflict. They also require training of all personnel handling prisoners, as well as prosecution of any violations.

7. Torture was prohibited in the context of war even before the Geneva Conventions. The Hague Convention Respecting the Laws and Customs of War on Land (Hague IV), October 18, 1907, Annex, for example, at Art. 4, requires all prisoners of war to be humanely treated.

Even when the United States refuses to sign a given treaty or protocol, it may be de facto bound by international customary law. As the United States Supreme Court has itself ruled, the customs and uses of the international community will be binding. "Like all the laws of nations, it rests upon the common consent of civilized communities. It is of force, not because it was prescribed by any superior power but because it has been generally accepted as a rule of conduct."[46]

In turn, it is beyond question that the ban on torture, accepted as it is by virtually all nations, constitutes binding international law. As stated by the Court of Appeals of the Second Circuit in the Filartiga case, involving torture and murder in Paraguay:

> In light of the universal condemnation of torture in numerous international agreements, and the renunciation of torture as an instrument of official policy by virtually all of the nations of the world (in principle if not in practice), we find that an act of torture committed

by a state official against one held in detention violates established norms of the international law of human rights, and hence the law of nations.[47]

As the above summary makes clear, international law prohibits the physical or mental torture or abuse of *any person*. Soldiers in an armed conflict form a special category of "persons" with additional protections specifically set forth in the Geneva Conventions. However, all other persons, including frightening and even dangerous criminals, may be detained, tried, and imprisoned, but they must remain free of torture and inhumane treatment. The Convention against Torture prohibits the torture or abuse of any person at any time and under any circumstances. The International Covenant of Civil and Political Rights also makes the prohibitions against torture and cruel and degrading treatment non-derogable, even during times of war. These protections apply even to persons accused of a crime. No "other" category of persons, for whom subjection to torture is permissible, exists in modern international law.[48]

Importantly, attempts to create a new category of "torture lite" fail as well. Torture, as well as inhumane, cruel, and degrading treatment, are *all* flatly forbidden by international law, as discussed above, even during times of war, and even for non-POWs accused of serious crimes. Period.

Why, then, can suit not be brought directly under these treaties? Because their terms and requirements are not self-executing. Congress must pass legislation establishing the victim's right to sue under these provisions. This was done in the two criminal statutes described above. Also, protective civil legislation in fact exists in the form of the Alien Tort Claims Act and the Torture Victims Protection Act. However, as discussed below, the Justice Department, even now, is urging in pending cases that these statutes are somehow inapplicable to U.S. officials.

The arguments and interpretations set out in the White House and Justice Department memorandums, urging the inapplicability of the Geneva Conventions, and distorting the definitions of torture, must now be evaluated in light of all of the above laws and treaties.

The Office of the Legal Counsel, Department of Justice memorandum of August 1, 2002, sets forth a "reinterpretation" of the definition of torture provided by the criminal statute 18 U.S.C. 2340 et seq. discussed above. According to the OLC, only a level of pain equivalent to that suffered during a serious physical injury, such as organ failure, loss of a body function, or death, would qualify as torture. Moreover, only psychological harm that lasts for months or even years would be covered by the provisions. These guidelines were echoed by Alberto Gonzales, former White House counsel to President Bush and now U.S. attorney general.[49]

To begin with, these interpretations are tantamount to legislation, as they add legal requirements and hurdles which Congress did not establish. Such additions do not lie within the authority of the Justice Department or the White House. Only our legislators have the power to legislate. Once again, deep flaws within our system of checks and balances are exposed here.

The interpretations, moreover, are untenable. With regard to duration of the mental harm, no one can seriously argue that the survivors of the Abu Ghraib abuses, or the many other similarly treated detainees, will ever fully recover from the trauma inflicted upon them. Anyone familiar with post-traumatic stress syndrome can speak to that issue. So can the survivors from Latin America. As for physical pain intensity, the proffered standard is rather meaningless. Many forms of death itself are far less painful than some of the torture methods utilized. Execution by injection, or the instantaneous death caused by a broken neck, are but two examples. By contrast, Professor Dershowitz's sterile needle under the fingernail will cause a horrifying level of pain. So, too, do the more "refined" methods, such as carefully placed electrical shocks and the use of excruciating positions. Prolonged sleep deprivation has devastating physical impact and has been again and again declared a form of torture.[50] Our intelligence agencies, especially the CIA, have long worked to perfect these methods. The goal has been to create pain and suffering beyond any human endurance. They have excelled in their tasks, but they are locked in a headlong collision with domestic and international law.

Similarly, the memorandums give a rather bizarre analysis of the intent requirements. To be sure, as stated in the memos, a perpetrator must normally have criminal intent in order to be found guilty. An accident does not constitute murder. However, the administration attorneys have suggested in their correspondence that since the ultimate objective of interrogation is intelligence, as opposed to torture, that the statutory requirement of specific intent would not be present. They cite the example of a person who robs a bank, then dawdles instead of hurrying to escape, because he seeks to be returned to prison and treated for alcoholism.[51] In that case, the robber did not in fact intend to keep the money.

Attempting to apply this logic to torture by U.S. interrogators becomes quite twisted. Our agents fully intend to carry out torture, and that is precisely what they have done. They did not intend to simply frighten the prisoners, while stopping short of inflicting any actual pain and suffering. The man who hires a hit man to murder his wife cannot claim that he is innocent because his real objective was to collect the insurance money.

Next, the memorandums urge that the Geneva Conventions are inapplicable, and thus any liability under the War Crimes Act as well. In part this is based on the argument that the president of the United States, as commander in chief, has the power to simply set these provisions aside. In short, President Bush was declared to be above the law. This argument certainly came as a shock to most attorneys and lawmakers.

More disturbing still, in many ways, were the pat claims that the conventions somehow did not apply in Afghanistan or Iraq, and that as a result, the torture methods used by the CIA and others were somehow legitimate. Moreover, even when the administration agreed to comply with the conventions, as in Iraq, many of the protections were simply discarded with all too facile arguments. U.S. Attorney General Alberto Gonzales, then counsel to the White House, described the protections as "quaint" and "obsolete." Historically, those very protections were drawn up not by naïve liberals, but by government leaders fresh from the experiences of the Bataan Death March and the Gestapo interrogation methods practiced on captured spies and resistance members. It is no coincidence that it was Colin Powell, a general, and other seasoned military officers who vehemently protested the evisceration of the conventions. Senator McCain, himself a much abused POW in Vietnam, has been fierce in his criticisms as well.

In order to properly evaluate the legal requirements, it must be remembered at the outset that there are *two* conventions in question here. The Third Geneva Convention deals with prisoner of war issues, and the Fourth Geneva Convention provides protections for civilians. These two documents must be read together.

At the outset of the war in Afghanistan, the Bush administration decreed that the detainees, as "terrorists," were somehow not entitled to these protections. Torture, however, cannot be carried out against any person at all. If a given prisoner does not fall within the legal definitions of a "prisoner of war" under the Third Convention, the Fourth Convention still prohibits any inhumane treatment of persons engaged in espionage, sabotage, or activities hostile to an occupying power.[52] Both the Third and Fourth Geneva Conventions forbid the inhumane treatment of a person participating in an internal armed conflict.[53] In short, whether a soldier in a formal army, a "guerrilla" style combatant, or a dangerous saboteur such as a suicide bomber, all detainees are entitled to humane treatment at all times. A denial of prisoner of war status in no way legitimates the use of torture or other abuses.

The following discussion sets forth the Geneva Conventions requirements applicable during various phases of the war on terror.

AFGHANISTAN UNDER THE TALIBAN

Both the United States and Afghanistan are signatories to the Geneva Conventions, and they are both fully bound by its terms. During the initial stage of the war, while the Taliban was still the government in power, all captured Taliban soldiers were entitled to prisoner of war status and protections. So, too, were any volunteer units forming part of that army.[54] Thus many al-Qaeda members fighting together with the Taliban may also have been eligible.

If there was any doubt as to the status of a particular detainee, then full prisoner of war protections had to be provided until a competent tribunal determined the matter.[55] Under Articles 3 and 13, all prisoners of war must be treated humanely. They cannot be placed in danger by any act or omission, subjected to violence, intimidation, insults, or public scrutiny. Full respect must be given to their honor and their persons (Article 14). They cannot be mentally or physically coerced or tortured in order to force them to divulge information (Article 17). They must be placed in prisoner of war centers, not prisons (Article 22). They cannot be sent to third nations unwilling to comply with the protections of the conventions (Article 12). All guards must be taught about the conventions' requirements (Article 39). No prisoner may be secretly detained (Article 69). Any death or injury to a prisoner of war must be fully investigated and a report must be made. Any guilty persons are to be prosecuted (Article 121).

In short, virtually all of the interrogation methods carried out against the Taliban soldiers first captured during the U.S. invasion, were illegal. So, too, were the extraordinary renditions and use of "ghost prisoners." Moreover, Camp X-Ray in Guantánamo should not have received any POWs until its conditions met fully with convention requirements. The punitive and long-term interrogation of vast numbers of detainees, without any adequate hearing as to their POW status, was also unlawful. A large percentage of such detainees were later determined to be innocent of any wrongdoing. Many, for example, had been denounced by neighbors seeking rewards or personal revenge. Others were simply at the wrong place at the wrong time. All of the violations are the full responsibility of the detaining powers, regardless of any individual responsibility of the interrogators or MPs.[56]

Some within the Bush administration had urged that the Taliban was a "failed state" and thus did not merit the protections. Yet this is a dangerous argument. Given the intense resistance in both Iraq and Afghanistan even now against the U.S. allied governments, those governments, too, could be described as "failed." Moreover, as further discussed below, under Common Article 3, even in the context of an internal conflict, torture cannot be utilized.

If a prisoner of war commits a crime, then he or she may be tried by a court with proper protections, and if guilty, disciplined.[57] However, the court must be properly impartial and independent, and offer adequate procedural safeguards.[58] Article 102 states, moreover, that "A prisoner of war can be validly sentenced only if the sentence has been pronounced by the same courts according to the same procedure as in the case of members of the armed forces of the Detaining Power." Corporal punishments, imprisonment without daylight, and any form of torture or cruelty, are prohibited.[59] No prisoner may be coerced to confess.[60]

Significantly, on November 8, 2004, the United States District Court in Washington, D.C., ruled that the military tribunals in Guantánamo could not try Mr. Sayed Hamdan until he was first given a hearing on his prisoner of war status. The tribunal lacked the appropriate rules and procedures to give Mr. Hamdan the required protections for any prisoners of war.[61]

It can be argued that al-Qaeda members, and other non-Taliban combatants, were not eligible for prisoner of war status. If so, they were nevertheless protected by the Fourth Geneva Convention. This treaty covers any persons who "find themselves, in the case of a conflict or occupation, in the hands of a party to the conflict or occupying power of which they are not nationals."[62] They are entitled to respect for their persons, honor, family rights, and customs.[63] No physical or moral coercion can be used to force them to divulge information, and they may not be subjected to physical suffering, including murder, torture, corporal punishments, and any other acts of brutality.[64] The wounded and sick are given special protections.[65] They cannot be transferred to other countries where the conventions are not observed.[66]

Although the Fourth Convention refers to civilians, this category includes persons committing violent acts. Specifically, persons detained as spies or saboteurs, or for having committed actions hostile to the security of the occupying power, may, where necessary, be deemed for a time to have waived their rights of communications, but still must be treated with humanity and provided with a fair trial.[67] Moreover, they should be afforded all civilian protections as soon as security permits. Thus al-Qaeda members, even if correctly denied POW status, could not be tortured, abused, or held as long-term ghost prisoners.

POST-TALIBAN AFGHANISTAN

Once the Taliban was overthrown, and the new U.S.-backed Afghan government established, the analysis changes somewhat, but the basic protections for all detainees still apply.

For any Taliban and other fighters refusing to recognize the new government, and instead giving continued loyalty to the fallen Taliban, the prisoner of war status and privileges should still hold.[68] The ongoing warfare at this stage may also be deemed an internal conflict, similar to the insurgencies throughout Latin America. Once again, torture, degradation, or similar abuses of any detainees in such circumstances are banned (see Common Article 3).[69] Given that the United States is fully participating in combating these insurgents, together with the new Afghan government troops, it, too, is bound to treat all detainees in accordance with the conventions.

If the continuing war is seen as a de facto occupation by the United States, then the detainees are covered by the Fourth Convention and must be treated as civilian saboteurs or hostile actors as discussed above.

IRAQ UNDER SADDAM HUSSEIN

All Iraqi soldiers captured in the early phase of the war, while Saddam Hussein remained in power, were entitled to the full protections of prisoners of war. As discussed above, none could be mistreated in any way, and all retained full POW status and protections until a competent tribunal determined otherwise. Those believed to have committed a crime could be subjected to a full and fair trial, and punished accordingly, but never tortured to extract information or to retaliate for their allegiance. Hence all of the abuses during this period in various detention centers represent rampant violations of the Geneva Conventions. So do the extraordinary renditions.

IRAQ UNDER U.S. OCCUPATION

Once Saddam fell and the United States became an occupying force in Iraq, persons continuing to fight against U.S. troops fall into two possible categories. Once again, those insisting on recognizing Saddam Hussein's regime would be protected as POWs by Article 4 of the Third Convention, as would any soldiers who laid down their arms at the end of the hostilities. Those who continue even now to carry out bombings, ambushes, and similar activities would be treated as civilian saboteurs and persons carrying out hostile actions under the Fourth Geneva Conventions (Articles 4 and 5). As such, they too are fully protected from any acts of torture and degradation, as discussed above. Nor may they be punished for any suspected crime without a full and fair trial first (Article 71). They may be turned over to a military court, but only within the occupied country, that is, not in Guantánamo or other third nations known to engage in torture (Article 66).

Civilian saboteurs or insurgents charged with a crime, even a deadly one, may call witnesses and be represented by a lawyer, and they have the right to appeal (Article 70 et seq.). A convicted person can only be detained in Iraq, and must serve out his or her sentence there (Article 76). The conditions of their prison must be equivalent to lawful prison conditions within the United States, including healthful, hygienic conditions, food, and medical and religious attention. They at all times have the right to visits from the Red Cross (Article 76). At the end of the occupation, these prisoners are to be released to the new government (Article 77). The convention protections apply for as long as the United States continues to exercise government functions there (Article 39).

Even after the new government became technically independent, if the attacks continue as part of an internal conflict, then Article 3 of both the Third and Fourth Conventions becomes applicable, and torture will still be banned. As long as the U.S. military is involved, it remains bound.

DETAINEES SEIZED IN OTHER COUNTRIES

Many suspects have been seized by the United States in other countries as well. Mr. Khaled Mohammed, allegedly a high-level associate of Bin Laden, for example, was seized, detained, and tortured by the CIA in Pakistan, and others have been arrested throughout various regions of the Middle East and Southeast Asia as well.

Because Bush has defined this war as being worldwide, and against any member of a terrorist network wherever he or she may be found, then such pockets of suspected terrorist networks in friendly nations would constitute an internal insurgency, and thus be eligible for protections from any form of abuse under Common Article 3. Since the United States is participating in these arrests and interrogations, it is also subject to the conventions. (In the alternative, of course, even if there is no war ongoing, the prohibitions of the Convention against Torture and other treaties apply.)

GENERAL PROVISIONS OF THE GENEVA CONVENTIONS

Every signatory nation must see to it that persons responsible for detainees during wartime possess copies and understand the terms of the Geneva Conventions.[70] The parties to the conventions are bound to give unlimited access to all prisoners, in all places of detention, to the International Red Cross.[71] The parties must also include the study of the conventions in their military courses and assure that all persons responsible for the detainees have special instruction.[72] As the White House and Justice Department memorandums, together with the statements of the young MPs left facing court-martials, make clear, these provisions were not respected.

Crucially, the conventions require all parties to enact legislation providing penal sanctions for anyone violating, or ordering the violation of, the provisions.[73] Moreover, such violators, including intellectual authors, must be brought to trial.[74] Grave breaches include not only torture but the willful deprivation of a fair trial.[75] No party nation may absolve itself of liability.[76] A nation may denounce the convention, but even then it expressly remains bound to fulfill "the principles of the law of nations, as they result from the usages established amongst civilized peoples, from the laws of humanity and the dictates of public conscience."[77] The Third and Fourth Convention contain very similar provisions on these issues.

Thus the very failure and refusal of the Justice Department to bring to trial high-level CIA and other intelligence officers and agents, is in and of itself a serious breach of the Geneva Conventions.

Perhaps in the end the only solution is the one the CIA officials fear the most—a Pinochet-style criminal case filed against them abroad under the doctrine of universal jurisdiction. Although the doctrine is quite sound, and rooted in centuries of jurisprudence,[78] it is unlikely that the United States would permit extradition of any officials or agents, let alone respect a foreign court ruling. Yet the growing trend in international law requires states to prosecute, extradite, or turn a torturer over to an international criminal tribunal. Under these concepts, persons like Donald Rumsfeld could in theory be arrested in France or Germany. Given the current realpolitik, this will not occur. However, as the global community grows ever smaller and is increasingly bound by international law, and as the United States frays its long-standing alliances and drifts towards isolation, who is to say what the future holds? If we do not clean house, we will eventually force our neighbors to do it for us.[79] As discussed below, already a number of CIA kidnapping and abuse cases are under investigation in Italy, Sweden, and Germany.

MILITARY LAW

What about the U.S. military? They, too, carry out virtually all of their activities abroad, often under the exigent circumstances of war. Moreover, military leaders must work constantly with very young and often inexperienced servicemen and -women. When they break the laws and treaties of the United States, do they operate with the full freedom from legal consequences that seems to shield the CIA? Or are they subject to certain limits and discipline, as in the case of the FBI?

Not surprisingly, the U.S. military is in fact highly disciplined, and its members are subject to many legal restrictions and sanctions, not just for disregarding rules of internal obedience and order, but for other forms of misconduct as well.

To begin with, all military personnel are subject to the provisions of the Military Code of Justice. These provisions cover many forms of misconduct—including rape, sodomy, assault, murder, and maiming—and provide for court-martial and punishment, including prison terms, for serious violations. This is precisely what is happening to the MPs involved in the cases out of Iraq and Afghanistan. Although these young soldiers are unjustly bearing the brunt of the punishment for crimes which they hardly invented, at least some justice is being carried out. This is certainly having a healthy effect on other uniformed men and women, who have commented often on the question of illegal orders and the Geneva Conventions since the scandal broke.

When the CIA engages in wartime efforts and works closely on the ground with the military, are its agents not subject to this code? The answer is no. The CIA is a civilian agency and hence its agents and officers cannot be court-martialed. It is assumed they will be prosecuted under civilian law, but as discussed above, this does not happen. This has the odd result of low-level MPs in Iraq being sent to prison under harsh but justified military laws, while CIA agents committing even worse abuses in the same place face no sanctions at all.

This was noted with disapproval by retired Special Operations major F. Andy Messing, who stated that the CIA agents in El Salvador were "on their own wavelength.... You have two parallel chains of command and one could end up doing what they feel like doing."[80]

The Military Extraterritoriality Act, 18 U.S.C. § 3261, provides yet broader avenues of relief and deterrence. The act permits the concurrent prosecution of any military person, or any person employed by or accompanying the armed forces, outside the United States, if such a person commits a crime punishable by over a year's imprisonment. This has rarely been utilized, and would again be up to prosecutorial discretion. However, all private contractors working with the military, if found to have committed torture or other abuses, could be subject to prosecution in the United States. Once again, this results in a strange situation; a CACI contractor working with the army can stand trial under this act, while a colleague working with the CIA will not.

There is also the Military Claims Act, 10 U.S.C. § 2734, which establishes a procedure for informal settlements of claims against the military by any foreign inhabitant, for wrongful (but noncombat) acts resulting in loss of property, personal injury, or death. If the victim lives within a country at war with the United States, he or she may still file if determined to be friendly to the U.S. This is a highly discretionary system and does not apply to combat-related activities. But it does represent some attempt to treat local residents fairly when harm occurs. As stated by the act, the purpose is to maintain friendly relations through prompt settlements. Under these provisions, detainees at Abu Ghraib and other areas, who were later freed for lack of any evidence against them, could present claims.

There is, of course, yet one more factor which serves to bind members of the military to appropriate human rights standards, and that is the matter of reciprocity. Any serviceman or woman who has ever worn a uniform is all too aware of the possibility of capture and abuse by the enemy. Senator John McCain is a living example of precisely this peril. For this very reason, members of the armed forces have traditionally safeguarded and respected the Geneva Conventions and other norms of warfare. Although CIA agents certainly run risks, they are nowhere near as high as those faced by the uniformed ranks during times of war. It is thus not surprising that General Powell and Senator McCain have been particularly vociferous on the matter.

CONSIDERATIONS

In the end, it would seem that the CIA has a level of impunity for serious illegal acts that neither the FBI nor the military has, despite their similar and at times even identical roles, risks, and responsibilities. Are there other considerations which would justify such extraordinary protections for the CIA alone?

The agency itself urges again and again that in order to obtain needed intelligence, it must pay and work with unsavory characters. As discussed above, this is true in part, and false in part, and bears close consideration here. Needless to say, placing a cash premium on information obtained from a detainee for all practical purposes puts a price on that prisoner's head. Paying for information both encourages and rewards torture.

When it comes to obtaining information from an enemy organization, such as al-Qaeda, the CIA will obviously have very little leverage, and would be unable to insist on respect for human rights or any other related matters. The agency, by purchasing intelligence, will not be attempting to support and strengthen al-Qaeda, as in the case of CIA collaboration with General Pinochet or the Central American military regimes throughout the Dirty Wars. Presumably, such limited payments would be made as bribes to those within the enemy organization willing to sell information about planned attacks, prisoner whereabouts, and similar matters. In short, the payments would be made in order to save lives only. As long as the contact is not being paid to torture another person for the information, as in the Central American cases, such preventative payments would seem reasonable enough.

Needless to say, the past close collaboration with military death squads in violent coup d'etats and devastating counterinsurgency campaigns against civilians in Latin America presents quite a different situation. In that context, the CIA was in fact acting to impose its own foreign policy decisions on sovereign nations, and to aid, abet, and assist in rampant torture and massacre campaigns in order to achieve these goals. Funding was not given to save American lives. Indeed, no American lives were at risk, other than those of persons like Sister Dianna, who might fall into the hands of the CIA's own partners. Moreover, the CIA and other U.S. agencies had enormous control and authority over the local death squads, as the above testimonies reflect. They could very easily have curbed the ongoing abuses, but chose not to. Instead, they encouraged and promoted torture by continuous payments and by shielding the perpetrators from all legal and political consequences.

When faced with accusations in this regard, the CIA has always urged that it had to "maintain its relationships" in order to keep up the flow of information. This is rather specious. We owned these armies. We continued to fund, equip, and shield the death squads because we liked what they were doing—protecting a political and economic status quo favorable to the United States. In cases like this, the CIA should be required to enforce all human rights norms among its partner organizations. This would be quite feasible. With corrupt military organizations such as the Guatemalan army, money speaks volumes, as does its cessation. Cooperation will always go to the highest bidder. For precisely this reason, I survived my hunger strikes in Guatemala, while thousands of locals were murdered for far less defiant acts. The army did not want to lose its U.S. tax dollars and feared the growing congressional scrutiny.

There are, of course, intermediate situations, nations in which the CIA hopes to gain a foothold among networks neither friendly nor hostile. Once again, money certainly speaks volumes. However, there is no real reason why funding should not be accompanied by pressure to respect human rights requirements. If a given operative is willing to risk treason charges, or worse, in return for cash, he or she is not likely to run away if the matter of torture is raised. Pressure should be commensurate with the payments made. If the United States wishes to claim the title of moral leader of the world, then it needs to put its money where its mouth is.

There can be little doubt that the current status quo—which gives the CIA de facto impunity for crimes against humanity while requiring parallel military and law enforcement agencies to respect domestic and international human rights laws and treaties—is highly skewed. Moreover, it is outright dangerous. We are looking not at a few rogue operators, but rather at an entire rogue agency that has seized powers it was never granted and, as outlined above, has placed itself above the law. This is precisely what our system of checks and balances and open records acts was designed to prevent, for few developments are more corrosive to a genuine democracy. Once again we must act to set our house straight, and swiftly, before it collapses on top of us.

But what can be done? Certainly a number of basic reforms could be passed by the legislature that would help to restore needed balance and protections. These are straightforward enough:

1. All government files concerning cases of torture or extrajudicial executions should be automatically declassified, including the names of the perpetrators, any involved or knowledgeable U.S. agents, and the relationship, financial or otherwise, between the perpetrator and the United States. The CIA should be permitted to withhold real names of involved agents only if it as-

signs such person a code name and agrees to present him or her at any congressional or court proceedings. Failure to properly declassify such information should constitute a felony.

2. If torture is credibly alleged, as certified either by the International Committee of the Red Cross, the U.N. Committee against Torture, or any officer or agency of the United Nations, such case should be promptly referred to a grand jury for investigation and indictment under the relevant statutes.

3. The Federal Tort Claims Act should be amended so that all acts of torture or murder, or any cruel, inhumane, or degrading treatment by any U.S. officials, agents, or contractors, are covered, whether carried out within the United States or abroad.

4. The Torture Victims Protection Act should be amended to expressly include actions by U.S. officials, agents, and contractors acting abroad.

5. The Alien Tort Claims Act should be amended to include a waiver of sovereign immunity.

Would these changes completely prevent any future abuses? Sadly, the answer is no. It is all too easy for covert operatives to carry out secret actions. The victims don't live to speak, and the agents' identities are never known. However, these reforms would be a major advance in ending the secret practice of torture.

CHAPTER FIVE
PAYING THE PRICE

Despite everything, leaders in the Bush administration still insist that the only proper response to the September 11 attacks is a show of strength, in short, brutality.[1] Perhaps in the end we must recognize that many members of the American public may to some degree condone the use of torture, although they do not wish to be confronted with the grim details. How can this possibility be squared with the reaction of utter outrage that greeted the Abu Ghraib disclosures? Fear is the answer.

The horrors of September 11 have left many of us traumatized and desperate for assurances of safety. Certainly the Bush administration has played this card to the maximum, telling us again and again that we are in grave danger and that security will only come from the "tough guy" approach. This sounds comforting somehow. Perhaps most of us know better, and are appalled by the thought of torture. However we see no other solution, no other way to escape from the burning towers etched in our subconsciousness. Humans have always resorted to barbaric practices when they feel that their way of life is threatened. This has always resulted in disaster, yet globally we have evolved very little in this regard. When frightened, we tend to turn to murder and brutality instead of thought, compromise, or conflict resolution.

Perhaps the time has come, however, when more thinking and less violence is the only genuine path to security. Perhaps the obvious "violence begets violence" is in fact true, and our harsh approach to the detainees will only result in more attacks and more backlash against U.S. citizens. Given the devastating capacity of nuclear weapons and their proliferation worldwide, we had best examine all of the possibilities. Playing ostrich will not save us, and may well kill us all.

As with any serious analysis, we must start with a clear and full complement of facts. We should first weigh the true human costs of torture and other abuses, not just with regard to the actual victim, but to family members, the community as a whole, and even the torturers themselves. Next we should evaluate the claimed justifications for torture. Does it work? Does it in fact lead to good intelligence? What about the oft repeated ticking bomb story? What alternatives are there? Finally, we should attempt to learn a bit from history. Certainly we are not the first nation to face possible attacks, including those carried out against civilians. Others have long faced the very fears and issues that confront us now, and of those many have sought security through heightened violence against potential perpetrators. Has this worked or backfired? We have to look squarely at these realities if we truly wish to find a solution.

THE HUMAN COSTS

It is clear from reading the White House and Justice Department memorandums that none of the authors had the vaguest concept of the human costs of torture. The writings reflect no awareness of the devastating and long-term effects on the victims, their families, and society as a whole. Rather, it is simply assumed that extraordinarily high levels of pain and degradation, so long as no permanent physical injury results, can simply be shrugged off. Nothing could be further from the truth, and we must take care to understand the long-term consequences of our actions. False assumptions can be dangerous.

With regards to the survivors, it must be recognized from the outset that the harm inflicted is both permanent and severe. Long after the body physically heals, the mind continues to suffer. As Sister Dianna has stated publicly, "One never heals from torture. One merely learns to cope with the aftermath."[2]

There have been a number of clinical reports on just what this "aftermath" entails. The list includes insomnia, nightmares, flashbacks, chronic anxiety, inability to trust others, deliberate self-injury, violent behavior, substance abuse, inability to concentrate, depression, and paranoia.[3] The Center for Victims of Torture, in Minneapolis, adds paranoia, guilt, suspicion, sexual dysfunction, and memory loss to the list. Moreover, the survivors will often try to numb the continuing pain in any way possible, including drug or alcohol abuse and even self-injury or thoughts of suicide.[4] These symptoms can and do torment the victims for decades or for the rest of their life. As victims of post-traumatic stress, the risk of suicide can be high for torture survivors, just as it was for many returning Vietnam veterans. A study of American POWs who had been held in Japan during World War II showed a 50 percent increase in deaths from cirrhosis of the liver, "accidents," and tuberculosis as well as a 30 percent higher suicide rate.[5] Some memories are nearly impossible to live with; the doomed heroine in *Sophie's Choice* comes to mind as a good illustration.

Researchers also believe that when the victim is bound and helpless, "torture not only harms the body, but it also corrupts the portion of the brain that screams at the body to fight back or flee ... when the body is restrained and can do neither."[6] Thus Prof. Van De Kolk of Boston University Medical School suggests that torture results in deeper and more permanent trauma than that suffered by survivors able to flee, such as those who escaped the World Trade Towers. Because those survivors were able to at least run and save themselves, they have a far better chance at recovery than persons who were tied down and able to do nothing.[7]

What does this mean in real life terms? I remember only too well watching the excruciating recovery process of my friend, Sister Dianna. The unbearable nightmares made sleep impossible for her for many years, leaving her pale and hollow-eyed. Huge bruises would mark her arms and hands from when she flailed them against the walls and bedside at night, trying to escape the tormentors in her dreams. Every time she tried to tell her story, the horrors would come rushing back as flashbacks and she would be attacked by fits of weeping. Cigarette smoke made the 111 healed burns throb as if new, and the sudden bark of any dog would terrify her. Rapid-fire and unfriendly questioning was very upsetting, reminding her of those who burned and beat her no matter how she responded to their questions. Men in uniform unnerve her still. For years she felt contaminated, somehow guilty, and suffered near crippling bouts of depression. Images of the woman killed with the machete haunted her. For a long time, her life seemed of little value to her, but she hung on and somehow survived. Slowly, she healed. What is remarkable about Sister Dianna is that she was able to recover enough of her faith and sense of self to become an international spokesperson and a healer of others.

Sister Dianna is hardly alone with regard to such nearly unbearable trauma symptoms. When "David," whose story is set forth in chapter 3, first spoke with me about his torture, he involuntarily held his arms up as if tied to a cross, and his eyes rolled back as he relived the horror. "The pain!" he gasped. He held his breath for a few moments, then collapsed into despairing tears. It took a while for him to return to the present, to notice my hand on his arm. We did not speak of this again for a long time to come. The Salvadoran doctor who was tortured as a young man can speak only occasionally of what occurred, and even then only for a little while before he begins to weep and cannot go on. Twenty years has eased nothing. A survivor of the "killing fields" of Cambodia reported chronic headaches and other problems some twenty-five years later. A medical study of more than a hundred blind women from Cambodia showed that they were not organically blind, but had been forced to witness the torture or murder of others. While psychosomatic blindness is usually temporary, the women's condition seemed to be permanent.[8] Auschwitz survivors in Israel sheepishly admitted to me that even at their bountiful kibbutz, they still hide a bit of bread under their pillows at night. As the son of two Holocaust survivors said, "My parents woke up howling almost every night. For a long time as a child I thought all parents did."[9]

At least some of these people have managed to somehow go on with constructive lives, despite the pain. Others have been less fortunate. Moreover, the damage to the person has been equally devastating in cases of pure mental torture. One young Guatemalan I will call "Pablo" was eleven years old when his entire village was massacred by the military. He managed to hide in a hollow tree stump and somehow escaped detection as scores of men, women, children, and elderly persons were raped, beaten, and hacked to death around him, including members of his own family. In the middle of the night he fled across the field of cadavers, back up the mountainside toward his home. Along the way he saw friends and neighbors lying dead outside their huts. He decided he would bury his own relatives, then turn himself in to be killed as well. To his amazement, a few relatives had survived. A young Mayan soldier, in quiet rebellion, had burst into their home and warned them to lie down and play dead. He then told the other soldiers that he had "taken care of things."

Pablo was about twenty when he came to Washington to give his testimony. He wanted to speak with all his heart, to win some kind of justice for his lost community. He did well enough at the hearing, although he was clearly reliving every moment of the slaughter and suffering greatly. For the rest of the day he was silent and remote from all of us, and that night he vanished from his bed. We searched frantically for him but it was several days before he reappeared. He had been hiding in the public parks, fleeing every police officer, terrified of the passing helicopters. He thought he was back there, in Guatemala, during the massacre. Although he survived this crisis, his life has been very difficult.

In 1971 a number of IRA prisoners were subjected by the British to torture methods that, none too coincidentally, closely mirror the techniques used recently by the United States in Iraq and Afghanistan. The young men were hooded and deprived of sleep and food for a week. Throughout their ordeal, they were forced to stand spread-eagled against a wall with most of their weight on their arms. If they fell or dropped their arms they were beaten severely. Strange sounds blasted incessantly at different decibels. They were not allowed to use the toilets. By the end many were hallucinating. One stumbled in saying his name and could barely count to ten. Most were unable to use their hands even to feed themselves. Although they physically recovered with time, the trauma symptoms plagued most of them for the rest of their lives. Many died before the age of fifty-five. One survivor suffered recurring blackouts for years, one was unable to work, and most suffered flashbacks, severe anxiety, insomnia, nightmares, and irritability.[10]

As a wife of one of the IRA prisoners said, "When he came out we had a terrible life. I couldn't turn on the Hoover. If you were turning a page in the newspaper it affected him. If you dropped a spoon on the floor he went mad. He never slept. He twisted, turned, shouted, bawled at night. I was scared of him. After he came out he used to put a gun to my head and threaten to shoot me."[11]

In short, survivors of physical and mental torture may literally survive, but they bear heavy and sometimes crippling scars which haunt them for the rest of their lives.

THE SUFFERING OF FAMILY MEMBERS

In evaluating the long-term impact of torture, many tend to forget the extreme hardships and trauma also inflicted on relatives of the victims. As the above description of daily life by an IRA survivor's wife makes clear, family life is very much affected and often damaged for a long time to come. This difficult situation is further illustrated by a Danish study of eighty-four children of Chilean survivors.[12] Thirty-four had insomnia and nightmares, five had tics, twelve had chronic stomach pains, thirteen suffered headaches, fifteen wet their beds, thirteen had anorexia, four had memory problems, and sixteen showed behavioral problems.

Perhaps the most difficult of all, however, is the endless wait ing and searching for the "disappeared," including the CIA's current "ghost prisoners." The shock of the initial capture is traumatic enough for any family. By way of illustration, we have Mirna Anaya's account of standing in a small shop in El Salvador with her family when heavily armed men dragged her husband away in broad daylight. Her little girl began to scream, "They've taken my Daddy!" and they all knew at once he would be severely tortured and probably killed. In fact, thanks to international outcry, he survived that kidnapping only to be shot to death on his front lawn a year later. Sometimes the abductions themselves are excessively brutal in order to instill terror into the local population as well as the family itself. I remember a friend telling me of her husband's kidnapping by the security forces in Guatemala many years ago. He was leaving a bank when he was assaulted by a large group of masked men with automatic rifles. They beat him ferociously but still he resisted. In the end they broke both of his legs forcing him into the vehicle. Years had past and she knew he must be dead. Yet still she was desperate, subject to crying fits, and unable to sleep. What if he were still alive, in pain, and needing help?

As discussed above, the abductions in Latin America were heavily backed by theUnited States throughout the Dirty Wars. Moreover, a number of the "captures" in Iraq and Afghanistan have been extremely violent and frightening, as documented and protested by a number of human rights organizations.[13] The circumstances have not justified the excessive force and degradation utilized. Worse yet, these actions will leave inevitable scars on the relatives who witnessed the abuses. As noted by journalist Michael Hirsh well before the Abu Ghraib scandal broke, "The question is, do these tactics only further the cycle of vengeance, creating as many insurgents as are being arrested?"[14]

It is, however, the eternal uncertainty that a loved one might still be in pain or danger that is the most intolerable. The relatives want to leap to the rescue, but meet only with official obstacles or worse. Yet another Guatemalan friend of mine once left her two lit-

tle girls with her father while she ran some errands. When she returned, the security forces were hosing down the floors. Twenty
years later she was still engaged in an agonized search for her children. Were they alive? Sold into adoption? Suffering in a child pros-
titution ring or worse? No one can hear her story without weeping.
How many could bear to live the reality?

Perhaps we would like to think that such terrible acts could
never be carried out by U.S. officials today in Iraq or Afghanistan.
But then again, what of the Afghan prisoner whose two school-age
children have been kept "accessible" to the U.S. military?[15] What of
the Iraqi general who was forced by U.S. agents to watch his young
son shivering with cold? What of the families of the "ghost prisoners," still unaccounted for by the CIA? What of the all cases we have
not been allowed to hear about? In these situations what we don't
know may well hurt us in the future.

Even when children are not the targets, the anguish caused by a
loved one's "disappearance" is unendurable. I certainly got a personal sense of this pain during my three-year search for Everardo,
and I cannot begin to describe it. I can say, though, that it is always with me. I still wake up at night, certain that I have heard his
voice, telling me that he is cold. Yet others have suffered so much
more. One young friend I met long ago in Guatemala was missing
more than ten family members, several of them children. A gentle
older woman there is still searching for her son, decades after he
vanished in a rural area. I stayed at her house years ago when the
death threats came too often. Every morning she rose at 4 A.M. and
to iron her son's shirts. As Sister Dianna explained, you don't recover, you just learn to live with it.

This unique form of anguish was discussed by Amnesty International in its November 30, 2000, briefing to the U.N. Committee
against Torture: "There is a trend towards recognizing that to make
someone disappear is a form of prohibited torture or ill treatment,
clearly as regards the relatives of the disappeared person." Moreover, "The relatives of those whose whereabouts are unknown and

whose fate has never been clarified have therefore suffered long-term mental anguish. It is the view of Amnesty International that this long-term uncertainty as to the fate of the 'disappeared'. . . constitutes one of the cruelest forms of psychological torture."

In this address, Amnesty cited numerous official statements in support of this position, including the following: "The Committee understands the anguish and stress caused to the mother by the 'disappearance' of her daughter and by the continuing uncertainty as to her fate and whereabouts. . . . In these respects she too is a victim";[16] and "Disappearances violate the rights of the family members to be free of torture and cruel and degrading punishments."[17] In short, the very act of leaving the family to wonder if their loved ones are alive, suffering, delusional, or lost, and how to find, assist, or give them burial is itself psychological torture.

THE TORTURERS

When considering the enormous and long-term harm inflicted upon torture survivors and their family members, it is difficult to conceive of the torturers themselves as anything but monolithic and abnormal brutes. In many ways, it is comforting to convince ourselves that most human beings are incapable of such acts, and that the torturers must be a rare and frightening kind of psychopath. Unfortunately, this is not usually the case. While it is certainly true that a "born sadist" or psychopath might be drawn to certain positions of power, it is equally true that the majority of torturers were utterly normal, perhaps even boring, human beings before being assigned to their grim tasks. This was certainly true in the Nazi context, a fact that Hannah Arendt has famously described as the "banality of evil." It is also true of the torturers in Latin America, as well as U.S. torturers in Vietnam and, more recently, Iraq.

John Conroy, in researching his book *Unspeakable Acts, Ordinary People,* interviewed a number of former torturers from many different regions of the world.[18] For the most part, they were average human beings who had never engaged in such actions before joining their military unit, and who had learned to torture through intensive basic training and the instillation of a particularly cohesive "team" mentality. In some cases this sense of "team" consisted of pride in being a member of a prestigious and privileged unit. In others, such as the case of a white Rhodesian, there was a siege mentality based on race. Although none were predisposed to torture fellow human beings, they were all able to learn.

We would all like to think that this could never happen to us, or to others of reasonably sound moral character and intelligence. This, however, is a false assumption. A famous experiment that is no doubt familiar to many readers was carried out at Yale University by Prof. Stanley Milgram forty years ago, yielding rather startling results.[19] He obtained a number of volunteers from a broad cross-section of the community, and told them they would be participating in a learning experiment. A person was then strapped to a table, and the volunteer was instructed to give the "learner" shocks for every wrong answer, increasing the voltage with each incorrect response. Although the victim was in fact an actor, and not attached to any real cables, the volunteers did not know this. They could, moreover, hear the victims' screams and pleas as the voltage was increased to dangerous levels. A series of these experiments was carried out with many different groups of volunteers. As long as the "instructor" ordered the volunteer to administer the shock, more than 60 percent obeyed, no matter how distressing the situation. In a later survey, one man reported that his wife reacted to his story by saying, "You can call yourself Eichmann." A female volunteer, meeting her "victim" later on, after matters had been explained, said, "Oh my God, what he (the experimenter) did to me. I'm exhausted. I didn't want to go on with it. You don't know what I went through here. A person like me hurting you, my God. I didn't want to do it to you. Forgive me please . . . I wouldn't hurt a fly."[20]

The Department of Defense panel charged with investigating the abuses at Abu Ghraib noted a similar experiment carried out at Stanford University in the 1970s.[21] Twenty-four average male students were divided into two groups, one to act as prisoners and one to act as prison guards. Although scheduled to last for two weeks, the experiment was canceled after six days due to the frightening behavior of some participants. Although some of the guards were "tough but fair," and others were passive, a third group became increasingly aggressive and engaged in "creative cruelty." It was concluded that this phenomena was not the result of deviant personalities, but rather of the intrinsically pathological conditions. In short, the powerful position of "guard" brings out the worst in us all.

Intriguingly, the DOD panel noted other factors that can lead to abuse, including the use of euphemistic language and the dehumanization of the prisoners. Thus, although stripping a prisoner naked is intended to "soften him up," it may also soften up a guard's inhibitions about inflicting abuse. The more we dehumanize others, the more inhuman we ourselves become.

In short, we all have it in us. As human society has evolved over the centuries, we have learned to mask and control these grisly basic instincts. However, the protective shielding can swiftly be stripped away under the right circumstances. Certain positions of power, as well as dehumanization of the victims, can erode social controls all too quickly. Military training obviously offers optimal conditions for bringing out this grim side of human nature as well. Soldiers are taught to set aside their own questions, to obey all orders, and to maim and kill the enemy. With just a little extra negative conditioning, they can be taught to do much worse. Unfortunately, so can most humans. The real question here is whether or not such dangerous psychological conditions should ever be permitted to develop.

One need only look at the deeply depressed expressions on the face of Lynndie England and the other MPs today, as they face the uproar over the Abu Ghraib abuses, to recognize the emotional torment they too are now enduring. This is not merely because they face punishment. It is because they must now face their own actions. Having been conditioned, taught, and even ordered to abuse, they are suddenly back in the "normal" world where such actions are unthinkable. One can only imagine the sense of confusion, self-loathing, alienation, and betrayal that they must now be suffering. Should they be punished? Of course. They did something very wrong. Was something wrongful done to them? Definitely. They were molded into torturers by our intelligence community.

Perhaps of greatest concern are those persons who, once trained to torture, cannot "unlearn" these tactics and become a serious problem on their return to civilian society, as discussed below. How many of us would want such a person for a next-door neighbor?

There is, of course, yet another category of torturers that deserves mention here because they, too, have suffered from the long-term effects of their experiences. These are the "unwilling" abusers, typified by a number of young Mayan soldiers in Guatemala. Many of these young soldiers were virtually kidnapped ("forcibly recruited") when a military vehicle simply drove into their village and dragged them from the streets and soccer fields. They suffered particularly brutal and dehumanizing experiences at boot camp, where they were mocked and beaten for being indigenous. During many of the massacres, these young recruits were forced to carry out the actual slaughter. Those who refused were killed along with the villagers. The others simply complied when they had to, and lived with the sickening memories. After the first few times their feelings grew numb. A protective wall in their minds built up against the horror. Yet once they returned home to civilian life, those walls came tumbling back down. For many, this transition has been an excruciating process.

Former torturers have spoken about these issues, albeit sparingly. Their memories are not happy ones, and for the most part they are deeply grieved by their own behavior. Some have put the memories behind them and simply gone on with their lives as best they can. Others have sought to somehow make amends. An Argentine pilot came forward to report the practice of flinging the *"desaparecidos"* into the sea from helicopters. Florencio Caballero, once his family was safely in Canada, spoke out again and again, trying to assist relatives of the "disappeared" and press for human rights in Honduras. Was he able to live with his own past? This is unclear. He died abruptly in Canada of rather mysterious ailments. Many believe he was murdered. Others insist that he swallowed lye.

Over the years I have met with some of Everardo's torturers face to face, most of them at the Inter-American Court trial in Costa Rica for his murder. This was not an easy experience. Certainly some of them are now psychotic, and may well have been "born sadists." Whichever the case may be, they have never returned to any normal life and are now quite frightening.[22] Though the war is long over, they continue to kill and terrorize the public. For others, the matter is far more complex. Some suffer from severe emotional breakdowns, others are so remote from other humans that they can barely speak.

Yet another former soldier was involved in a well-documented massacre in Guatemala. He thought little of it at the time, as the slaughter had become so routine. But after a while he felt sickened and fled the country. Driven to despair now, twenty years later, by his memories, he seeks refuge in the bottle and in God. He would like to speak out in public but has no way of protecting his relatives back home from army retaliation.

Perhaps the saddest case was that of a young indigenous soldier I met in Guatemala. Like many others, he had been forcibly recruited at the age of fifteen, and somehow survived a particularly brutal basic training. After his first battle, the sergeant had become enraged and dragged a young boy out of a nearby village, beating him and demanding to know where the weapons were hidden. The soldier quickly realized that they boy did not understand Spanish. The sergeant then tied him to a tree and ordered the soldiers to take turns burning his feet with flaming logs. The young soldier refused, but was told to obey or take his own boots off and suffer the same treatment. He burned the boy's feet.

Everyone was upset afterward, but slowly their protective mechanisms began to form. The young soldier's did not. He felt he would lose his mind, and at the next battle he lay down and played dead. Afterwards he stripped off his uniform and ran naked to a nearby village to beg for help. The locals understood and smuggled him to a church in the capital. A priest asked if I could help, but by the time I arrived the young man had gone quite mad and was in the basement, barking like a dog.[23]

HARMS TO SOCIETY AS A WHOLE

Surely few of us would argue that human society benefits from having our sons and daughters turned into torturers. I rather suspect that most of us, having spent our lives trying to teach our offspring right from wrong, would put up quite a fuss if this were to happen to a child of our own. Who among us would enjoy seeing a son or daughter leering back at us from photos like those from Abu Ghraib?

In a similar vein, I suspect that few military leaders believe that this form of corruption of their uniformed ranks is beneficial. Most military leaders who have served time under combat conditions tend to be highly disciplined and firmly believe in the Geneva Conventions. Many have not been pleased at all with the disclosures from Abu Ghraib. This not only shames the entire armed forces, justly or not, but it in fact endangers the others who serve. The soldiers who daily risk their lives in battle count on the Geneva Conventions to protect them should they fall captive. When those protections are lost, they are the first to suffer. Just ask Senator John McCain. It comes as no surprise that those who most vigorously protested the White House and Justice Department memos were Gen. Colin Powell and a number of military judge advocates, as discussed above. In the end however, the military forces were not the only ones harmed. No sector of our society can afford the level of corruption that those abuses represent.

The spread of officially sanctioned torture, moreover, has dev-

astating effects on the impacted community. Its systematic use fo-
ments public terror and paralysis, which in turn often leads to the
complete breakdown of civilian institutions, such as the courts and
legislature. If a judge or lawmaker must risk torture or assassination, he or she is highly unlikely to function well. Meanwhile, many
of the most skilled civilians, fearing the worst and seeking safety
for their children, will head into exile, resulting in what the Guatemalans commonly call the "brain drain." With the silencing of
public debate and dissent, economic and social growth will stag-
nate, giving rise to yet a greater exodus of refugees. The economy
in Guatemala, much like Iraq today, was once favored by the United
States as a showcase for capitalism and democracy. It is in a shambles still today.

Where the official use of terror has been widespread, the entire
community will suffer collective trauma. This manifests itself in
many ways, including high rates of alcoholism and domestic violence, as well as widespread apathy and distrust toward community
affairs or matters of public interest. While peasant cooperatives
once flourished in Guatemala as an ideal way for impoverished
workers to share scarce resources, these organizations were singled
out for repression during the war. Today, in many areas, many people refuse outright to work with the new programs, or insist that
the term "cooperative" never be used. Meanwhile, violent street
crime, once unusual, is now at frightening levels. The suppressed
collective rage is palpable everywhere. In rural regions where I once
walked the trails without a thought, knowing that the villagers
would treat me with kindness only, the people now erupt periodi-
cally into violent mob lynchings. To be sure, the attacks have been
led by local military liaisons. However, twenty years ago this would
have been impossible. Community violence was inconceivable.

Moreover, as discussed above, the survivors, their families, and
even the torturers themselves will find the transition back to normal life a difficult one. In many ways the genie cannot be put back
in the bottle. Persons who were taught to carry out acts of brutality on a daily basis do not so easily deprogram themselves. While

some, as discussed above, reject their pasts or slowly manage to transition back to normal civilian life, others do not. Between January 2002 and June 2004, more than a thousand women were raped and killed in Guatemala, their bodies bearing signs of horrific abuse and mutilation. This number is extraordinary when compared to the three hundred women killed in the last decade in the notorious Juárez situation. Although many officials have brushed off the killings as gang- and drug-related murders, relatives of the victims insist that this is nonsense. Many suspect the government is somehow implicated. Moreover, the brutal methods evident in the killings are all too familiar and, according to the Guatemalan Women's Group, simply reflect a continuation of the past abuses.[24] In short, certain death squad members have acquired some rather nasty tastes.

INTERNATIONAL HARM

One of the greatest harms to arise from the use of torture by the United States in Iraq and Afghanistan is the extraordinary signal it has sent to repressive regimes around the world. With a flourish of the pen, Mr. Ashcroft and Mr. Gonzales have in effect reauthorized the Dirty Wars and erased the human rights advances of decades, if not centuries.

To begin with, since the horrors of World War I and World War II, the global community has struggled mightily to impose humanitarian limits on the battlefield and beyond. Given that murder and destruction are inherent parts of any war, this has been no easy task. And yet much to their credit, many nations have agreed upon carefully considered and well-defined restraints. As a result, the use of poisonous gas and weapons of mass destruction is now prohibited. Prisoners of war and resistance fighters may not be degraded or tortured for their information. Civilians must be respected and protected. Hiroshima is not to happen again. These hard-won advances should be proud symbols of human evolution. Instead, our leaders have tossed them aside as if they were nothing.

Moreover, as discussed at length above, during the Dirty Wars throughout Latin America hundreds of thousands of persons were kidnapped, tortured, and murdered by abusive military regimes. The vast majority of the victims were civilians. Those who were involved in armed uprisings were not engaged in any acts against the civilian populations or other "terrorist" conduct. Rather, they were involved in traditional combat efforts in the context of civil war and internal uprisings. Instead of working with the police or turning the prisoners over to the courts or to legitimate prisoner of war camps, the military leaders took matters into their own hands, displacing the local judiciary and legislature, scorning the rule of law, and inflicting terror on their own population for decades on end. The long-term devastation has yet to be fully measured.

Little by little advances were made by the human rights community towards ending the Dirty War phenomenon. General Pinochet was indicted for war crimes by the Spanish courts, and other similar cases swiftly followed in Europe. Civil suits were brought under the Alien Tort Claims Act in the United States against death squad leaders. Harsh reports and condemnations have been issued by international truth commissions. The Inter-American Court on Human Rights of the OAS made truly historic contributions, bringing case after case to trial in Costa Rica, and ruling repeatedly against the military perpetrators of human rights crimes. In 2000, the court issued a lengthy and unanimous decision declaring that all of the military actions taken against Everardo constituted severe violations of humanitarian law. His status as a URNG commander in no way negated such fundamental rights as a fair trial and freedom from torture. This came as startling news to many a Latin American military official.

Now we have regressed and given a virtual green light to such Dirty Wars tactics. The United States has unilaterally declared that its own military and intelligence forces can decide who may have committed a "crime" or been involved in acts of terrorism. Suspicion alone can justify the arrest and prolonged detention of a person before any charges are brought or hearings offered. Thus many an innocent prisoner has suffered at Abu Ghraib and Guantánamo before finally being heard and released. For a long time, attorneys and the courts here in the United States were shut out of the process entirely, and the scope of their role remains unclear even now. In short, with regard to the detainees, our defense and intelligence communities seek to displace our judiciary. Although several recent court decisions on these matters offer us hope, crucial issues still remain undetermined. Worse yet, it is clear that once a person is deemed "suspect" by the army or the CIA, he or she will be subjected to torture. For survivors of the Dirty Wars, the déjà vu is overwhelming.

Many of us had dared to hope that the Dirty Wars were at last behind us. Now they have been legitimized at the highest levels of our executive branch. In Latin America the message has been received and the results are already evident. On a recent trip to Guatemala to remind the military of outstanding court orders to return Everardo's remains, I was answered with leers. Things are different now, I was told. After all, doesn't my own government say so? A few weeks later my witness called me, weeping. His cousin had been shot dead in Guatemala: three bullets to the head and nothing stolen. The army was responding to my inquiries.

THE "TICKING BOMB"?

If the societal costs are so high, why, then, would torture ever be tolerated? Some of our officials insist that such "tough" (read that brutal) measures are necessary under certain extreme circumstances. Specifically, they might be needed to protect the public from an imminent and catastrophic attack upon civilians. The hypothetical cited again and again by our defense and intelligence leaders is the so-called ticking bomb situation. In that scenario, as outlined in brief in chapter 4, it is discovered that a devastating bomb, perhaps even a nuclear one, is about to go off in a crowded place, such as Grand Central Station. Many thousands of civilian lives are at stake and at the last minute, a suspect is captured. He is frantically questioned by law enforcement officers but refuses to speak. An intelligence agent reluctantly but bravely tortures the man and he gives the information. New York City is saved.

After the September 11 attacks, the American public was bombarded with these "what if?" situations, as our national leadership geared up for war and decided that most forms of de facto torture were to be deemed legal. Certainly the examples we heard on the radio and television were terrifying enough. But has this situation ever actually occurred? To date it has not. The stories we were told were in fact hypothetical, and not based on actual history. We cannot make appropriate national decisions if we are frightened into them with make-believe. Nor do we need to change the law, as discussed above. Moreover, there are a number of additional issues, such as the potential future response to our tactics, that require careful evaluation.

We must look at the question of whether or not torture actually works. Will it result in good intelligence? Most seasoned intelligence experts tell us that it does not. As one former Operation Phoenix veteran stated, "We had people who were willing to confess to anything if the [South Vietnamese] would just stop torturing them."[25] The U.S. Army's own handbook makes this same point, noting that useful intelligence has been gained in the past from prisoners treated humanely, whereas information obtained through torture has proven unreliable.[26] Linda Houk, a military interrogator during the first Gulf War, confirms that torture is considered neither ethical nor a source of reliable information.[27] Even an internal CIA memo notes that physical abuse is counterproductive because the prisoner will say anything to stop the torture, and also will be far less likely to cooperate in the future.[28] Mr. Baker, a sixteen-year veteran of the CIA and now chief of a private security company operating in Iraq, agrees, as do many other experts.[29] Apparently even mild forms of torture can result in a false confession.[30] Of course, all of these statements square with our civilian law enforcement experiences. For precisely these reasons, our courts reject all coerced confessions. The accuracy of the contents cannot be trusted.

Don Dzagulones, the interrogator who served in Vietnam with the Phoenix program, is especially vehement on this issue. As he stated to John Conroy:

> If it happened I am not aware of it. Like prisoner X comes in, you beat the living snot out of him. He tells you about a Viet Cong ambush that is going to happen tomorrow, you relay the information to the infantry guys, and they counter-ambush and the good guys win and the bad guys lose, all because you tortured a prisoner. Never happened. Not to my knowledge. And you don't get any more functional an interrogator than I was. I mean I was bottom rung. . . . This is the front line for interrogators, that's where I was. So my experiences aren't universal, but they were at the nitty-gritty level, down at the base.[31]

Retired U.S. Army colonel Carl Bernard agrees, noting the extensive use of torture by the Operation Phoenix members in Vietnam. "We imitated the French army's torturing and killing of captured revolutionaries in Algiers in Vietnam. It did not work. We knew almost nothing of our so-called enemy; we knew very little more of our supposed allies beyond what we assumed to be common goals."[32] Experienced interrogators are equally adamant about the humiliations carried out at Abu Ghraib. As one Israeli expert says, "This is stupidity. . . . It's not useful, in fact it's harmful. After a man's humiliated like this, if there was a chance he'd open up, now there's no way."[33]

Certainly all of this is confirmed by the few persons who have survived torture. Sister Dianna Ortiz, during her long interrogation with burning cigarettes, tried to confess to whatever her torturers asked, simply to escape further burns on her body. No matter what her answers, however, they kept burning her. The Iraqi detainee, Mr. Aboud, admitted under torture that he was Osama Bin Laden in disguise. María Guardado decided she was going to die anyway and said nothing at all. Everardo, with a defiance born of five hundred years of repression against the Mayans, apparently gave bits of information, all of which turned out to be false.[34] A surviving friend in Guatemala sadly admits that with time he told everything he knew, plus a great deal more that he made up out of desperation. The fact that this doubtless caused the deaths of innocent people haunts him still.

Many interrogators nonetheless insist that the strong measures do work. As one Special Forces officer told journalist Mark Bowden in 2003, "I'll tell you how to make them talk. You shoot the man on his left and the man on his right. Then you can't shut him up."[35] Former Marine captain Bill Cowan says that electrical clips "worked like a charm" on a prisoner in Vietnam. The security rules of the underground in Guatemala required everyone to move, change codes and safe houses *immediately* when a key person was captured. Not everyone talked under torture, but no one could wait around to find out the hard way. Michael Kouby, an Israeli interrogator, insists that almost all prisoners will break and talk in the end, and he gives some examples of small attacks that were prevented.[36]

Doubtless this question will be the subject of heated debate for years to come. The truth probably lies somewhere in between. Common sense should tell us that most people will certainly say something under torture, simply to stop the pain. In fact, they will say anything at all, as most torture survivors will confirm. As a result, the interrogator is left with large quantities of information, most or even all of which may be false. This will inevitably lead to delays, confusion, and even attacks against innocent parties. Moreover, the longer the abuse continues, the more likely the prisoner is to break mentally or become detached or resistant. Once again, the goal of good intelligence is not well served.

In evaluating the harsh measures used by the United States throughout the war on terror, it is difficult to say that there have been enormous intelligence advances as a result. Certainly the most

abusive measures conceivable have been used on Khaled Mohammed, who has suffered water-boarding and knows that his wife and
children are captives as well. Yet Osama Bin Laden remains at large
and many intelligence specialists doubt that Khaled has really given
much crucial information.[37]

The ticking bomb scenario raises other special considerations
which should also be taken into account here. If there really was
an extraordinary plan to detonate a powerful bomb under Grand
Central Station, then information about this plan would be re-
stricted to clandestine leaders at the very highest levels. The "need
to know" standards apply to all clandestine activities, including
the CIA's. Moreover, the participants themselves would have been
carefully selected and submitted to long and meticulous training.
Our intelligence agents would thus have a very small potential pool
of informants to begin with, and would have to actually locate and
arrest one of them before the explosion occurred.

Once the capture was accomplished, still more basic rules of security common to all clandestine organizations would come into
effect. The prisoner would be well prepared for precisely this possibility, and well trained to either withstand the first twenty-four
hours of torture in silence, or else to give false or irrelevant information. Indeed, the disinformation to be given during that first
period of torture would doubtless have been planned and agreed
upon far in advance of any activities. Meanwhile, a key person in
such an extraordinary effort would be carefully monitored by colleagues. In all likelihood, the person could not be seized without
quite a dust-up, to say the least. Moreover, the suspect's security
team would be responsible for knowing where he or she was at all
times, and would have an elaborate periodic check-in program. It
would be known within an hour or less that the operative was missing. With the first missed check-in, the explosive would be moved,
all apartments or places of operation abandoned, all files destroyed
or relocated, and all participants rushed out of the city. The bomb
might still go off, but not where the prisoner thought it would.

In short, in most efforts at this level of sophistication, torture will not work even if the captive decides to talk. The program will be designed submarine-style. Doomed persons in damaged areas will simply be sealed off. Meanwhile, the campaign will continue as planned somewhere else.

What interrogation methods do work, then? The long-time, tried-and-true methods worked out by U.S. law enforcement agencies. FBI reports note that suspects are more likely to confess to an investigator who treats them with respect. "As any cop or reporter will tell you, most people want to tell their story, given the right incentive."[38] Jerry Giorgio of the NYPD says, "You want a good interrogator? Give me somebody who people like and who likes people. Give me somebody who knows how to put people at ease."[39] Moreover, the traditional techniques of incentives—good cop/bad cop, pushing emotional buttons, flattery, and outright trickery—have long proven productive.[40] Apparently the FBI had been using slow but fruitful techniques on overseas suspects for nearly a decade, but lost the turf battle to the CIA after 9/11, with the now obvious results.[41] Perhaps cultural awareness, as opposed to brutality, is a better approach to interrogation in the current war on terror. Intriguingly, the Saudis now use Muslim religious leaders to work with particularly militant prisoners, in an effort to deprogram them.[42] Unfortunately, these methods can take time, but in the end they are far more effective.

So what, in the end, is the answer to the ticking bomb question? Clearly the solution does not lie in torture. Rather it lies in earlier detection, which in turn requires the improved coordination and refined intelligence gathering and analysis recommended by so many in the wake of September 11. As stated by retired Maj. F. Andy Messing, "If you are so desperate that you need to torture somebody it means you've failed in your general mission."[43] Perhaps the best advice of all came from within, with whistleblowers like longtime FBI agent Coleen Rowley, who recommended a total restructuring and change of leadership of the agencies.[44]

It is rather significant that while the CIA and other intelligence branches were carrying out their own sociopolitical agenda in Central and South America, where no genuine threats to the U.S. were presented, many crucial indications of very serious security threats in other regions were missed altogether. Millions of U.S. taxpayers' dollars and countless intelligence agents were committed to hunting down and wiping out Church leaders, student activists, peasant movements, labor unions, and other dissidents for decades on end. Had our funding and personnel instead been limited to purely defensive matters, would the development of the nuclear bomb in India, the missed spies, and even the September 11 attack have been detected in advance?

We must still address the question posed: Should torture be legalized for the rare ticking bomb situations, in case they ever do occur in the future? Admittedly, torture is unlikely to work for all the reasons discussed above. But if the bomb is about to go off, shouldn't our legal system allow our agents to do whatever they can? The answer is that it already does. As discussed above in chapter 1, our laws and jurisprudence already provide for extraordinary situations. Any police officer who literally saved the world by torturing an individual prisoner is a very unlikely candidate for prosecution. The concept of prosecutorial discretion was developed for just such compelling circumstances. Even if the officer stood trial, it is unlikely that the judge would assign any prison time at the penalty phase, and if such a sentence were required, a presidential pardon or grant of clemency would be virtually guaranteed.

Hence any agent or officer truly facing this situation would know that he or she would not face punishment. More importantly, though, any officer or agent facing a less compelling situation but still tempted to use torture, would know that he or she would have to explain things to a judge and jury. This has a very healthy deterrent effect. Torture remains strictly illegal. Any person found guilty of inflicting torture had better have some very good reasons. Will this give an agent pause before using torture? Definitely. Is this a good thing or a bad thing? A very good thing.

Alan Dershowitz has argued that since torture will be used

whether we like it or not, strict legal standards should be established to limit its use, and the interrogators should be required to obtain the equivalent of a "torture warrant" from the courts. An elephant-sized hole in this logic is the fact that the CIA, as we have seen above, has remarkable expertise in deceiving and circumventing fellow members of the U.S. government. Why would it not, then, deceive the U.S. courts as well?

Worse yet, once torture is made permissible for certain circumstances, intelligence experts will invariably tumble down the slippery slope of definitions, as discussed above in chapter 4. We have just witnessed this result with the disastrous aftermath of the White House and Justice Department memos. Limits are impossible to establish, let alone enforce. How imminent must an attack be to warrant the use of torture? A few hours? Why not a few weeks? How big must the bomb really be? In Israel torture may have prevented a few small-scale attacks. Should we, too, permit this? This would be a very different scenario from that now being urged upon the public. How much does the suspect have to know? Would it not be appropriate to also torture the suspect's relatives to make the prisoner talk? [45] Somehow, with this line of thinking, torture soon becomes acceptable on a vast scale. We don't need it, and we cannot control it, as recent events have made painfully clear. More to the point, our legal system has already taken care of it.

The experience in Israel, where ticking bombs are a very real daily threat, is quite relevant to us here. The Landau Commission in 1987 had permitted interrogators to use moderate physical pressure on prisoners, if needed to prevent an imminent terrorist attack. The result, predictably, was that the exception swallowed the rule. A key report issued by B'Tselem, an Israeli civil rights organization, showed that 85 percent of all Palestinian detainees, some 850 to 1,200 per year, were being physically abused. The situation was so extreme that in 1999 the Israeli Supreme Court banned the practices altogether. To be sure, the abuses are still widespread, but now the interrogators risk being taken to court. The words of the Israeli Supreme Court bear repeating here:

The decision opens with a description of the difficult realities in which Israel finds herself security-wise. We shall conclude this judgment by readdressing that harsh reality. We are aware that this decision does not ease dealing with that reality. This is the destiny of democracy, as not all means are acceptable to it, and not all practices employed by its enemies are open before it. Although a democracy must often fight with one hand tied behind its back, it nonetheless has the upper hand. Preserving the Rule of Law and recognition of an individual's liberty constitutes an important component in its understanding of security. At the end of the day, they strengthen its spirit and its strength and allow it to overcome its difficulties.[46]

BACKLASH

A critical factor in evaluating the torture issue is the question of backlash. If we permit our own agents to engage in torture, will we be able to obtain better information and thus win the war against terror? Or will such actions simply fan the flames of popular rage so high against us that we become ever more deeply imperiled?[47]

We have a preliminary answer, of course, from the people of Iraq themselves. For a few bright days early on in the war, some Iraqis were pleased with the fall of Saddam Hussein, and threw flowers at U.S. troops. Those were the days, but unfortunately they were numbered. Discontent and anger began to fester as a war of supposed liberation became an obvious occupation by non-Muslims. Devastating bombs, such as the one that destroyed the U.N. headquarters, became increasingly frequent. However, there is little doubt that with the Abu Ghraib scandal, a major turning point was reached. Within days U.S. citizen Nicholas Berg was decapitated, his killers expressly citing the prison abuses as their justification. By the fall of 2004, bombings against the U.S. military and its allies had increased to thirty to fifty per day, and international solidarity with the insurgents was clearly rising in the Islamic world.

More important than the reaction of Muslim militants, however, is the outraged response from the general public in Iraq, the very people whose hearts and minds we supposedly sought to win. As one Iraqi stated in response to the Abu Ghraib photographs, "It is wrong, wrong, 100 percent and a crime. You came here to liberate us from an unjust dictator who killed and tortured us."[48] Mr. Mowafak Sami, who was arrested with his father and two brothers and abused, commented later that this treatment "makes me feel aggressive against the coalition forces."[49] As Abu Ahmad, who had personally suffered the abuses at Abu Ghraib, told the *New York Times,* "The Americans are an occupation force, not liberators, and we should fight to drive them out."[50] As described in chapter 1, Saddam Saleh Aboud was also tortured and humiliated at Abu Ghraib. Although his body healed and he was released, his rage has not cooled. When asked if he was planning to join the insurgents, he responded, "What would you do if I occupied your country, tortured people, and violated all the laws of your country? Would you resist me?"[51] All said and done, the message from the Iraqi public seems clear enough.

Worse yet, the abuses have caused fellow Muslims from surrounding countries to join up with the Iraqi insurgents. Several young Muslim citizens of France have died in the Iraqi insurgency against the United States.[52] The brother of a young Saudi computer technician who also died in the Iraq fighting, said, "America's unjust policy towards Muslims is the main reason. Everyone feels this humiliation; he's not alone, there are so many young men who wish they could cross over into Iraq to join the Jihad but they can't."[53]

None of this should come as a surprise to us. "Historical data show a strong correlation between U.S. involvement in international situations and in increase in terrorist attacks against the United States."[54] If we ourselves were occupied by a foreign power and then systematically abused, I suspect our reaction would be as Mr. Aboud predicted. We would, of course, fight like hell. Thus we should not expect those we vanquish with pure military might to respond any differently. As stated by one expert, "Violations of the Geneva Conventions can turn a people against the United States and toward the guerrillas or terrorists."[55] This has certainly been true in the past. As John Conroy noted of the Irish reaction to British torture in 1971, "People started walking through the doors of the IRA begging to join. In the year after the torture was exposed, the number of deaths rose by 268 percent."[56] Clearly our own military leadership knew exactly what reaction to expect; as one U.S. officer stated, "We will be paid back for this."[57] So far, the prediction has been quite accurate.

As a matter of logic, it does seem rather unlikely that torture and repression could ever result in world peace. This rather obvious thought is certainly borne out by recent history. Although the "tough guy" approach may temporarily quell an uprising, in the end it only fans the flames higher and is always be fatal to the original government objectives.

Clearly the old South Africa provides a good illustration. Although the white apartheid regime was notoriously brutal and did not hesitate to use torture on its suspects and detainees, in the end, it did not survive. The extremely harsh methods used during the internal conflict only prolonged the war and intensified the human suffering on all sides. But it also unified the opposition by sowing hatred and despair. In the end, the apartheid government was overthrown, and Nelson Mandela became the president of South Africa, after enduring decades of imprisonment.

Great Britain's harsh crackdown on the IRA in Ireland over many generations has certainly never yielded the desired submission. Indeed, as noted above, the harsher the repression, the more the outraged population tended to support the resistance efforts. After the torture cases of 1971, IRA membership rose sharply, as did the local violence. Despite Great Britain's greatly superior military might, Ireland has never been subdued.

Similarly, the Mayans of Guatemala were never fond of the terrifying Spanish Inquisition methods that arrived with the conquistadors. These harsh traditions were handed down from generation to generation within the wealthy landowning class, and were later reinforced with special techniques brought in by the CIA. The result has been an indigenous uprising every single generation. The most recent civil war lasted for more than thirty-five years. Given the ongoing repression, another war in the future is inevitable.

The experience of the United States in Vietnam is much the same. We sought to force our way of life, uninvited, on a very different society. When we met with resistance we were willing to utilize very brutal methods, including direct torture as well as torture by proxy. Vietnam became a living hell for all involved for more than a decade, but in the end the under-armed but quite determined locals drove us out. The Soviets, in trying to subdue the Afghans, stumbled in the same way with the same disastrous results.

Perhaps the most on-point historical example is the Algerian revolution. As it also involved a Muslim Arab population, similar religious and cultural issues were presented. The National Liberation Front (FLN) did not initially have a broad base of popular support, nor did it have great military might in comparison to the French army.[58] Accordingly the FLN choice of weapons, as in Iraq today, was the bomb. Former French resistance fighter Gen. Paul Aussaresses and Indochina veteran Col. Roger Trinquier, worked closely together to quell the uprising, and admittedly utilized widespread torture and extrajudicial executions. For a while, the methods seemed successful, and the bombings diminished. In the end the strategy was obviously a complete failure. The furious Algerians, already angered by years of colonial rule, united with the FLN and drove the French from their country.

Regrettably, the United States did not learn from French history—Aussaresses served as French liaison at the infantry school at Fort Benning in the early 1960s, while Trinquier's writings on counterinsurgency were apparently influential with members of Operation Phoenix.[59] Obviously, the no-holds-barred methods favored by these officers were equally disastrous in Vietnam as they had been in Algeria.

VIOLENCE BEGETS VIOLENCE

The statement that violence begets violence should be self-evident. Yet the entire post September 11 strategy of our administration is based on the assumption that the "tough guy" and "shock and awe" approach will somehow be most effective. As discussed above, this assumption is deeply flawed. Unfortunately, the word "tough" is euphemistic at best. We have hit the people of Iraq and Afghanistan with nearly everything we have in our extraordinary arsenal of military equipment and weaponry. This was hardly a fair fight between parties of equal strength. Moreover, although we insist that smart bombs and precision targeting techniques were utilized, it is clear that civilian casualties and suffering have been heavy indeed.

For those on the ground during the horrific bombing of Baghdad, any sense of shock and awe quickly yielded to rage and the urge to fight back. This has only been intensified by our harsh search and arrest methods and by the denial of fair hearings, practices which have been repeatedly decried by human rights organizations. Our brutal interrogation techniques, including torture and sexual humiliation, and our interference with medical care in areas like Fallujah, can only doom our efforts to win the people's "hearts and minds." Clearly, we have not learned our history lessons.

Moreover, using sanitized language like "stress and duress" and "collateral damage" to lull the conscience of the American public does not create true security for anyone. This only leaves us, ostrichlike, with our head in the sand. Rather than averting our eyes from disturbing realities, we must take a long, hard look. Better yet, we should take that long and hard look from the viewpoint of the Afghan and Iraqi people. If we do not understand them, we can neither effectively defend ourselves nor, better yet, wage peace. Instead we are left dangerously blind-sided. We made this error in Vietnam. Why are we repeating such painful mistakes?

We are creating a nation of trauma survivors in both Iraq and Afghanistan. As discussed earlier, combined trauma and humiliation will result in long-term and devastating injuries. Moreover, subjecting any person to extreme trauma, especially at a young age, greatly increases the likelihood of violent behavior by the victim in the future. The sad fact that battered and abused children will often later batter their own children or engage in violent acts against others, is both well known and well documented. If we remember the difficult return of our own servicemen and -women from Vietnam, it is clear that adults may well respond in a similar fashion. As noted by one expert on terrorism, "People who have been traumatized are more likely to use violence to solve conflict or relieve stress."[60] Moreover, as discussed above, survivors of extreme trauma such as torture are often excellent candidates for suicide, self-abuse, and early deaths. "At the extremes, the trauma victim either commits suicide or homicide."[61]

Historically, traumatized and humiliated communities have often responded with collective rage and violence. The colonized Third World certainly made this clear. Moreover, the Europeans were no exception to the rule. The people of Germany, devastated and humiliated after their defeat in World War I, were susceptible to Hitler's raging leadership. In Colombia, as the seemingly endless agony escalates, so too does the mutual violence. Moreover, the two thousand years of deadly pogroms, ending with the horrors of the Holocaust, surely explain in part the excessively harsh methods of the Israeli defense forces. For better or worse, humans tend to do unto others as was done to them. Those of us here in the United States, before we get too smug on this matter, should take a close, post–September 11 look in the mirror ourselves.

"Fear, hate, and rage are produced by trauma and traumatized people have the fuel for starting and continuing violent conduct."[62] In short, violence does indeed beget violence.

Does this mean that every trauma survivor is a danger to society? Obviously not. We made this foolish mistake in our own recent history when all Vietnam veterans were stereotyped as mentally unstable as a result of post-traumatic stress. This was an enormous injustice to them all. The vast majority of trauma survivors, albeit scarred, manage to slowly heal themselves and continue with productive lives. Although the pain never leaves them, they learn to live with it. Some, in fact, become extraordinary and compassionate leaders. Anyone who has met the near angelical Sister Dianna Ortiz would hasten to agree. Certainly Senator John McCain, a very different persona, deserves our great respect and admiration. Elie Wiesel, a survivor of Auschwitz, has managed to devote his entire life to human rights issues. These remarkable people are but a few examples. The millions of other survivors quietly leading their lives, caring for their children, supporting human rights, and contributing to their communities, are true unsung heroes as well.

What we must learn from the statistics gathered by medical professionals is that shame, violence, and trauma create the conditions for later violence in some cases. Although most will resist, be it through therapy, family and community support, or sheer will, for some the urge will become irresistible. Depending on their surroundings and the sociopolitical context, they will respond differently, but with violence. It takes only a few bombs to create great tragedy. We should be thinking carefully about these realities when we inflict mass trauma on the entire populations of Iraq and Afghanistan. After reflecting on these issues, I became curious about the young Palestinian suicide bombers, referred to by many as "Martyrs." Doesn't the tragic conflagration within Israel and the Occupied Territories offer us a close and current paradigm to learn from? Why would so many suicide bombers give up their lives at so young an age? The claims of religious fanaticism, or the alleged beliefs that they would be rewarded with dozens of virgins in Paradise, struck me as both foolish and racist.[63] Again, if we do not attempt to understand those whom we fear, then we will never reach safety. To demonize or oversimplify these people is to hide our head in the sand.

In the spirit of such mutual understanding, we must recognize that in the crucible of today's Israeli-Palestinian conflict, civilians on both sides are suffering greatly. We cannot decry the one and ignore the other. Since I was born in 1951, I grew up steeped in the images of the Holocaust, and the rightful insistence on "never again." In this I still believe. My heart went out to the kindly Israeli physician who helped train U.S. emergency personnel for future terrorist attacks, then returned home for his daughter's wedding, only to perish with her in a suicide bombing. Looking at this case, the cries for revenge against the "terrorists" are only too easy to understand. These civilians had done nothing to deserve such terrible deaths.

It is crucial, however, that we not look at the events in Israel-Palestine only through a one-way glass. The available studies show that the young Palestinians who become suicide bombers are not psychopaths or otherwise suicidal or mentally ill. Nor are they poorly educated, or weak, or easily influenced by an overly dominant religion. To the contrary, most have had a reasonable level of education. They have never been involved in random violence, such as domestic assaults, drunken brawls with locals, or common crime. Nor have they shown any suicidal tendencies in the past. In other words, they have thought about matters, they believe their actions are morally correct, and they are willing to sacrifice their lives for those beliefs. Their battered home communities agree. For this reason the suicide bombers are called "Martyrs," and not terrorists, by the Palestinians. We need to listen very carefully to this message. While Westerners may ultimately disagree with and flatly reject the actions taken, the motivations must still be heard and understood. Listening to the other side does not dishonor the innocent victims. Failing to listen will lead to more bombings and more victims. Negative stereotypes and dogma, moreover, only stoke the fires of violence on both sides.

If we are painfully honest with ourselves, the motivations for the young suicide bombers, right or wrong, are not so difficult to understand. Virtually all of them would be of an age to have witnessed some of the first intifada and the devastating security crackdown that followed. Drs. Rona Fields, Salman Elbedour, and Fadel Abu Hein, in their joint article "The Palestinian Suicide Bomber,"[64] report that two thousand Palestinian children under the age of sixteen were killed and twenty-five thousand injured during those bitter years.[65] The current suicide bombers would doubtless have lost friends and family in the violence, and might well have been injured or imprisoned themselves, or subjected to collective punishments. Imprisoned friends and relatives would in all likelihood have been tortured and humiliated. The suicide bombers would, moreover, have seen houses bulldozed, roadways closed to them, and educational and economic opportunities lost as a result of the security measures. These systematic abuses have long been documented by numerous human rights groups, including the remarkable works of B'Tselem.[66]

On my recent travels to the West Bank and Gaza, I found a de facto ghetto population, locked in and treated with great harshness at all checkpoints. Given the obvious importance of personal dignity within the Muslim community, and the kindness lavished automatically on all guests, the disrespect and public humiliations suffered at those checkpoints was startling in contrast. Family and medical visits, and even work-related travel, moreover, were extremely difficult and often impossible. In Gaza, especially, it seems that every street bears signs of Israeli bulldozers and bullets. The playgrounds are empty of children, and no one stands near the windows. People live in daily fear of sudden raids and long "administrative" detentions. Although beaches are nearby, many are denied access despite the sweltering heat. Shops are closed and half empty. The rage and humiliation was palpable everywhere I went, like a bomb about to explode.

In short, we are looking at a highly traumatized Palestinian society. Does this somehow mean that the victims of the suicide bombings deserved to die? Of course not. These were innocent people, and many may well have been artists, teachers, human rights advocates, or compassionate medical and social workers. But civilian men, women, and children within the Palestinian communities also deserve to live, and far larger numbers are being killed and maimed by Israeli military actions. Little has been done to ameliorate this reality. What all this does mean is that the harsh security methods being used by the Israeli Defense Forces (and now also by the United States) may in fact be creating conditions that generate a violent response. It also means that the young suicide bombers were not acting mindlessly, but in fact had reasons for their actions. Given the enormous inequality of military strength and resources, for many, the suicide bombings seem like the only way to make their cries for justice and humanitarian treatment heard. If locked into an impossible situation, and denied all reasonable avenues of redress, would not most humans consider blasting their way free? History answers in the affirmative.[67] We can disagree with the reasons for the bombings, but we cannot pretend those reasons do not exist. It is highly significant, moreover, that top Israeli defense leaders have recently criticized aggressive government decisions and actions against the Palestinians.[68]

In sorting through the many available profiles of these young men and women, I found glaring omissions in the questions asked. Most of the documentation addressed basic matters such as age, gender, family structure, education, religion, and economic status. Nowhere could I find adequate treatment of the obvious trauma factor. Certainly trauma would not be the only factor behind a decision to engage in a suicide attack.[69] Yet it may prove to be one of several common denominators in profiles that are becoming ever more diverse. If so, this is important information. However, in much of the professional literature it was either missing or insufficient.

Drs. Fields, Elbedour, and Abu Hein did address the trauma factor in their thoughtful joint article, "The Palestinian Suicide Bomber."[70] They carefully evaluated nine of the suicide bomber cases with the following findings. All nine experienced the first intifada in Gaza. Of those, five were injured during the uprising. Eight were imprisoned—three once, four twice, and one three times. All eight were tortured in prison, one severely. Eight had their homes entered by Israeli commandos during that period. Of those, five families had members beaten or humiliated during the raid.[71] These findings are highly significant, but clearly more extensive documentation was still needed.

Dr. Ariel Merari of the Department of Psychology at Tel Aviv University also offered important findings in his report, "Suicide Terrorism."[72] Dr. Merari discards "revenge" as a motive, but his data in this regard is intriguing. Although he discusses a number of different movements in various regions, he carefully evaluated the cases of thirty-four of the thirty-six Palestinian suicide bombers who carried out attacks from 1993 to 1998. Of the thirty-four, one had lost a close family member as a result of Israeli Defense Forces (IDF) security actions, and eleven had had a friend killed. In seven cases a close relative (a father or brother) was jailed. Fifteen of the suicide bombers had been beaten during demonstrations, and eleven of those were injured. Eighteen had been put in jail, though most for short time periods. Most had been active during the intifada itself. "In most cases, therefore, a high level of militancy preceded a personal trauma, although such trauma might later add to the already existing hatred and desire for revenge."[73] Significantly, Dr. Merari also found that none of the suicide bombers were suffering from "ordinary" suicidal tendencies, or despair at the individual level, although in some cases their actions might have been motivated by despair at the national or community level.[74] "In the suicide's notes and last message the act of self-destruction was presented as a form of struggle rather than as an escape. There was no sense of helplessness-hopelessness. On the contrary, the suicide was an act of projecting power rather than expressing weakness."[75]

Not surprisingly, it was Palestinian-born Prof. Basel A. Saleh of Kansas State University who first stressed the importance of the traumatic environment created by the IDF security measures, as well as the failure of the various studies to adequately address this issue. He carefully compiled a database on some eighty-seven cases of suicide bombings and shooting attacks by Palestinians, rang-ing from the 1990s through 2002, and documented serious "grievances" in forty-four cases. "Simply, recent research on Palestinian suicide militants has failed to consider the full range of stressors leading to the suicide attacks. Restricting attention to only economic factors or level of education has resulted, for example, in no understanding of why young Palestinians carry out suicide attacks.... The existing research is responsible for providing moral support to militarily aggressive policies against the general population.... However, the evidence presented in this chapter suggests that force will only force more attacks."[76]

The changes reflected in the data and related information about the suicide bombers of the second intifada are sobering indeed. It must be remembered that this new generation of Martyrs grew up amidst the chaos, suffering, and extreme security measures of the first intifada, and the repression and security restrictions that followed. The number of suicide attacks between late 2000 and early 2004 jumped to 149, and have increased throughout this last year. This represents an enormous increase from the first intifada. Even if Martyrs are strictly defined to include only those wearing explosive belts or driving car bombs, the number is still 127, nearly triple the total of the first intifada.[77] Moreover, nineteen of the "Martyrs" were from Gaza, thirty-one from Nablus, eighteen from Jenin, nine from Hebron, nine from Tulkarem, and thirteen from Bethlehem. In short, large clusters of the suicide bombers grew up in the most harshly repressed Palestinian communities.

Working closely with local community members, I drew up a simple questionnaire which included inquiries about trauma-related issues, including personal battery or imprisonment, or the death, battery, or imprisonment of a close relative or friend. I then asked the local partners to meet quietly with the families of the "Martyrs" and carry out the interviews. At the time of this writing, the research project is incomplete; but the information gathered from areas where the interview process has been completed, specifically from Jenin and Nablus, is very telling.

In Jenin, seventeen families were interviewed. Of those, fourteen reported highly traumatic events in the lives of their deceased son or daughter. In the case of the young woman attorney, Hanadi Taysir Abdelmalik Jaradat, for example, her brother and cousin were seized by the Israeli Special Forces and killed in front of the family home in June 2003. Her father had spent two years in prison during the 1970s and remained psychologically affected long afterward. She killed twenty-one Israelis in a Haifa restaurant on October 4, 2003, when she detonated a bomb concealed on her person. Abdulkarim Issa Khalil Tahaina had an equally difficult personal background. He was shot in the abdomen during the second intifada, and was frequently called in for interrogations. Two of his cousins were killed by the Israeli Defense Forces, and three brothers were imprisoned during the first intifada. In only two cases did the families deny any traumatic events. In a third, the young man lost his job as a result of the travel restrictions, and the family was unsure as to any trauma other than the ongoing problems of the occupation.

Twenty-nine families were interviewed in Nablus, and three in Ramallah. Of the Nablus families, only two did not report traumatic events in the life of the "Martyr." In most cases the trauma was very severe. Jamad Abd AlGhani Rashid Nasser was beaten by Israeli soldiers in front of his own home when he was eleven years old. His father and brother were repeatedly arrested and subjected to humiliating treatment. Another relative was shot to death. Anassem Youssef Mohammed Rihan's brother was shot to death in front of the family home, and a friend was killed by an Apache missile attack. Three brothers and a number of other relatives were imprisoned. Wafa'a Ali Adris was a thirty-one-year-old woman working for the Red Crescent. She herself had been badly injured by a rubber bullet, and once transported a wounded friend to a hospital, only to have his brains fall out onto her hands. Her brother had been repeatedly imprisoned. Ashraf Sobhi El Said watched as two men were shot in front of his small juice shop.

TRUTH, TORTURE, AND THE AMERICAN WAY

The interview results speak for themselves.[78] Clearly trauma is very much a common denominator among the Palestinian suicide bombers. Some say that this is not a meaningful factor, since virtually all young Palestinians will have some IDF-related trauma in their background. This is a non sequitur. It is precisely because most young Palestinians have suffered serious trauma that the number of suicide bombings has so greatly increased.

Certainly the Jewish citizens can tell us of just as many agonizing losses on their side of the embattled borders. This is precisely the problem. In the end it seems that Israelis and Palestinians, brothers and sisters since the days of the Old Testament, are two highly traumatized societies now locked into an ever escalating cycle of violence and terror.

Yet even with so clear an example unfolding tragically before our very eyes, our own country is responding in precisely the same way to our own national trauma, September 11. We are reacting out of fear instead of thinking our way through the difficult process of conflict resolution. In the end, our use of violence and repression can only sow seeds of hatred and trauma, which in the end will produce ever greater violence against us.

CONCLUSION
REFLECTIONS ON OUR FUTURE

STILL DRIVING IN THE WRONG DIRECTION

Despite the scandal and the mounting backlash in the Middle East, the CIA and other intelligence networks continue to utilize torture as an interrogation tool.[1] If anything, the Bush administration seems focused on the protection of those practices rather than on their eradication. Investigations are still promised, and formal public declarations against torture are still issued. But the torture of the detainees is continuing, business as usual. We are moving steadfastly ahead in the war against terror, but we are moving in the wrong direction.

Alberto Gonzales is our new attorney general, despite his notorious White House memo authorizing torture and declaring the Geneva Conventions to be quaint and obsolete. He is now defending the ongoing use of extraordinary renditions, even as many officials declare that the practice has become "an abomination."[2] Gonzales has also stated that CIA officers and agents are not bound by President Bush's 2002 pledge to treat all prisoners humanely.[3] Meanwhile, John Negroponte, who as ambassador to Honduras long concealed the increasing military atrocities from the U.S. Congress, is now the chief of intelligence. Porter Goss has been appointed director of the CIA, and claims that all current CIA interrogation techniques, including water-boarding, are within professional and legal limits. What methods would constitute torture in his opinion has yet to be clarified. When the Senate passed legislation including strong measures prohibiting the abuses, White House opposition was so vehement that the provisions were finally dropped.[4]

Instead of enforcing the laws and treaties of the United States, many officials are engaged in ongoing efforts to conceal evidence and avoid prosecutions. A number of detainees claim they were forced to sign false statements that they were well treated. One prisoner reports that during an interrogation session his nose was broken and his arms dislocated by American agents. He was also subjected to a mock execution. He withdrew his charges after being told he would otherwise never be released.[5] Photographs have been erased, and investigators have hurriedly closed cases on the grounds of insufficient evidence instead of properly gathering the facts.[6] A serious assault case, although confirmed by medical records, was closed when the interrogator simply denied the charges.[7]

Meanwhile, our international alliances are fraying. The administration continues to press other nations for full immunity for U.S. agents, exempting them from prosecutions in the International Criminal Court. Uncooperative governments like Bolivia are threatened with the withdrawal of financial aid and trade rights. Nonetheless, some fifty governments have refused to sign.[8] Our European allies, too, are growing restless with our intransigence, and a number of governments are taking action. Investigations into CIA kidnappings and abuse are underway in Sweden, Germany, and Italy.[9] For the first time, the United Nations Commission on Human Rights is being urged to condemn the United States for its torture practices.[10] If we do not set our own house straight, and soon, then the international community must and will do it for us. Meanwhile, as we procrastinate, the rage against us in the Middle East is rising to unprecedented levels.

What should be done? How should the war against terror be fought? Are there other alternatives? The answers may lie in our own unique collective history.

REFLECTIONS ON OUR FUTURE

The United States Constitution and the Bill of Rights hold a near-sacred position in our national heritage. That is as it should be, for the ideals expressed in those documents—from the recognition of human equality, to the right to basic justice, to the outright ban on wanton official cruelty—are fine ones indeed. Of course we were not the only ones to pursue these lofty goals, nor were we fully able to comply with them. Even as the words "All men are created equal" rang across the land, many leading citizens, including Thomas Jefferson, owned slaves, and Native peoples perished in army massacres. Equal rights for women was not yet a concept. Although the rack and the screw were outlawed, brutal acts by government officials remained commonplace.

Our history, thus, has been one of a long struggle to live up to our own values, to insist upon our national ideals, to put our money where our mouth is. Again and again we have proven ourselves to be all too human, and have fallen short or gone astray in this regard. Yet in the end we have tried, at least, to set ourselves straight, to correct our errors and start anew. Slavery was abolished. Women were enfranchised. The extraordinary civil rights work of Dr. Martin Luther King and hundreds of others changed the face of American society forever. Our Supreme Court has repeatedly upheld the right to a fair trial, most recently by declaring that not even President Bush is above the law when it comes to the Guantánamo detainees. Slowly, too, our society has rejected the official infliction of pain and suffering, from public whippings and hangings, to police brutality, to intolerable prison or institutional conditions.

In short, when it comes to keeping matters in order within our own country, we have been able to evolve, to change, to permit needed reforms. Certainly we have a ways to go in upholding our ideals; one need merely visit Pine Ridge Reservation or review the evidence in the cases of Rodney King or Abner Louima to determine that. But in the end, perhaps our greatest strength lies in the fact that we are willing to struggle with our own collective soul and slowly work to achieve our proclaimed goals. Apparently, we still believe. In the end it is this same stubborn public belief—that our country can and must live up to its ideals—that allows us to grow and resolve our problems.

Was this vital national faith destroyed along with the World Trade Center on September 11? For a while, it seemed so. As we plunged into the all too human cycle of grief, fear, rage, and revenge, we veered perilously close to discarding our core values outright. Certainly the Bush administration was able to exploit the national mood and toss aside our historical ban on torture and the basic requirements of a fair trial. In the end, though, the public reacted properly to the photographs of prisoner abuses at Abu Ghraib. The unanimous response was one of outrage and repudiation. In short, when the realities are clearly presented to us, we can still hear our national conscience shriek. Our country, as we have always known it, still has a pulse.

The problem, of course, lies with the realities concealed from us. This has always been the case. While the American public has slowly grappled with ongoing injustices visible within our own borders; it has long failed to discover and correct our government's abuses abroad. There are many reasons for this, including the obvious linguistic and geographical barriers. Moreover, many of the worst U.S. overseas practices are kept highly secret. Press investigations, so crucial in Vietnam, slowed in Central America and dropped off sharply with the policy of "embedded" journalists in Iraq.[11] Meanwhile, we as a people have a great weakness for wishful thinking. If we are not confronted outright with clear evidence of U.S. human rights violations abroad, we tend to assume they do not exist. We ignore the warning signals. When we do see violations, we vociferously protest, but we allow ourselves to be lulled with light assurances that it was just a few bad apples.

It is precisely this national weakness that has permitted agencies like the CIA to long usurp powers never granted by Congress, and to routinely carry out illegal practices such as torture with full impunity. In turn, this has badly damaged our system of checks and balances, skewed our declared foreign policy, weakened our international treaties and alliances, and created enormous resentment against us throughout the world. This is no small amount of damage, and deal with it we must. In doing so we must finally recognize that the acts of torture we have witnessed are not merely matters of individual error or excess. Rather, they are evidence of a secret official policy carried out for decades by the CIA and other intelligence agencies. Legal responsibility goes all the way to the top.

This is not a problem we can cure with a few quick court-martials, a promised investigation, or even a change of administration. We must delve much deeper than that, and it will be a sad and difficult process. Yet as a nation we have faced many difficult challenges before, from slavery and the Civil War, to the Great Depression, to the civil rights movement and Vietnam. When it comes to torture abroad, the actions being taken in our name and paid for with our tax dollars are our own responsibility. We should take heart and do what we have always done: roll up our sleeves and get to work.

On moral grounds alone, we should reject torture outright as an official practice. If we cannot bear the photographs, we must halt the reality. Moreover, in this era of suicide bombs and the war on terror, we need to think carefully about the consequences. Is the Bush administration's strategy of shock and awe, "ghost prisoners," and torture going to keep us safe? Or has it already greatly endangered us?

The operative word here, of course, is "think." It is all too human to respond to a threat with anger and violence. Our instinct for "flight or fight," after all, goes back to the caves. So does our tendency, when faced with a frightening enemy with a big club, to simply utilize a bigger club. This has been precisely our emotional reaction since September 11. Whether we admit it or not, we are frightened, and a show of military strength to "teach them a lesson so they don't come back" is just what we want. The bombing of Baghdad and the use of "stress and duress," for example, has doubtless spawned countless future suicide bombers, but it made us feel safe.

In short, we are not thinking. Instead, we are allowing our ancient survival instincts and corrupt national leaders to drag us toward a true apocalypse. We have been in similar situations before. The Cuban Missile Crisis, for example, comes to mind. As the world reeled toward a catastrophic nuclear war, it would have been all too human for either Kennedy or Kruschev to rush to press the little red button first. Indeed, many in the military urged precisely that. But both leaders were able to reason, to allow their minds to overrule the spiraling sense of fear and distrust. So, too, as world wars became a modern phenomenon, and weapons of mass destruction began to proliferate, the human race has been able to think its way to new humanitarian restrictions on the conduct of war itself. We saw the results of genocide when the gates at Auschwitz opened. After Hiroshima we understood only too well what Einstein meant when he said, "I know not with what weapons the third world war will be fought, but the fourth one will be fought with sticks and stones." We must continue to think.

What strategies, then, are available for creating world peace and security, if torture, brutality, and "ghost prisoners" are not the solution? An initial means of preventing another September 11, of course, lies in basic crime prevention work by law enforcement officials around the world. Finely coordinated international police efforts, involving many nations, is crucial to improving our intelligence gathering and allowing us to learn of attacks before they occur. We must work with those who know their communities, speak the local language, and truly understand the culture. We must engage in teamwork, as opposed to dominance, and we must set aside our own politics. As we learned in the case of the nonexistent Iraqi weapons of mass destruction, political goals can skew our analytical abilities and lead us far astray indeed. Again, these basic measures must go hand in hand with a serious "hearts and minds" campaign. The CIA has repeatedly noted the difficulty of obtaining sound intelligence in the Middle East. In the end money cannot buy everything.

Once an attack occurs, it must be answered. No one suggests that the United States should simply turn the other cheek to Mr. Bin Laden and await further terror. However, once again, the thinking response would be an intensive international police campaign supported, if truly necessary, by international surgical military efforts. The goal should not be shock and awe, but rather hearts and minds. This approach may not satisfy our lust for revenge or our fearful need for a show of strength. In the end, however, it may increase our safety. Instead, the U.S. use of horrific firepower, mass torture, and the denial of basic justice to detainees, has imperiled us for years to come.

Basic police methods are far too little and far too late. We should try, of course, to prevent organizations like al-Qaeda from forming in the first place. The long-term solutions, ironically, lie with the tactics most often scorned by our defense and intelligence communities. As the global community grows ever smaller and interdependent, we must turn to conflict resolution, mutual cooperation, international laws, and alliances as never before. We must evolve, and very swiftly, past the "big stick" concept and our pride in surviving in a "dog eat dog" world. Instead, all nations, including our own, must learn to understand each other's cultures and needs, and to respect our differences. We must accept the fact that we are indeed our brothers' and sisters' collective keepers. If we are indifferent to the basic human needs of others, then peace will always elude us. Suffering, when too long ignored, inevitably leads to conflagration.

It is not too late for our nation to turn back from the brink. The words of Dr. Martin Luther King, decades after his tragic murder, still offer us both eloquence and wisdom: "We can live together as brothers, or we will surely die together like fools."

ACKNOWLEDGMENTS

I wish to give special thanks to the Radcliffe Institute of Advanced Study for its support and generosity, and my admiration and affection to the brave survivors who have shared their stories with me, to my beloved *compas* in Guatemala, to my Texas teammates, and to my brothers and sisters in Coalition Missing. I especially appreciate the longtime support and advice of Sister Alice Zachmann and Patricia Davis; the wise and thoughtful advice of Ambassador Robert White, Dean Claudio Grossman, Dean Louise Richardson, Prof. Noam Chomsky, and Prof. Phillip Heymann; the keen literary analysis and compassion of Greg Bates; the courage and wit of Mike Wallace; and the invaluable friendship and commitment of the Unitarian Universalist family and the courageous staff of Beacon Press.

NOTES

INTRODUCTION: AN EARLY GLIMPSE

1. Everardo was his nom de guerre and the name his fellow URNG (National Revolutionary Union of Guatemala) members and I always used with him. His legal name was Efraín Bámaca Velásquez.
2. For a more detailed analysis of the cases of Everardo and Sister Dianna, see chapter 3.
3. Sister Dianna's extraordinary journey is chronicled in *The Blindfold's Eye: My Journey from Torture to Truth,* written with Patricia Davis (Orbis Books, 2002).
4. See *Harbury v. Deutch,* filed and pending in U.S. District Court, District of Columbia, 96-CKK-438.
5. The Torture Abolition and Survivor Support Coalition.
6. Commission for Historical Clarification (CEH), *Guatemala: Memory of Silence,* 1999 (also referred to herein as the United Nations Truth Commission Report).
7. This position was later softened, and it was supposedly agreed that the Geneva Conventions would be respected.
8. Professor Alan Dershowitz of the Harvard Law School, in one notorious statement suggested that under extreme circumstances torture could be authorized by special, court-issued "torture warrants," and suggested a sterilized needle under the fingernail as one possible technique. "Dershowitz: Torture Could Be Justified," *CNN,* March 4, 2003. See also Seth Kreimer, "Too Close to the Rack and Screw: Constitutional Constraints on Torture in the War on Terror," *Journal of Constitutional Law,* Vol. 6:2, Nov. 2003, p. 278.
9. See, for example, "U.S. to Reassess Intelligence Operations," *Reuters News Service,* Sept. 16, 2001. See also "Back to Guatemala," Editorial, *Texas Observer,* June 7, 2002.
10. See, for example, Matthew Brzezinski, "Bust and Boom," *Washington Post,* Dec. 30, 2001, regarding highly explicit information obtained in the Philippines six years before the attacks. See also National Commission on Terrorist Attacks, *The 9/11 Commission Report,* July 22, 2004.

11. See, for example, "FBI Whistleblower Describes 'Roadblocks,'" *CNN*, June 6, 2002, concerning FBI agent Coleen Rowley's statements to the U.S. Senate.

12. Eric Lichtblaus and David Sanger, "Bush Warned of Possible Attack on US, Official Says," *New York Times*, April 10, 2004. See also *CIA Warned of US Attack in 95*, CBS News, April 16, 2004.

13. For a detailed discussion of the Latin America cases, see chapter 3.

CHAPTER ONE: THE FALL OF ABU GHRAIB

1. Dana Priest and Barton Gellman, "U.S. Decries Abuse but Defends Interrogations," *Washington Post*, Dec. 26, 2002, p. A-1.

2. Babak Dehghanpisheh, John Barry, and Roy Gutman, "The Death Convoy of Afghanistan," *Newsweek*, Aug. 26, 2002, pp. 22–30.

3. Ibid., p. 28.

4. Ibid., p. 24.

5. Proffer of Facts in Support of Defendant's Suppression Motions, *U.S. v. Lindh*, Crim. No. 02 37 A, filed June 13, 2002, U.S. District Court, E. Div. of Virginia, at p. 18.

6. Priest and Gellman, "U.S. Decries Abuse." See also Dana Priest and Joe Stephens, "A Secret World of U.S. Interrogations," *Washington Post*, May 11, 2004, p. A-1.

7. Dehghanpisheh et al., "Death Convoy."

8. Jane Mayer, "Lost in the Jihad," *New Yorker*, March 10, 2003.

9. Proffer of Facts, *U.S. v. Lindh*, p. 10.

10. Ibid., p. 16.

11. Ibid., p. 21.

12. Mayer, *Lost in the Jihad*.

13. *Statement of Maher Arar*, Nov. 6, 2003; "His Year in Hell," *60 Minutes*, CBS, Jan. 21, 2004; "Canadian Man Deported by U.S. Details Torture in Syria," *Democracy Now*, Nov. 7, 2003.

14. Ibid.

15. Ibid.

16. *Statement of Maher Arar*.

17. 18 U.S.C. 2340 et seq.

18. Dana Priest, "Top Justice Aide Approved Sending Suspect to Syria," *Washington Post*, Nov. 19, 2003.

19. Ibid.

20. "His Year in Hell."

21. Dana Priest, "Man Deported After Syrian Assurances," *Washington Post*, Nov. 19, 2003.

22. DeNee Brown and Dana Priest, "Deported Terror Suspect Details Torture in Syria," *Washington Post*, Nov. 20, 2003, p. A-1.

23. Disturbingly, certain congressional members would later seek to pass leg-

islation legalizing deportation to nations utilizing torture, if such "assurances" were first obtained (House draft, H.R. 10. Nov. 2004).

24. Scandal broke out once again in November 2004 when journalists revealed that the Pentagon and the CIA had used a leased plane more than 300 times to drop off detainees, who were often drugged, gagged, and sedated, in Syria, Egypt, Uzbekistan, and other countries practicing torture. The jet always left from Washington, D.C., and had a total of 49 destinations, including Guantánamo (Amy Goodman, "U.S. Operating Secret 'Torture Flights,'" *Democracy Now,* Nov. 17, 2004). Two victims claim they were drugged by masked U.S. agents in Sweden and taken to Egypt, where they were tortured with electrical shocks (Farah Stockman, "Terror Suspects' Torture Claims Have Mass. Link," *Boston Globe,* Nov. 29, 2004, p. A-1).

25. Faye Bowers and Philip Smucker, "U.S. Ships Al Qaeda Suspects to Torture Using Arab States," *Christian Science Monitor,* July 26, 2002; Priest and Gellman, "U.S. Decries Abuse."

26. Douglas Jehl and David Johnston, "Rule Change Lets CIA Freely Send Suspects Abroad to Jails," *New York Times,* March 6, 2005. See also Dana Priest, "CIA's Assurances on Transferred Suspects Doubted," *Washington Post,* March 17, 2005.

27. Evan Thomas and Mark Hosenball, "Moving Targets," *Newsweek,* Dec. 1, 2003, p. 26.

28. Priest and Gellman, "U.S. Decries Abuse."

29. "His Year in Hell."

30. Dana Priest, "Jet Is an Open Secret in Terror War," *Washington Post,* Dec. 27, 2004, p. A-1. See also Jane Mayer, "Outsourcing Torture," *New Yorker,* Feb. 14, 2005.

31. Mayer, "Outsourcing Torture."

32. Brown and Priest, "Deported Terror Suspect."

33. 18 U.S.C. 2340, 2340A, et seq. See also discussion in chapter 4.

34. Priest and Gellman, "U.S. Decries Abuse."

35. According to IRA prisoners subjected to such "uncomfortable" positions, the pain was unbearable and for a long time afterward they were unable to use a fork or write their names. Latin American prisoners likewise found such treatment excruciating (John Conroy, *Unspeakable Acts, Ordinary People,* U. of California Press, 2000). See chapter 5.

36. Priest and Gellman, "U.S. Decries Abuse."

37. Kathy Gannon, "Prisoners Released from Bagram Say Forced to Strip Naked, Deprived of Sleep, Ordered to Stand for Hours," *AP World,* General News, March 14, 2003.

38. "U.S. Accused of Torture in Iraq," *CBS News,* July 19, 2003.

39. Priest and Gellman, "U.S. Decries Abuse."

40. Jess Bravin and Gary Fields, "How Do U.S. Interrogators Make a Captured Terrorist Talk?" *Wall Street Journal,* March 4, 2003.

41. Michael Hirsh, "Abu Ghraib: 'Breaking a General,'" *MSNBC Newsweek*, Sept. 6, 2004.

42. "Prisoners 'Killed' at US Base," *BBC News*, March 6, 2003.

43. Ibid.; and Carlotta Gall, "U.S. Military Investigating Death of Afghan in Custody," *New York Times*, March 4, 2003.

44. April Witt, "U.S. Probes Death of a Prisoner in Afghanistan," *Washington Post*, June 24, 2003, p. A-18.

45. "An Afghan Radio Diary," *NPR News*, Morning Edition, Dec. 12, 2003.

46. It was only in June 2004, after the Abu Ghraib scandal and intensive investigations began, that David Passaro, a U.S. "contractor," was charged with beating Mr. Wali with his flashlight. Passaro was a former Army Special Operations agent, and he had first served with a clandestine paramilitary team composed of Special Forces and CIA personnel responsible for capturing and interrogating Taliban and al-Qaeda prisoners. He remained with the CIA until Dec. 2002, when he became a contractor. (Susan Schmitt and Dana Priest, "Civilian Charged in Beating of Afghan Detainee," *Washington Post*, June 18, 2004.)

47. See, for example, "Assessing the New Normal," by the Lawyers Committee for Human Rights, Sept. 2003; "Enduring Freedom," by Human Rights Watch, March 8, 2004; "Iraq, One Year On the Human Rights Situation Remains Dire," by Amnesty International, March 18, 2004; "Report of the International Committee of the Red Cross on the Treatment by the Coalition Forces of Prisoners of War and Other Protected Persons by the Geneva Conventions in Iraq During Arrest, Internment and Interrogation," Feb. 2004; and Neil A. Lewis and Eric Lichtblau, "Red Cross Says That for Months It Complained of Iraq Abuses to U.S.," *New York Times*, May 7, 2004, p. A-10.

48. Robin Wright and Glenn Kessler, "Rejection of Prison Abuses Was Sought; Administration Was Reluctant," *Washington Post*, May 16, 2004.

49. Mary Mapes and Dan Rather, "Court Martial in Iraq," *60 Minutes*, CBS News, April 28, 2004.

50. Ibid., statement of Lt. Col. Cowan.

51. Ian Fisher, "Ex-Prisoners of G.I.s Offer More Claims of Mistreatment," *New York Times*, May 4, 2004, p. A-8.

52. Ian Fisher, "Iraqi Recounts Hours of Abuse by U.S. Troops," *New York Times*, May 5, 2004, p. A-1.

53. Maj. Gen. Antonio M. Taguba, *Article 15–6 Investigation of the 800th Military Police Brigade;* and Seymour Hersh, "Torture at Abu Ghraib," *New Yorker*, May 10, 2004. See also Mapes and Rather, "Court Martial in Iraq," and John Barry, Michael Hirsh, and Michael Isikoff, "The Roots of Torture," *Newsweek*, May 24, 2004, p. 27.

54. Barry et al., "The Roots of Torture," p. 28.

55. Scott Higham and Joe Stephens, "New Details of Prisoner Abuse Emerge," *Washington Post*, May 21, 2004, p. A-17.

56. Philip Shenon, "Officer Suggests Iraq Jail Abuses Were Encouraged," *New York Times*, May 2, 2004. See also Hersh, "Torture at Abu Ghraib."
57. Douglas Jehl and Eric Schmitt, "Dogs and Other Harsh Tactics Linked to Military Intelligence," *New York Times*, May 22, 2004, p. A-1.
58. Barry et al., "The Roots of Torture," p. 28, citing Darius Rejali.
59. Carl Hulse and Sheryl Stolberg, "Lawmakers See Iraq Images and Are Shaken by Scenes," *New York Times*, May 13, 2004, p. A-1.
60. Toni Loci, "Hidden Identities Hinder Probe," *USA Today*, May 28–31, 2004.
61. See, for example, Pauline Jelinek, "Were Abuse Photos Aimed at Getting Prisoners to Talk?" *AP*, May 11, 2004.
62. See chapter 3.
63. Ian Fisher, "Iraqi Tells of Abuse, from Ridicule to Rape Threat," *New York Times*, May 14, 2004, p. A-10, quoting Mr. Saddam Saleh Aboud and setting forth his story.
64. Ibid., citing Taguba, *Article 15–6 Investigation of the 800th Military Police Brigade*.
65. Ibid. See also James Risen, "Command Errors Aided Iraq Abuse, Army Has Found," *New York Times*, May 3, 2004, p. A-1.
66. James Risen, David Johnson, and Neil Lewis, "Harsh CIA Methods Cited in Top Qaeda Interrogations," *New York Times*, May 13, 2004, p. A-1.
67. Ibid.
68. Michael Hirsh, John Barry, and Daniel Klaidman, "A Tortured Debate," *Newsweek*, June 21, 2004, p. 50.
69. *Suspected Presence of Clandestine Cemeteries on a Military Installation*, Department of Defense, Combined Message, April 1994.
70. Hirsh et al., "A Tortured Debate."
71. Jehl and Schmitt, "Dogs and Other Harsh Tactics."
72. Bradley Graham, "Number of Army Probes of Detainee Deaths Rises to 33," *Washington Post*, May 22, 2004, p. A-17; Jehl and Schmitt, "Dogs and Other Harsh Tactics."
73. Thomas Ricks, "Documents Detail Abuse of Detainees," *Boston Globe*, Dec. 15, 2004.
74. Thomas Shanker, "U.S. Disciplines 4 for Abuses in Iraq," *New York Times*, Dec. 10, 2004.
75. Neil Lewis and David Johnson, "New FBI Memos Describe Abuses of Iraqi Inmates," *New York Times*, Dec. 21, 2004.
76. Tim Golden and Eric Schmitt, "General Took Guantanamo Rules to Iraq for Handling of Prisoners," *New York Times*, May 13, 2004, p. A-1.
77. Dana Priest and Joe Stephens, "Secret World of U.S. Interrogation," *Washington Post*, May 11, 2004, p. A-1.
78. James Risen and David Johnston, "Photos of Dead May Indicate Graver Abuse," *New York Times*, May 7, 2004, p. A-11.
79. Carlotta Gall, "Afghan Gives Own Account of U.S. Abuse," *New York Times*, May 12, 2004, p. A-1.

80. Stephen Graham, "Military Probing Report Afghan Detainee Killed in Custody," *Boston Globe*, Sept. 22, 2004, p. A-19.
81. Carlotta Gall and David Rohde, "New Charges Raise Questions on Abuse at Afghan Prisons," *New York Times*, Sept. 17, 2004, p. A-1.
82. Lianna Hart, "Afghan Detainee's Leg Was Pulpified, Witness Says," *Los Angeles Times*, March 23, 2005.
83. Carol Leonnig, "Further Detainee Abuse Alleged," *Washington Post*, Dec. 26, 2004, citing FBI memorandums obtained by the ACLU.
84. Lewis and Johnson, "New FBI Memos Describe Abuses"; Jim Lobe, "US Downplays Report on Guantanamo Prisoner Abuses," *Inter Press Service*, Dec. 1, 2004.
85. See "FBI Reports Guantanamo Abuse," *CNN*, Dec. 8, 2004, and "IRCR Accuses US Military of Abuse at Guantanamo Prison," *VOA News*, Nov. 30, 2004.
86. Leonnig, "Further Detainee Abuse Alleged."
87. Carol Leonnig and Dana Priest, "Detainees Accuse Female Interrogators," *Washington Post*, Feb. 10, 2005.
88. Dana Priest and Scott Higham, "At Guantanamo, a Prison within a Prison," Dec. 17, 2004, p. A-1.
89. Eric Schmitt, "Four Navy Commandos Are Charged in Abuse," *New York Times*, Sept. 4, 2004, p. A-5.
90. James Risen and David Johnson, "Photos of Dead May Indicate Graver Abuses," citing diary of Sgt. Ivan L. Frederick, *New York Times*, May 7, 2004, p. A-11.
91. Dana Priest and Joe Stephens, "The Road to Abu Ghraib," *Washington Post*, May 11, 2004, p. A-12.
92. Ibid., quoting Mr. Peter Probst.
93. According to *Washington Post* journalists Dana Priest and Scott Higham, "Under a presidential directive and authorities approved by administration lawyers, the CIA is allowed to capture and hold certain classes of suspects without accounting for them in any public way and without revealing the rules for their treatment." (Priest and Higham, "At Guantanamo, a Prison within a Prison.")
94. Ironically, although the prisoner was deemed to be of high intelligence value, he was interrogated only once in seven months (Eric Schmitt and Tom Shanker, "Rumsfeld Issued an Order to Hide Detainee in Iraq," *New York Times*, June 17, 2004, p. A-1).
95. Eric Schmitt and Douglas Jehl, "Army Says CIA Hid More Iraqis Than It Claimed," *New York Times*, Sept. 10, 2004, p. A-1.
96. Ibid.
97. Steven Lee Myers, "Military Completed Death Certificates for 20 Prisoners Only After Months Passed," *New York Times*, May 31, 2004, p. A-8.
98. Douglas Jehl, "Pentagon Will Not Try 17 GIs Implicated in Prisoners' Deaths," *New York Times*, March 26, 2005.

99. Priest and Stephens, "The Road to Abu Ghraib."

100. John Yoo, *Memorandum to President Bush, Re: Application of Treaties and Laws to al-Qaeda and Taliban Detainees*, Jan. 9, 2002.

101. Neil Lewis, "Justice Memos Explained How to Skip Prisoner Rights," *New York Times*, May 21, 2004, A-12.

102. Alberto Gonzales, *Memorandum to the President, Re: Decision Re Application of the Geneva Conventions on Prisoners of War in the Conflict with Al Qaeda and the Taliban*, Jan. 25, 2002.

103. U.S. Department of Justice, Office of Legal Counsel, *Memorandum for Alberto R. Gonzales, Counsel to the President, Re: Standards of Conduct for Interrogation under 18 U.S.C. §§ 2340-2340A*, Aug. 1, 2002; Department of Defense, *Working Group Report on Detainee Interrogations in the Global War on Terrorism: Assessment of Legal, Historical, Policy, and Operational Considerations*, March 6, 2003.

104. Neil Lewis and Eric Schmitt, "Lawyers Decided Bans on Torture Didn't Bind Bush," *New York Times*, June 8, 2004, p. A-1, citing memoranda listed above in nn. 100–103.

105. Dana Priest and R. Jeffrey Smith, "Memo Offered Justification for Use of Torture," *Washington Post*, June 8, 2004, p. A-1, citing memorandums listed above in nn. 100–103.

106. Ibid.

107. Despite the public furor caused when these memos were disclosed, the contents were not repudiated by the Bush administration until December 2004, when White House counsel Alberto Gonzales was nominated for the position of attorney general and faced withering questioning regarding his own memo, in which he described the Geneva Conventions as "quaint" and "obsolete."

108. Barry et al., "The Roots of Torture," pp. 26–34.

109. President Bush continues to press for bilateral immunity agreements as well, threatening to cut off aid to those nations not promising to hold the U.S. immune for any ICC prosecutions. See Jim Lobe, "U.S. Pushes War-Crimes Immunity in Foreign-Aid Bill," *Inter Press Services*, Nov. 30, 2004.

110. Ibid.

111. Ibid. According to *Newsweek*, these methods included intimidation with dogs, stressful positions, hooding for days at a time, the withholding of food, and naked isolation in cold, dark cells for more than thirty days at a time.

112. Walter Pincus, "Focus Shifts from Military Police to Intelligence," *Washington Post*, May 11, 2004, p. A-15, citing Taguba, *Article 15–6 Investigation of the 800th Military Police Brigade*.

113. Golden and Schmitt, "General Took Guantanamo Rules to Iraq."

114. Douglas Jehl, "Some Abu Ghraib Abuses Are Traced to Afghanistan," *New York Times*, Aug. 26, 2004, p. A-11.

115. Joel Brinkley, "Army Policy Bars Interrogations by Private Contractors," *New York Times,* June 12, 2004.

116. The CIA has proffered a memo suggesting that its agents were not to be present in any military interrogations utilizing force. However, the memo did not apply to the CIA's own detainees or practices. Moreover, as the above facts make clear, the CIA itself was already utilizing extraordinarily harsh methods. The memo thus seems rather hollow. See Douglas Jehl, "CIA Order on Detainees Shows Its Role Was Curbed," *New York Times,* Dec. 14, 2004.

117. Eric Schmitt, "Abuses at Prison Tied to Officers in Intelligence," *New York Times,* Aug. 26, 2004, p. A-1.

118. Jehl, "Some Abu Ghraib Abuses."

119. Ibid.

120. Chairman James R. Schlesinger, *Independent Panel to Review DOD Detention Operations,* Aug. 2004.

121. Eric Schmitt, "Abuse Panel Says Rules on Inmates Need Overhaul," *New York Times,* Aug. 25, 2004, p. A-1, citing the Schlesinger Panel Report (see n. 120).

122. Bradley Graham and John White, "Top Pentagon Leaders Faulted in Prison Abuse," *Washington Post,* Aug. 25, 2004, citing the Schlesinger Panel Report (see n. 120).

123. Evan Thomas and Mark Hosenball, "Bush's Mr. Wrong," *Newsweek,* May 31, 2004, pp. 22–32.

124. Several high-level military officers have supported a civil rights case brought against Mr. Rumsfeld for just these reasons (Bob Herbert, "We Can't Remain Silent," *New York Times,* April 1, 2005).

125. Some sanctions were brought, however, against certain marines and others in later disclosed abuse cases (see Shanker, "U.S. Disciplines 4 for Abuses in Iraq," and Ricks, "Documents Detail Abuse of Detainees"). However, the number of sanctions as compared to the number of cases of abuse remains woefully inadequate. In Afghanistan, for example, of six recently disclosed deaths, only two have led to legal action (Carlotta Gall, "Rights Group Reports Deaths of Men Held by U.S. in Afghanistan," *New York Times,* Dec. 14, 2004). Moreover, criminal charges are often avoided and administrative sanctions imposed instead (see R. Jeffrey Smith and Dan Egan, "New Papers Suggest Detainee Abuse Was Widespread," *Washington Post,* Dec. 22, 2004). Perhaps most importantly, the higher-up officials responsible for authorizing and promoting these systemic violations remain unscathed by any legal proceedings. Alberto Gonzales, for example, was promoted to the position of U.S. attorney general.

126. Carlotta Gall, "Mercenaries in Afghanistan Get 8 to 10 Years in Prison," *New York Times,* Sept. 16, 2004, p. A-12.

127. Ibid., quoting Edward Caraballo.

CHAPTER TWO: THE LESSONS OF LATIN AMERICAN HUMAN RIGHTS HISTORY

1. See discussion of applicable U.S. laws and treaties, chapter 4.
2. Jim Handy, *Gift of the Devil* (South End Press, 1984), p. 208, citing the 1950 and 1964 census reports.
3. Stephen Schlesinger and Stephen Kinzer, *Bitter Fruit* (Doubleday, 1982), pp. 54–56.
4. Ibid., pp. 105–129.
5. Ibid., p. 233.
6. The *Unidad Revolucionaria Nacional Guatemalteca.*
7. Commission for Historical Clarification (CEH), *Guatemala: Memory of Silence,* 1999 (also referred to herein as the United Nations Truth Commission Report), p. 15.
8. Handy, *Gift of the Devil,* p. 247.
9. 1984 interview by Jennifer Harbury with surviving villager, Chiapas refugee camps; see also AI Index: AMR 34/02/98 *GUATEMALA: All the Truth, Justice for All.*
10. 1985 interviews with members of the Grupo de Apoyo Mutuo, or "GAM," and other witnesses, and with Jean Marie Simon in Guatemala City, Guatemala; see also AI Index: AMR 34/02/98 *GUATEMALA: All the Truth, Justice for All.*
11. *Guatemala: Memory of Silence,* pp. 7, 14–16, 23–24, 30–31.
12. Ibid., pp. 14–15.
13. Ibid., p. 9.
14. Mark Weisbrot, "Clinton's Apology to Guatemala a Necessary First Step," *Knight Kidder/Tribune Media Services,* March 15, 1999; Andrew Reding, "A Genocide Tribunal for Guatemala," *Journal of Commerce,* March 18, 1999.
15. See chapter 3. See also Tim Wiener, "In Guatemala's Dark Heart, CIA Tied to Death and Aid," *New York Times,* April 2, 1995.
16. Allan Nairn, "The CIA and Guatemala's Death Squads," *The Nation,* April 17, 1995.
17. Intelligence Oversight Board (IOB), *Report on Guatemala,* June 28, 1996, p. 22.
18. Ibid., p. 4.
19. John Coatsworth, *Central America and the United States: The Clients and the Colossus* (Harvard U. Press, 1994), p. 168.
20. Michael Klare and David Anderson, *Scourge of Guns,* Federation of American Scientists, 1996; *Foreign Military Sales, Foreign Military Construction Sales, and Military Assistance Facts,* Deputy for Operations and Administration, Defense Security Cooperation Administration, Sept. 30, 1990 and Sept. 30, 2000; and Jeffrey Smith and Dana Priest, "Covert Aid, Intelligence Ties Undermined Public Outrage," *Washington Post,* April 2, 1995.
21. Coatsworth, *Central America and the United States,* p. 192.
22. Nairn, "The CIA and Guatemala's Death Squads."

23. IOB, *Report on Guatemala*, p. 20.
24. *The Guatemalan Military: What the U.S. Files Revealed*, National Security Archive, June 1, 2000, Doc. No. 1.
25. Ibid., Doc. No. 11.
26. Ibid., Doc. No. 3.
27. Ibid., Doc. No. 8.
28. Ibid., Doc. No. 19.
29. Ibid., Doc. No. 20.
30. Ibid., Doc. No. 30.
31. Ibid., Doc. No. 33.
32. Ibid., Doc. No. 37.
33. Ibid., Doc. No. 42. (Note: It is probable that Everardo was held at this base during his time as a clandestine prisoner of war.)
34. *CIA Report Re Capture of a Guatemalan Guerrilla Leader*, March 18, 1992.
35. Tom Barry and Deb Preusch, *Central America Fact Book* (Grove Weidenfeld, 1986), p. 199.
36. Ibid.
37. Ibid., citing Kenneth J. Grieb, "The United States and the Rise of General Maximiliano Hernández Martínez," *Journal of Latin American Studies*, Nov. 1971, p. 152.
38. Ibid., pp. 199–200.
39. Ibid., p. 200, citing Cynthia Arnson, *El Salvador: Revolution Confronts the United States* (Washington Institute for Policy Studies, 1982), p. 7.
40. Ibid., p. 201.
41. Ibid., pp. 201–202.
42. Commission on the Truth for El Salvador, *From Madness to Hope: The 12 Year War in El Salvador*, 1993.
43. March 1980 sermon given by Archbishop Romero in San Salvador.
44. *From Madness to Hope*, Part III, "Chronology of the Violence."
45. Ibid.
46. Ibid.
47. Ibid., "Massacres of Peasants by the Armed Forces."
48. Kevin Murray with Tom Barry, *Inside El Salvador* (Resource Center Press, 1995), p. 59.
49. *From Madness to Hope*, Part IV, "Cases and Patterns of Violence."
50. William Blum, *Killing Hope* (Common Courage Press, 1995), p. 357.
51. Ibid.
52. www.soaw.org.
53. *An Insider Speaks Out*, video produced by Linda Panetta, Veterans for Peace, 1998.
54. *Inside the School of the Assassins*, video by Richter Productions, 1997.
55. Statement of U.S. Rep. Esteban Torres, Sept. 4, 1997, 143 Cong. Rec. E1678-01.

56. *Inside the School of the Assassins;* see also Mark Matthews, "U.S. Manuals Taught Murder, Kennedy Says," *Baltimore Sun,* March 7, 1997, and Dana Priest, "U.S. Instructed Latins on Executions, Torture," *Washington Post,* Sept. 21, 1996.

57. Allan Nairn, "Behind the Death Squads," *The Progressive,* May 1984, p. 22.

58. Greg Walker, *At the Hurricane's Eye: U.S. Special Forces from Vietnam to Desert Storm* (Ivy Books, 1994), p. 90.

59. Blum, *Killing Hope,* p. 358.

60. Bradley Graham and Douglas Farrah, "With Honors Bestowed: U.S. Veterans of Salvadoran War Lift Their Silence," *Washington Post,* May 27, 1996, p. A-16.

61. Nidia Díaz, *I Was Never Alone: A Prison Diary from El Salvador* (Ocean Press, 1992), pp. 19–21. A Cuban working as a CIA agent has also claimed responsibility for her capture.

62. Philip Taubman, "Top Salvador Police Official Said to Be CIA Informant," *New York Times,* May 22, 1984, p. A-1.

63. Nairn, *Behind the Death Squads,* pp. 20, 23.

64. Affidavit of Kate Bancroft, Nov. 13, 2003, summarizing interviews with Mr. Joya Martínez. See also Bill Hutchinson, *When the Dogs Ate Candles: A Time in El Salvador* (Boulder: University Press of Colorado, 1998).

65. Barry and Preusch, *Central America Fact Book,* p. 253.

66. Ibid., pp. 251, 264.

67. Ibid., p. 253.

68. Ibid., pp. 254–255.

69. Father James "Guadalupe" Carney, *To Be a Christian Is to Be a Revolutionary: The Autobiography of Father James Guadalupe Carney* (Harper and Row, 1987). Note: English and Spanish editions are available through the Padre Guadalupe Carney Foundation, c/o Communication Center #1, 214 South Meramec Ave., St. Louis, MO 63105.

70. Barry and Preusch, *Central America Fact Book,* p. 258.

71. Leo Valladares Lanza, *The Facts Speak for Themselves* (Human Rights Watch, 1994).

72. Barry and Preusch, *Central America Fact Book,* p. 259.

73. Valladares Lanza, *The Facts Speak for Themselves,* p. 142.

74. Ibid., p. 143–145.

75. Gary Cohn and Ginger Thompson, "Unearthed: Fatal Secrets," *Baltimore Sun* Special Report, June 11–18, 1995.

76. Ibid.

77. Ibid.

78. Ibid.

79. Ibid.

80. Ibid.

81. Ibid.

82. Ibid.
83. Ibid.
84. Ibid.
85. Ariel Armony, *Argentina, the United States and the Anti-Communist Crusade in Central America, 1977–1984* (Center for International Studies, Ohio U., 1997), p. 59.
86. Cohn and Thompson, "Unearthed: Fatal Secrets."
87. Ibid.
88. Ibid.
89. Ibid.
90. Ibid.
91. Ibid.
92. Ibid.
93. Ibid.

CHAPTER THREE: FROM THE LATIN AMERICAN TORTURE CELLS

1. Jennifer Harbury, *Searching for Everardo: A Story of Love, War, and the CIA in Guatemala* (Warner Books, 1997). See also Jennifer Harbury, *Bridge of Courage* (Common Courage Press, 1994).
2. Everardo's legal name was Efraín Bámaca Velásquez.
3. Personal interviews with Santiago Cabrera López, 1993–1998.
4. Statement of G-2 Especialista Ángel Nery Urrizar to Jennifer Harbury in June 1995; see also Urrizar's testimony to the Inter-American Commission on Human Rights, Jan. 1996.
5. Intelligence Oversight Board (IOB), *Report on Guatemala*, June 28, 1996, pp. 2, 16. See also Allan Nairn, "CIA Death Squads," *The Nation*, April 17, 1995.
6. DEA memorandum of June 21, 1995, re DEA-6 by Stephen Green; as well as June 9, 1988 DEA memorandum and Aug. 25, 1988 DEA memorandum. See also CIA memo of June 1992.
7. CIA document of Oct. 1991 (signed by Thomas Twetton) and DOD document of Feb. 1995, "Perspective on Col. Julio Roberto Alpirez."
8. Sam Dillon and Tim Weiner, "In Guatemala's Dark Heart, CIA Tied to Death and Aid," *New York Times*, April 2, 1995; and "CIA Paid Guatemalan Officer Although It Knew of American's Slaying," *Washington Post*, reprinted in the *Dallas Morning News*, March 25, 1995.
9. Affidavit and interviews with John Doe.
10. Affidavit of, and conversations with, John Doe. Mr. Doe was also present, and described the man as tall and fair-haired with hairy arms, an oddity in Guatemala. He was wearing pilot's overalls with rolled-up sleeves, but notably, the required Guatemalan military insignia was nowhere on his clothing, leading Mr. Doe to understand that the man could not be Guatemalan. The man wore U.S.-made boots as well.
11. March 18, 1992 CIA bulletin.

12. As noted above, U.S. documents describe Alpirez as an unstable and violent man who excelled at liquidation efforts throughout the 1980s.
13. Letter of Oct. 15, 1997, and accompanying table of undisclosed documents, from John L. McPherson, assistant general counsel to the CIA, to Mr. Robert Loeffler, attorney for Jennifer Harbury.
14. Jeffrey Smith, "CIA Chief Fires 2 Over Scandal in Guatemala," *Washington Post*, Sept. 30, 1995.
15. 1993 CIA memo by Thomas Twetton.
16. DOD, *Suspected Presence of Clandestine Cemeteries on a Military Installation*, April, 1994.
17. DOD, *The Fate of Those Captured*, Nov., 1994.
18. This case history is based on my many lengthy conversations with my close friend, Sister Dianna Ortiz herself, in the years since we met in 1994, and on *The Blindfold's Eye*, written by Sister Dianna Ortiz with Patricia Davis (Orbis Books, 2003).
19. This case history is based on my personal conversation with "Miguel" in Guatemala in the fall of 2003, and on his signed statement of 2003.
20. Miguel knew the accent even then, from the many tourists, as well as radio, television, and film. He later lived many years in the United States, where he learned English well and confirms that the accent was that of a North American.
21. The case history of John Doe is based on my numerous conversations with him since 1997 through the present, as well as on his testimony to various human rights organizations and tribunals. I will not further identify him here, given the numerous security problems he has had to date.
22. This testimony is based on my interviews with "David" throughout 1994. Once again, a pseudonym is used to protect him and his family members from reprisals.
23. This case history is based on my personal interviews with María Guardado in Los Angeles, California, in the fall of 2003.
24. Chillingly, María spent time with the sanctuary and solidarity networks in Texas, where she encountered a great deal of resistance from one person, who repeatedly tried to silence her story and isolate her. It later became known that the network was very heavily infiltrated by FBI and other informants.
25. Once again, a pseudonym is used to protect the witness and his family from retaliation. This account is based on a personal interview with Marco by Jennifer Harbury, Sept. 2004.
26. Laurie Goodstein, "Church Worker Says Salvadoran Police Tortured Her: U.S. Vice Consul Allegedly Had 'Coffee with the Colonel' While American Was Interrogated," *Washington Post*, Nov. 30, 1989, p. A-16.
27. Ibid.
28. Personal interview with Andrés Pavón by J. Harbury in Honduras, fall of 2003.

29. Personal interviews with "Elena" by J. Harbury, 1998–2004. Again, a pseudonym is used to protect her and her family members.
30. See generally Father James "Guadalupe" Carney, *To Be a Christian Is to Be a Revolutionary: The Autobiography of Father James Guadalupe Carney* (Harper and Row, 1987).
31. Correspondence from Joe Connolly to J. Harbury, Oct. 2004.
32. Joseph Mulligan, S.J., "What Happened to Father Carney? Missing Priest Alert," *Christian Century*, May 21–28, 1997.
33. George Black and Anne Nelson, "The U.S. in Honduras : The Mysterious Death of Father Carney," *The Nation*, Aug. 4–11, 1984, p. 82.
34. Statements of Florencio Caballero to Carney family members.
35. Black and Nelson, "The U.S. in Honduras."
36. Ibid., p. 84.
37. Affidavit of Joseph Connally, June 20, 2004, based on personal interviews with Florencio Caballero.
38. George Black, "The Many Killers of Father Carney," *The Nation*, Jan. 23, 1988.
39. Carney, *To Be a Christian*, p. 549.
40. Vernon Loeb, "The CIA Won't Name Hondurans Suspected of Executing Rebel," *Washington Post*, Nov. 4, 1998.
41. Walter Pincus, "CIA Again Eyes Abuses in Honduras," *Washington Post*, Dec. 23, 1996.
42. Gary Cohn and Ginger Thompson, "Unearthed: Fatal Secrets," *Baltimore Sun* Special Report, June 11–18, 1995.
43. Ibid.
44. Ibid.
45. Ibid.; citing statement of Richard Stolz, DDO of the CIA, to Select Committee on Intelligence, June 17, 1988.
46. Anne-Marie O'Connor, "Who Was Mr. Mike and Why Did He Aid Honduran Torture?" *Atlanta Journal and Constitution*, March 13, 1994.
47. Lt. Cmdr. Michael J. Walsh and Greg Walker, *SEAL!: From Vietnam's Phoenix Program to Central America's Drug Wars* (Pocket Books, 1994).
48. Ibid., p. 265.
49. Ibid., p. 276.
50. Ibid., pp. 278–279.
51. Ibid., p. 149.
52. Thomas Hauser, *The Execution of Charles Horman* (Harcourt Brace Jovanovich, 1978), p. 39.
53. Ibid., pp. 23–28.
54. Ibid., pp. 55–60; see also Peter Kornbluh, *The Pinochet Files* (New Press, 2003).
55. Hauser, pp. 95–103; Kornbluh, ch. 5.
56. Hauser, pp. 96, 98–103; Kornbluh, ch. 5.
57. Hauser, pp. 130, 217; Kornbluh, ch. 5.

58. R.V. Fimbres, Department of State document, Aug. 25, 1976.
59. Vernon Loeb, "CIA May Have Had Role in Journalist's Murder," *Washington Post,* Oct. 9, 1999; see also Kornbluh, *The Pinochet File,* ch. 5.
60. Philip Agee, *Inside the Company: CIA Diary* (Penguin Books, 1975).
61. Hauser, *The Execution of Charles Horman,* pp. 135–142.
62. Ibid., pp. 135–142.
63. Diana Jean Schemo, "FBI Watched an American Who Was Killed in Chile Coup," *New York Times,* July 1, 2000.
64. Hauser, *The Execution of Charles Horman,* pp. 208–209.
65. William Blum, *Killing Hope: U.S. Military and CIA Interventions Since World War II* (Common Courage Press 1995), pp. 163–172.
66. In 1968 one-third of the OPS officers in the Dominican Republic were in fact CIA officials; see A.J. Langguth, *Hidden Terror* (Pantheon Books, 1978), p. 124.
67. Langguth, *Hidden Terror,* pp. 145–165.
68. Ibid., pp. 162–163.
69. Ibid., pp. 164–165.
70. Ibid., pp. 208–216; Mr. Arruda also confirmed this to J. Harbury, telephone interview, Oct. 2004.
71. Ibid., p. 251.
72. Ibid., pp. 286–287.
73. Ibid., p. 253.
74. Manuel Hevia Cosculluela, *Pasaporte 11333: Ocho Años con la CIA* (Havana, Cuba: Editorial de Sciencias Social, 1978), pp. 279–287.
75. Langguth, *Hidden Terrors,* p. 253.
76. Hevia Cosculluela, *Pasaporte 11333,* p. 284.
77. *Inside the School of Assassins,* video by Richter Productions, 1997.
78. John Marks, *The Search for the Manchurian Candidate* (Times Books, 1979).
79. Langguth, *Hidden Terrors,* p. 225.
80. Ibid., p. 25.
81. John Conroy, *Unspeakable Acts, Ordinary People: The Dynamics of Torture* (Knopf, 2000), pp. 113–120.
82. Nick Schou, "Operation Phoenix Rises from the Ashes of History," *Orange County Weekly,* Jan. 16, 2004, www.ocweekly.com/ink/04/19/news-schon.php citing 1971 congressional testimony of Mr. Bart Osborn.
83. Richard Ehrlich, "Death of a Dirty Fighter," *Asia Times,* July 8, 2003, quoting Phillip Smith, executive director of the Center for Policy Analysis.
84. The case of José Rubén Carrillo Cubas in El Salvador was unusual.
85. See, for example, the CIA's *Human Resources Exploitation Training Manual, 1983,* analyzed in Gary Cohn, Ginger Thompson, and Mark Matthews, "Torture Was Taught by the CIA," *Baltimore Sun,* Jan. 27, 1997.
86. U.S. files confirm the use of such a pit there.
87. Gary Cohn, Ginger Thompson, and Mark Matthews, "Torture Was Taught

by CIA," *Baltimore Sun*, Jan. 27, 1997, citing KUBARK and *Human Resources Exploitation Manual of 1983*.
88. Charlie Savage, "CIA Resists Request for Abuse Data," *Boston Globe*, Dec. 27, 2004.

CHAPTER FOUR: WHAT CAN BE DONE: THE LAW

1. *Culombe v. Connecticut*, 367 U.S. 568, 581 n. 23 (1961), quoting Patrick Henry, in 3 Elliot's Debates (2d ed. 1891), 447–448.
2. *Culombe v. Connecticut*, 367 U.S. 581, 584 (1961), concerning the coerced confession of a mentally retarded suspect.
3. *Culombe*, id.
4. *Glass v. Louisiana*, 471 U.S. 1080, "Thus in explaining the obvious unconstitutionality of such ancient practices as disemboweling while alive, drawing and quartering, public dissection, burning alive at the stake, crucifixion, and breaking at the wheel, the Court has emphasized that the Eighth Amendment forbids 'inhuman and barbarous' methods of execution that go at all beyond 'the mere extinguishment of life' and cause 'torture or a lingering death.'" In re Kemmler, 136 U.S. at 447. It is beyond debate that the Amendment proscribes all forms of "unnecessary cruelty" that cause gratuitous "terror, pain, or disgrace." Wilkerson v. Utah, 99 U.S. 130, 135–136 (1879), n9.
5. *Farmer v. Brennan*, 511 U.S. 825 (1994).
6. *Ruiz v. Estelle*, 503 F. Supp. 1295 (S.D.Tx. 1980).
7. *Farmer v. Brennan*, 511 U.S. 825 (1994).
8. *Estelle v. Gamble*, 429 U.S. 97 (1976).
9. *Hudson v. McMillian*, 503 U.S. 1 (1992).
10. *Tennessee v. Garner*, 471 U.S. 1 (1985).
11. *Youngstown v. Romeo* 457 U.S. 307 (1982).
12. *U.S. v. Verdugo-Urquidez*, 494 U.S. 259 (1990).
13. *Rasul v. Bush*, 159 L.Ed. 2d 548 (2004). See also *Hamdi v. Rumsfeld*, 159 L.Ed. 2d 578 (2004).
14. Martin Edwin Anderson, "Is Torture an Option in War on Terror?" *Insight*, May 27, 2002, quoting retired Maj. F. Andy Messing.
15. See, for example, Michael Hirsh, John Barry, and Daniel Kleidman, "A Tortured Debate," *Newsweek*, July 21, 2004.
16. Federal Tort Claims Act, 28 U.S.C. S 1346(b) and other provisions.
17. *Sosa v. Alvarez-Machain*, 124 S. Ct. 2739 (2004).
18. *Harbury v. Deutch*, 96-CKK-438, U.S. District Court, District of Columbia.
19. See *Eisenfeld v. The Islamic Republic of Iran*, 172 F.Supp.2d 1, 8 (D.D.C. 2000), "It is beyond question that if officials of the United States, acting in their official capacities, provided material support to a terrorist group to carry out an attack of this type, they would be civilly liable and would have no grant of immunity."

20. The CIA was established in 1947 by the National Security Act, Ch. 343, 61 Stat. 495 (1947), codified at 50 U.S.C. 401-405 (1982).

21. Aug. 12, 1949, 6 U.S.T. 3516, 75 U.N.T.S. 287.

22. *Filartiga v. Pena-Irala,* 630 F.2d. 876, at 880 (2nd Cir. 1980). See also *Siderman v. Republic of Argentina,* 965 F.2d 699, 717 (9th Cir. 1992), cited by the Court in Memorandum Opinion of March 13, 2001, "The right to be free from official torture is fundamental and universal, a right deserving of the highest status under international law, a norm of jus cogens . . . To subject a person to such horrors is to commit one of the most egregious violations of the personal security and dignity of a human being."

23. General Counsel of the CIA (Houston) to director of CIA, memorandum, Sept. 25, 1947, concerning CIA authority to perform propaganda and commando type functions (http://academic.brooklyn.cuny.edu/history/johnson/65ciafounding2.htm).

24. See Plaintiff's Supplemental Presentation of Requested Evidence, Dec. 2003, pp. 39–41, citing CIA directives and instructions requiring respect for human rights.

25. As noted above, international law does not permit sovereign immunity to shield those who commit crimes against humanity, including torture. Surely the same standards should apply in civil cases.

26. Convention against Torture, Art. 14.

27. Amnesty International, *Universal Jurisdiction: The Duty of States to Enact and Enforce Legislation,* 2001, Ch. 14, Part VIII. http://web.amnesty.org/pages/uj-memorandum-eng

28. Federal law makes the actions taken in Iraq and Afghanistan subject to criminal prosecution directly under the War Crimes Act, and under 18 U.SC. 2340, discussed below, as well.

29. Faye Bowers and Philip Smucker, "U.S. Ships Al Qaeda Suspects to Torture Using Arab States," *Christian Science Monitor,* July 26, 2002.

30. See discussion of extraordinary rendition in chapter 2.

31. See policy discussion in chapter 5.

32. Neil Lewis, "Broad Use of Harsh Tactics Is Described at Cuba Base," *New York Times,* Oct. 17, 2004, p. A-1.

33. Human Rights Watch, *U.S. State Department Criticism of "Stress and Duress" Interrogation around the World,* 2004.

34. U.N. Committee against Torture, CAT/C/SR.297/ADD.1, Conclusions, para. 6–4, cited in B'Tselem, *Routine Torture: Interrogation Methods of the General Security Service,* Feb. 1998, p. 37. (NOTE: the similarity to the U.S. techniques reinforces the conclusion that these are not random violations but rather carefully developed and ordered official practices.)

35. 18 U.S.C. § 2441.

36. In fact, the Bush administration is threatening cuts in aid to any countries refusing to sign bilateral immunity agreements, which would prevent ICC

prosecutions of U.S. officials. See Jim Lobe, *US Pushes War-Crimes Immunity in Foreign-Aid Bill, Inter Press Services,* Nov. 30, 2004.

37. Adam Liptak, "Who Would Try Civilians from the U.S?" *New York Times,* May 26, 2004.
38. The American Convention on Human Rights, Art. 5, prohibits torture and cruel, inhuman, or degrading punishments. Although many rights may be suspended during times of war, this prohibition, as well as the right to life and to a fair trial, are non-derogable (Art. 27). Similar provisions may be found in the European Convention for the Protection of Human Rights and Fundamental Freedoms, Art. 3 and 15. Although the United States is not a party to these two conventions, their provisions do form part of customary international practice, which does bind the United States as discussed below.
39. ICCPR, Art. 4.
40. Convention against Torture, Art. 1.
41. Ibid., Art. 2.
42. Ibid., Art. 3.
43. Ibid., Art. 4.
44. Ibid., Art. 16.
45. Ibid., Art. 10.
46. The Paquete Habana, 175 U.S. 677 (1900).
47. *Filartiga v. Pena-Irala.*
48. Thus the Inter-American Court on Human Rights of the OAS found the Guatemalan army responsible for severe violations of the human rights of my husband, Everardo, despite his status as a URNG leader and combatant. See *In Re Bámaca* decision, 2000.
49. Despite this extraordinary memo by Alberto Gonzales, describing the Geneva Conventions as "quaint" and "obsolete," President Bush nominated him for the position of attorney general in December 2004. Shortly before the congressional hearings on the nomination, a new memo was coyly released, revoking the previous ones, establishing a more normal definition of torture, and insisting that the White House rejected all forms of torture (R. Jeffrey Smith, "Justice Dept. Memo Redefines Torture," *Washington Post,* Dec. 31, 2004.)
50. See United Nations Committee against Torture, CAT/C/SR.297/ADD.1, Conclusions, para. 6–4, and Human Rights Watch, *U.S. State Department Criticism of "Stress and Duress" Interrogation around the World,* 2004.
51. Memorandum for Alberto R. Gonzales, Office of Legal Counsel, Aug. 1, 2002, p. 4, citing Gonzales.
52. Fourth Geneva Convention, Aug. 12, 1949, U.N.T.S. No. 973, vol. 75, p. 287. Art. 4 and 5.
53. Third and Fourth Geneva Conventions, Common Art. 3.
54. Third Geneva Convention, Art. 4.

55. Third Geneva Convention, Art. 5.
56. Third Geneva Convention, Art. 12.
57. Third Geneva Convention, Art. 83–85.
58. Third Geneva Convention, Art 82–86.
59. Third Geneva Convention, Art. 87.
60. Third Geneva Convention, Art. 99.
61. *Hamdan v. Rumsfeld,* Civ. Action 04-0519, Nov. 8, 2004 Opinion.
62. Fourth Geneva Convention, Art. 4.
63. Fourth Geneva Convention, Art. 27.
64. Fourth Geneva Convention, Art. 31, 32.
65. Fourth Geneva Convention, Art. 16.
66. Fourth Geneva Convention, Art. 45, 49.
67. Fourth Geneva Convention, Art. 5, 37.
68. Third Geneva Convention, Art. 4, Part 3.
69. Third and Fourth Geneva Conventions, Art. 3.
70. Third Geneva Convention, Art. 39.
71. Third Geneva Convention, Art. 126; Fourth Geneva Convention, Art. 143.
72. Third Geneva Convention, Art. 127; Fourth Geneva Convention, Art. 144.
73. Third Geneva Convention Art. 129; Fourth Geneva Convention, Art. 146.
74. Third Geneva Convention, id., and Fourth Geneva Convention, Art. 147.
75. Third Geneva Convention, Art. 130; Fourth Geneva Convention, Art. 147.
76. Third Geneva Convention, Art. 131; Fourth Geneva Convention, Art. 148.
77. Third Geneva Convention, Art. 142; Fourth Geneva Convention, Art. 158.
78. Amnesty International, *Universal Jurisdiction*, Sept. 1, 2001.
79. The Center for Constitutional Rights of New York City has filed precisely such a complaint with the German authorities, as of Nov. 30, 2004.
80. Anderson, "Is Torture an Option in War on Terror?"

CHAPTER FIVE: PAYING THE PRICE

1. The invasion of Fallujah in Nov. 2004, for example, was decried around the world, as ambulances and hospitals were seized by U.S. troops and civilians were prevented from leaving the embattled city.
2. Steve Friess, "What Makes the Effects of Torture Linger?" *USA Today,* June 28, 2004.
3. Advocates for Survivors of Torture and Trauma, www.astt.org.
4. Sister Dianna Ortiz, TASSC executive director.
5. John Conroy, *Unspeakable Acts, Ordinary People* (Knopf, 2000), p. 182, citing G. W. Beebe, "Follow-up Studies of World War II and Korean War Prisoners," *American Journal of Epidemiology,* vol. 92, no. 2, 1970.
6. Ibid.
7. Friess, "What Makes the Effects?"
8. Conroy, *Unspeakable Acts,* p. 181.
9. Ibid., p. 179, quoting Art Spiegelman, *New York Times,* Oct. 6, 1992.
10. Ibid., ch. 13.

11. Ibid., p. 188.
12. Ibid., p. 181, citing Cohn et al., "A Study of Chilean Refugee Children in Denmark," *Lancet*, Aug. 24, 1985.
13. Human Rights Watch, *Enduring Freedom*, Vol. 16, March 2004; see also, for example, Michael Hirsh, "Blood and Honor," *Newsweek*, Feb. 2, 2004.
14. Hirsh, *Blood and Honor*.
15. Jess Bravin and Gary Fields, "How Do U.S. Interrogators Make a Captured Terrorist Talk?" *Wall Street Journal*, March 3, 2003, B-1.
16. Human Rights Committee, Communication 107/1981, case of Maria del Carmen Almeida de Quinteros (Uruguay) paragraph 14.
17. European Court of Human Rights, Report of Judgments and Decisions, 1998-III No. 74, *Kurt v. Turkey*.
18. Conroy, *Unspeakable Acts*, ch. 8, citing Stanley Milgram, *Obedience to Authority* (Harper and Row, 1974).
19. Ibid., pp. 96–102.
20. Ibid., citing Milgram, *Obedience to Authority*, pp. 79–84.
21. C. Haney, C. Banks, and P. Zimbardo, "Interpersonal Dynamics in a Simulated Prison," *International Journal of Criminology and Penology*, 1973, pp. 169–97, cited by the Independent Panel to Review DOD Detention Operations, 2004, Appendix G.
22. I met a number of these people face to face during the 1998 trial in Everardo's case at the Inter-American Court of the OAS in San José, Costa Rica. They had been subpoenaed to attend and testify. While all were hostile and some were nervous, two were quite frightening. One hissed like a snake when he spoke, and tried to intimidate the court. The other was so alienated he could make no eye contact and could barely connect with the questioning attorney to speak. He grunted monosyllabic answers in a flat monotone. The effect on the audience was palpable.
23. Jennifer Harbury, *Bridge of Courage* (Common Courage Press, 1993).
24. Marion Lloyd, "Guatemalan Activists Seek Justice as Women Die," *Boston Globe*, June 14, 2004.
25. Martin Edwin Andersen, "Is Torture an Option in War on Terror?" *Insight on the News*, posted May 27, 2002 (www.insightmag.com).
26. Statement of Senator Patrick Leahy, Jan. 6, 2005, during conference hearings on the nomination of Alberto Gonzales.
27. Jeff Kass, "Former Army Interrogator Offers a Peek inside Psychological Tactics," *Rocky Mountain News*, March 26, 2003.
28. CIA Memorandum for Inspector General, *Investigation of New York Times Articles Allegations of CIA Involvement with Honduran Officials Accused of Human Rights Abuses*, Aug. 24, 1988.
29. James Glanz, "Torture Is Often a Temptation and Almost Never Works," *New York Times*, May 9, 2004; see also Peter Brookes (CIA and Naval Intelligence veteran), "The Rule of Pain," *Chicago Tribune*, May 9, 2004.
30. Brad Knickerbocker, "Can Torture Be Justified?" *Christian Science Monitor*,

May 19, 2004, quoting Steven Welsh of the Center for Defense Information in Washington, D.C.

31. Conroy, *Unspeakable Acts*, p. 113, quoting Mr. Don Dzagulones.
32. Andersen, "Is Torture an Option?"
33. Mitch Frank, "A Pattern of Abuse?" *Time*, May 17, 2004, p. 45.
34. Everardo may also intentionally have led one platoon into an ambush, according to certain files. CIA reports at first sound thrilled about his "cooperation," but after a year or so become rather testy.
35. Mark Bowden, "The Dark Art of Interrogation," *Atlantic*, Oct. 2003, p. 60.
36. Ibid., pp. 58, 65.
37. Ibid., p. 56.
38. Frank, "A Pattern of Abuse?" p. 45.
39. Bowden, "The Dark Art of Interrogation," p. 69, quoting Mr. Giorgio.
40. Peter Brookes, "The Rule of Pain," *Chicago Tribune*, May 9, 2004, p. 1.
41. Milt Bearden, "Torture: As Futile As It Is Brutal," *Los Angeles Times*, May 23, 2004, p. 1.
42. Dana Priest and Joe Stephens, "Secret World of U.S. Interrogation," *Washington Post*, May 11, 2004, p. A-1.
43. Andersen, "Is Torture an Option?"
44. See, for example, James V. Grimaldi, "Two FBI Whistle-Blowers Allege Lax Security, Possible Espionage," *Washington Post*, June 19, 2002, p. A-10.

Prof. Alan Dershowitz insists that there is at least one instance in which the use of torture did save the day; see Alan M. Dershowitz, *Why Terrorism Works* (Yale U. Press, 2002), citing Matthew Brzezinski, "Bust and Boom" *Washington Post*, Dec. 30, 2001, p. W-9. This occurred in the Philippines, when local agents discovered a plot to blow up 11 airliners and assassinate the pope. That case was certainly frightening, but the facts actually point the other way. A simple search of the suspect's home gave the Philippine police most of the key evidence about the assassination and bombing plan. Police found proof, moreover, that a housemate had been involved in the first attack on the World Trade Center. Thus most of the needed evidence was gathered before interrogation even began, and was turned over at once to the CIA and the FBI.

The prisoner was then tortured for 67 days. Given this time span, the attack was clearly not "imminent," and the coconspirators' plans had obviously been put on hold as soon as the arrest occurred, as discussed above. Under torture, the prisoner did admit to a plan to bomb the passenger jets, and also to fly a Cessna or other plane into CIA headquarters. Would time-tested police interrogation methods, or the Saudi approach of using local Muslim religious leaders, have been even more fruitful? Probably, and with much less backlash as a result. Sadly, the U.S. took little action on these startling disclosures, and after the September 11 attacks, Philippine investigators were openly critical. "We told the Americans about the plans to turn planes into flying bombs as far back as 1995. Why didn't they pay attention?" In short, the plot was not "foiled" thanks to the use of torture. Instead, the plans were simply adjusted by al-Qaeda leaders to another time and another place, specifically, September 11 in New York City. Worse yet, the intelligence was received by U.S. agents but never properly utilized.

45. These very problems were eloquently discussed by Jessica Montell of B'Tselem, an Israeli human rights group, with Mark Bowden; see Bowden, "Dark Art of Interrogation," op. cit.

46. *Public Commission against Torture v. Israel*, 38 Int'l Legal Materials 1471, 1489 H.C. 5100/94. The Israeli Court is not alone in the struggle to keep to the moral high ground under difficult circumstances. In the 1970s in Italy, former prime minister Aldo Moro was kidnapped by Red Brigade Commandos. One officer sought permission to torture a suspect. Gen. Carlos Alberto Della Chiesa denied permission. "Italy can permit itself to lose Aldo Moro. What it cannot allow is the practice of torture"; see Andersen, "Is Torture an Option?" op. cit.

47. An early warning to the U.S. military prior to the Abu Ghraib disclosures warned of the abuses and suggested that this could feed the Iraqi insurgency by "making gratuitous enemies" ("Report Warned on Abuse," *Boston Globe,* Dec. 1, 2004, p. A-12).

48. Anderson Cooper, "Will Apparent Torture of Iraqis by U.S. Troops Lead to More Bloodshed?" *CNN,* April 30, 2004.

49. Ian Fisher, "Ex-Prisoners of GIs Offer More Claims of Mistreatment," *New York Times,* May 4, 2004, p. A-8.

50. Ibid.

51. Ian Fisher, "Iraqi Tells of Abuse, from Ridicule to Rape Threat," *New York Times,* May 14, 2004, p. A-10, quoting Mr. Saddam Salch Aboud and setting forth his story.

52. Scheherezad Faramarzi, "Leaving Slums of Paris, Two Muslim Teens Turn to Waging Jihad," *Boston Globe,* Nov. 26, 2004, p. A-48.

53. Neil MacFarquhar, "Saudis Support Jihad in Iraq, Not Back Home, *New York Times,* April 23, 2004, A-1.

54. Kurt Nimmo, "Alan Dershowitz and the Ticking Bomb," *Information Clearing House,* March 5, 2003, quoting the Defense Science Board, *1997 Summer Task Force on DOD Response to Transnational Threats.*

55. Brad Knickerbocker, "Can Torture Be Justified?" *Christian Science Monitor,* May 19, 2004, quoting Ivan Eland of the Independent Institute of Oakland, California.

56. Shankar Vedantam, "The Psychology of Torture, Past Incidents Show Abusers Think Ends Justify the Means," *Washington Post,* May 11, 2004, quoting John Conroy.

57. Ibid., statement of Lt. Col. Cowan.

58. See generally Martha Crenshaw, *Revolutionary Terrorism: The FLN in Algeria, 1954–1962* (Hoover, 1978).

59. Andersen, *Is Torture An Option?*

60. Timothy Gallimore, "Unresolved Trauma: Fuel for the Cycle of Violence and Terrorism," in *The Psychology of Terrorism*, vol. 2, ed. Chris Stout (Praeger, 2002), p. 152.

61. Ibid., p. 153.

62. Ibid., p. 148, citing T. J. Scheff, "The Shame-Rage Spiral," in *The Role of Shame in Symptom Formation* (Erlbaum, 1987), pp. 109–140.

63. Dr. Eyad Sarraj and other professionals from the Gaza Community Mental Health Project have been pointing this out for years, but few have listened.

64. Rona Fields, Salman Elbedour, and Fadel Abu Hein, "The Palestinian Suicide Bomber," in *The Psychology of Terrorism*, vol. 2, ed Chris Stout (Praeger, 2002), p. 193.

65. Ibid., p. 207.

66. See, for example, *Routine Torture: Interrogation Methods of the General Security Service,* report issued by B'Tselem, an Israeli civil rights organization, 1998. Other B'Tselem reports include *Policy of Destruction,* 2002; *Trigger Happy,* 2002; and *Standard Routine: Beatings and Abuse of Palestinians by Israeli Security Forces during the Al Aqsa Intifada,* 2001.

67. Pine Ridge and Watts certainly come to mind as U.S. examples.

68. Greg Myre, "Four Israeli Ex-Security Chiefs Denounce Sharon's Hard Line," *New York Times,* Nov. 15, 2003, p. A-3. See also Ramit Plushnick-Masti, "Israeli Army Chief Blasts Hard Line on Palestinians," *Associated Press,* Oct. 31, 2003: "The dispute was set off by Lt. General Moshe Yaalon, the army chief of staff, who said Israel's tough policies are increasing Palestinian hatred towards Israel and fostering sympathy for the very groups Israel is trying to destroy."

69. No evidence has been offered, for example, that would suggest that the suicide bombers of the September 11 attacks had suffered any earlier trauma. Rather, their actions would seem to have been based on other motivations, such as political militance.

70. Fields et al., "The Palestinian Suicide Bomber."

71. Ibid., p. 212.

72. Prof. Ariel Merari, "Suicide Terrorism," Report, Department of Psychology, Tel Aviv University.

73. Ibid., p. 7.

74. Ibid., p. 9.

75. Ibid., p. 10.

76. Basel A. Saleh, "Economic Conditions and Resistance to Occupation in the West Bank and Gaza Strip: There Is a Causal Connection," Kansas State University, Manhattan, Kansas, 2003, unpublished research.

77. I thank both Mr. Basel A. Saleh and Ms. C. for their kindly assistance in providing me with these very hard to obtain numbers and information.

78. This information is available on the Torture Abolition and Survivors Support Coalition International Website, www.tassc.org.

CONCLUSION

1. Richard Serrano, "Marines Tortured Prisoners Before and After Abu Ghraib," *Los Angeles Times,* Dec. 15, 2004.
2. Jane Mayer, "Outsourcing Torture," *New Yorker,* Feb. 14, 2005.
3. Eric Lichtblau, "Gonzales Excludes CIA from Rules on Prisoners," *New York Times,* Jan. 20, 2005.
4. Douglas Jehl and David Johnston, "White House Fought New Curbs on Interrogations, Officials Say," *New York Times,* Jan. 12, 2005.
5. Suzanne Goldenberg and James Meek, "Papers Reveal Bagram Abuse," *Guardian* (U.K.), Feb. 18, 2005.
6. Charlie Savage, "Files Suggest That U.S. Troops Tried to Hide Abuses," *Boston Globe,* Feb. 18, 2005.
7. Ibid.
8. Luis Bredow and Jim Schultz, "U.S. Threatens Bolivia in an Effort to Secure Criminal Court Immunity," *Pacific News Service,* March 3, 2005.
9. Craig Whitlock, "Europeans Investigate CIA Role in Abductions," *Washington Post Foreign Service,* March 13, 2005.
10. "U.S. May End Up in Dock at U.N. Human Rights Meeting," *Reuters,* March 13, 2005.
11. There have of course been extraordinary reporting efforts by many, including but not limited to Dana Priest of the *Washington Post,* the *60 Minutes* disclosures about Abu Ghraib, and *Democracy Now* programming.

INDEX

Aballi, Dureid Al, 10
Aballi, Khraisan Al, 9–10
Abd, Hayder, 12
Aboud, Saddam Saleh, 14–15, 163, 170
Abu Ghraib prison scandal, 11–17, 18, 104, 129, 161, 163; backlash from, 169, 170; CIA role in, 13, 15, 16, 18–19, 22–23, 25, 29; human rights organizations and, xxv–xxvi; MPs in, 13, 14–15, 16, 139, 153, 154; public reaction to, 1, 157, 186
Administrative Procedure Act, 110
Adris, Wafa'a Ali, 181
Afghanistan, war in, xxv, 102, 103, 109, 121; Geneva Conventions and, 20, 131; prisoner massacres in, 2–4, 4–5; prisoner-of-war status in, 132–34; Soviets and, 172; Taliban, xxiii, 5, 21, 132–34; torture of prisoners in, 10–11, 17; trauma survivors in, 173
Afghan Organization of Human Rights, 3
Agee, Philip, 91
Ahmad, Abu, 12, 170
Akbar, Hyder, 10–11, 17
Algeria, 172
Alien Tort Claims Act (ATCA), xxi, 110–11, 112, 115, 128, 143, 160
Allende, Salvador, 90

Almalki, Abdullah, 6, 7
Alpirez, Julio Roberto, xv, 58; as CIA paid informant, xvi, 36–37, 38, 54, 60, 61, 101
al-Qaeda, xxiii, 7, 21, 132, 134, 140; Bin Laden and, xxiv, 189
"Al-Qaeda Determined to Attack Inside the United States" (bulletin), xxiii
Alvarado, Pedro de, 40
Álvarez Martínez, Gustavo, 49, 50, 51, 85, 86
American Civil Liberties Union (ACLU), 17, 103
American Declaration of the Rights and Duties of Man, 126
Amnesty International, 11, 42, 151–52
Anaya, Herbert, 75–76, 150
Anaya, Mirna, 75, 150
Arar, Maher, 6–8, 9, 22, 123
Arbenz, Jacobo, 33, 34
Arendt, Hannah, 152
Arévalo, Juan José, 33
Argentina, torture methods training and employment in, 49, 50, 52, 58
Argueta, Juan, 76
Armony, Ariel, 52
Army Field Manual 34-53, 21
Arruda, Marcos, 94
Ashcroft, John, 5, 159

of, xix–xx, 31; in El Salvador, 40,
45–47; Everardo and, xvi, 60,
62–65, 69–70; extraordinary
rendition and, 2, 8, 22, 117; FBI
compared to, 118–19, 140, 166;
Geneva Conventions and, 20;
"ghost prisoners" of, 18–19, 103,
150; Guatemalan death squads and,
xvii, 32, 34, 39; in Honduras, 47,
48, 51, 52–53, 85–86; human rights
abuses by, xviii; intelligence in
Middle East and, 189; kidnappings
by, 184; Latin American death
squads and, 28, 30, 32, 45–47, 54,
115–16, 118, 141; military and, 24,
138; and MKULTRA program, 96,
100; as rogue agency, 142; SOA and,
44; sovereign immunity of, 109–10,
116, 124; torture by proxy and, 117;
in Uruguay, 95; in Vietnam, 97;
whistleblowers in, xxiii. *See also*
North American (CIA) torturers
CIA paid informants ("assets"),
xx, xxiv, 64–65, 99, 109–10, 117;
Alpirez as, xvi, 36–37, 38, 54, 60, 61,
63, 101; in El Salvador, 46, 47; Everardo and, 56, 63; human rights
abuses by, xxiv, 30, 55; "ticking
bomb" scenario and, 118–19
circuit court, 115, 127
civilian casualties, 173. *See also*
massacres
civilian contractors, 117
civil law, 106–16; Alien Tort Claims
Act (ATCA), xxi, 110–11, 112, 115,
128, 143, 160; Federal Tort Claims
Act (FTCA), 109, 111, 113, 115, 143
civil wars, 41, 159–60; in Guatemala,
34, 45, 172
Clinton, Bill, xvii, 36, 60, 125
coerced confessions, 6, 15, 77, 106,
162–64
Cohn, Gary, 50

COINTELPRO, 119
Colombia, 174
Comando, The, 60–61
Commission for Historical
Clarification of Guatemala
(CEHG), 34–36
Committee in Defense of Human
Rights in Honduras (CODEH), 49
confessions, coerced, 6, 15, 77, 106,
162–64
Congress, U.S., xviii, 59, 106, 128, 129;
Abu Ghraib prison scandal and,
12; CIA and, 112, 113, 186; death
squads and, 54; House Intelligence
Committee, 2; Patriot Act and,
xxiii; search for Everardo and,
xv, xvii, 65
Conroy, John, 152, 163, 171
constitutional protections, 106–9, 185
Contras (Nicaragua), 32, 47, 50, 52,
85, 99
Convention Against Torture (U.N.),
xx–xxi, 9, 115, 121, 124, 126–27, 128
corruption, 157
Cosculluela, Manuel Hevia, 95
Costa Rica, 82–83, 156, 160
counterinsurgency training, 45
counterterrorism: in Guatemala, 38
court-martial, xxvi, 13
Cowan, Bill, 164
criminal law, 116–25; CIA practices
and, 117–19, 121, 123, 124; and Convention against Torture, 121, 122,
124; and "ticking bomb" scenario,
118, 119–20
Cuban Missile Crisis, 188
Culombe v. Connecticut, 106
cultural awareness, 166

D'Aubuisson, Roberto, 44
DCI Watch Committee Report, 39
death squads: CIA relationship with,
28, 30, 32, 54, 100, 118, 141; disap-

Against Torture, 122, 143, 151; resolutions of, 126–27; Truth Commission, 34–36, 41. *See also* Convention Against Torture (U.N.)

Universal Declaration of Human Rights, 126

universal jurisdiction, doctrine of, 137

Unspeakable Acts (Conroy), 152

URNG (Guatemalan guerrilla movement), xxi, 34, 71; Everardo and, 36, 57, 61, 160

Uruguay, 93, 95–96, 99, 100

U.S. Army homicide investigations, 19–20

U.S. Embassy, xiv, xvi, 61, 67, 80, 95; in Chile, 91, 92, 93

U.S. government: *See* Congress, U.S.; Senate; Supreme Court. U.S.; White House; *specific administrations*

U.S. v. Verdugo-Urquidez, 109

USAID report, 38

USA Patriot Act (2001), xxiii

Vaky, Vyron, 38

Valladares Lanza, Leo, 49, 87

Valle, José, 52

Van De Kolk, Professor, 146

Van Der Weid, Jean Marc, 93–94

Velásquez, Efraín Bámaca. *See* Everardo

Vietnam War, 96–97, 103, 146, 172; Operation Phoenix in, 88–89,

99, 162, 163, 172; post-traumatic stress syndrome and, 174

violence: backlash and, 144–45; mob, 158; trauma and, 173–74, 175

Wali, Abdul, 10–11

Walker, Greg, 45

Walsh, Michael J. ("Mr. Mike"), 53, 86, 87–90, 99, 100

War Crimes Act (1996), 116, 123, 130

Warner, John, 14

war on terror, xxiii, xxiv, 136, 160, 164–65, 183, 187; policy questions and, 118; suicide attacks in, xxvi; "tough guy" approach to, 120

Washington Post, 2, 9, 19, 80

weapons of mass destruction, xxv, 159, 188

Wiesel, Elie, 175

"wink and nod" approach to intelligence gathering, 88, 118

Winters, Don, 51

Wohlstetter, Peter, 92–93

Woods, Carolyn, 22

World Court, 125

World Trade Center attack, xxi–xxii. *See also* September 11 attacks

World War II, 146

Yale University torture study, 153

Yoo, John, 20

Zubaida, Abu, 2, 10